Sound Bytes from Reviews of
Secrets of a Super Hacker

"*Secrets of a Super Hacker* is a fascinating hacker cookbook that reveals the ease of penetrating even the most stalwart computer system."
> — **The San Francisco Chronicle**

"Not often do the contents of a book match its cover hype, but here is one book that comes closer than most. *Secrets of a Super Hacker,* by The Knightmare, is billed as 'every security manager's worst nightmare.' It does, indeed, descend into the realm of security managers' darkest fears."
> — **Infosecurity News**

"...step-by-step instructions in meaningful hacking [using] a personal computer."
> — **Booklist**

"Excellent. This work will appeal to many, especially business professionals as the networks and e-mail become more commonplace."
> — **The Reader's Review**

"...the most specific, detailed, general-purpose guide to electronic shenanigans I've seen. Recommended."
> — **Reading for Pleasure**

"All 205 pages are loaded with clear, concise, and very devious information. It is well-written, sprinkled with wit and the Knightmare's own personal experiences."
> — **Selected Book Reviews**

"Sysops may find it necessary to read this one, especially if their callers read it first."
> — **BBS Magazine**

"It's readable, interesting, informative, balanced, and accurate, with a nice spirit of fun and swashbuckling!"
> — **<solmaker> on alt.books.reviews**

"*Secrets of a Super Hacker*...should be read by anyone who has the crazy notion that his data is safe."
> — **ComputerWorld**

Secrets of a
Super Hacker

by The Knightmare

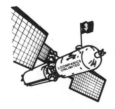

Loompanics Unlimited
Port Townsend, Washington

Secrets of a Super Hacker
© 1994 by Dennis Fiery

Introduction © 1994 by Gareth Branwyn

Cover by Bart Nagel

Illustrations by Dan Wend/MEDIA Graphics

Published by:
Loompanics Unlimited
P.O. Box 1197
Port Townsend, WA 98368

Loompanics Unlimited is a division of Loompanics Enterprises, Inc.

ISBN 1-55950-106-5

Library of Congress Catalog Card Number 93-86568

Contents

PART TWO
During Hack

PART THREE
After Hack

APPENDICES

Introduction:
Hackers: Heroes or Villains?

by Gareth Branwyn

Hacking in the Village
"Where am I?"
"In the Village."
"What do you want?"
"Information."
"Whose side are you on?"
"That would be telling. We want... information... information... information."
"Well you won't get it."
"By hook or by crook, we will!"

Remember the '60s TV show *The Prisoner*? Created by and starring Patrick McGoohan, this surrealist series was basically a platform for McGoohan to explore his own fears of modern surveillance/spy technology, behavioral engineering, and society's increasing ability to control people through pacifying pleasures. He was convinced that all this might soon mean the obliteration of the individual (expressed in the defiant opening shout: "I am not a number, I am a free man!"). McGoohan's #6 character became a symbol of the lone individual's right to remain an individual rather than a numbered cog in the chugging ma-

chinery of the State. McGoohan, a Luddite to be sure, despised even the TV technology that brought his libertarian tale to the masses. He saw no escape from the mushrooming techno-armed State short of out-and-out violent revolution (it was, after all, the '60s!). As prescient as *The Prisoner* series proved to be in some regards, McGoohan failed to see how individuals armed with the same tech as their warders could fight back. The #6 character himself comes close to revealing this in a number of episodes, as he uses his will, his ingenuity, and his own spy skills to re-route #2's attempts to rob him of his individuality.

One doesn't have to stretch *too* far to see the connection between *The Prisoner* and the subject at hand: hacking. With all the social engineering, spy skills, and street tech knowledge that #6 possessed, he lacked one important thing: access to the higher tech that enslaved him and the other hapless village residents. Today's techno-warriors are much better equipped to hack the powers that be for whatever personal, social or political gains.

In the last two-part episode of the series, #6 finally reveals why he quit his intelligence job: "Too many people know too much." Again, this expresses McGoohan's fear that the powers that be were holding the goods on him and everyone else who was bucking the status quo at that time. He probably didn't mean "people" as much as he meant "governments." It is this fact, that "too many [governments/megacorps/special interest groups] know too much" that has provided an important motivation to many contemporary hackers and has fueled the rampant techno-romantic myths of the hacker as a freedom of information warrior.

Let's look at a number of the mythic images of the hacker that have arisen in the past decade and explore the reality that they both reflect and distort:

The Hacker as Independent Scientist

The first image of hackerdom to emerge in the '60s and '70s was of the benevolent computer science student pushing the limits of computer technology and his/her own intellect. Computer labs at MIT, Berkeley, Stanford and many other schools hummed through the night as budding brainiacs sat mesmerized by the promise of life on the other side of a glowing computer screen. These early hackers quickly developed a set of ethics that centered around the pursuit of pure knowledge and the idea that hackers should share all of their information and brilliant hacks with each other. Steven Levy summarizes this ethic in his 1984 book *Hackers*:

"To a hacker a closed door is an insult, and a locked door is an outrage. Just as information should be clearly and elegantly transported within the computer, and just as software should be freely disseminated, hackers believed people should be allowed access to files or tools which might promote the hacker quest to find out and improve the way the world works. When a hacker needed something to help him create, explore, or fix, he did not bother with such ridiculous concepts as property rights."

While this ethic continues to inform many hackers, including the author of the book you are holding, it has become more difficult for many to purely embrace, as the once-innocent and largely sheltered world of hackerdom has opened up onto a vast geography of data continents with spoils be-

yond measure, tempting even the most principled hackers. The Knightmare weaves his way in and out of these ethical issues throughout *Secrets of a Super Hacker*.

The Hacker as Cowboy

The cowboy has always served as a potent American myth of individuality and survivalism in the face of a harsh and lawless frontier. It is no accident that William Gibson chose cowboy metaphors for his groundbreaking cyberpunk novel *Neuromancer* (1984). Case and the other "console cowboys" in the novel ride a cybernetic range as data rustlers for hire, ultimately sad and alone in their harsh nomadic world. They are both loner heroes and bad-assed predators of the law-abiding cyber-citizenry they burn in their wake. I don't think I need to tell readers here what impact Gibson's fictional world has had on fueling hacker fantasies or what potent similarities exist between Gibson's world and our own.

Like the cowboy tales of the wild west, the myth of the hacker as cowboy is undoubtedly more image over substance (as are most of the myths we will explore here), but there are some important kernels of truth: a) hackers are often loners, b) there are many nomadic and mercenary aspects to the burgeoning cyberspace of the 1990s, and c) it is a wide-open and lawless territory where the distinctions between good and bad, following the law and forging a new one, and issues of free access and property rights are all up for grabs (remember the Indians?). Not surprisingly, Electronic Frontier Foundation co-founder John Perry Barlow (a Wyoming cattle rancher himself) chose frontier metaphors when he wrote his landmark essay "Crime and Puzzlement" (*Whole Earth Review*, Fall 1990). The first section of this lengthy essay that lead to the birth of the EFF was entitled, "Desperadoes of the DataSphere."

The Hacker as Techno-Terrorist

When I was a budding revolutionary in the '70s, with my Abbie Hoffman and Jimi Hendrix posters and my cache of middle class weapons (.22 caliber rifles, .12 gauge shotgun, hunting bows), I, like McGoohan, was gearing up for the Big Confrontation. With a few friends (who seemed more interested in firearms than revolutionary rhetoric), I used to do maneuvers in the woods near my house. We would fantasize how it was all gonna come down and what role we (the "Radicals for Social Improvement") would play in the grand scheme of things. It doesn't take a military genius to see the futility of armed force against the U.S. military on its own turf. The idea that bands of weekend rebels, however well trained and coordinated, could bring down "The Man" was pure romance. Part of me knew this — the same part of me that was more interested in posture than real revolution and in getting laid more than in fucking up the State. My friends and I were content to play-act, to dream the impossible dream of overthrow.

One of the first "a-ha's" I had about computer terrorism in the late '80s was that the possibilities for insurrection and for a parity of power not based on brute force had changed radically with the advent of computer networks and our society's almost complete reliance on them. There was now at least the possibility that groups or individual hackers could seriously compromise the U.S. military and/or civilian electronic infrastructure. The reality of this hit home on November 2, 1988, when Robert Morris, Jr., the son of a well-known computer security researcher, brought down over 10% of the Internet with his worm (a program that self-propagates over a network, reproducing as it goes). This event led to a media feeding frenzy which brought the heretofore computer underground into the harsh lights of television cameras and sound-bite journalism. "Hacker terrorists," "viruses," "worms," "computer espionage"...all of a sudden, everyone was looking over their shoulders for lurking cyberspooks and sniffing their computer disks and downloads to see if they had contracted nasty viruses. A new computer security industry popped up overnight, offering counseling, virus protection software (sometimes with antidotes to viruses that didn't even exist!), and workshops, seminars and books on computer crime.

Hysteria over hacker terrorism reached another plateau in 1990 with the execution of Operation Sundevil, a wide-net Secret Service operation intended to cripple the now notorious hacker underground. Like a cat chasing its own tail, the busts and media coverage and additional busts, followed by more sensational reportage, created a runaway loop of accelerating hysteria and misinformation. One radio report on the "stealing" (copying, actually) of a piece of information "critical to the operations of the Emergency 911 system" for Bell South opined: "It's a miracle that no one was seriously hurt." Of course, the truth turned out to be far less dramatic. The copied booty was a very boring text document on some management aspects of the Bell South system. For a thorough and lively account of this and many of the other arrests made during Operation Sundevil, check out Bruce Sterling's *The Hacker Crackdown* (Bantam, 1992).

Whatever the truth of these particular incidents, computer crime is here big time and the boasts of even the most suspect hacker/cracker are usually at least theoretically possible. Computer terrorism has yet to rear its head in any significant fashion, but the potential is definitely there. This is very unsettling when you think how many people can gain access to critical systems and how many loony tunes there are out there armed with computers, modems, and less-than-honorable intentions. Wireheads of every gauge would do well to study volumes like *Secrets of a Super Hacker* to stay abreast of the game and to cover their backsides should the proverbial shit hit the fan.

The Hacker as Pirate

Next to "cowboy," the most potent and popular image of the hacker is that of a pirate. Oceanographic and piracy metaphors are equally as common in cyberculture as ones about lawless frontiers and modem-totin' cowboys and cowgirls. People talk of "surfing the edge," and the "vast oceans of the Internet." Bruce Sterling's near-future novel about data piracy was named *Islands in the Net*. In it, third world countries and anarchist enclaves operate data havens, buying and selling global information through the world's wide-bandwidth computer networks.

Anarchist theorist and rantmeister Hakim Bey penned an essay called "Temporary Autonomous Zones (or T.A.Z.)" inspired by Sterling's data islands. Bey sees in the rapidly growing technosphere of our planet the possibilities for a new form of nomadic anarchic culture that might resemble the sea-faring pirate societies of the 18th century. Using all the resources of the global nets, individual cybernauts can come together to form temporary and virtual enclaves. These bands can wreak havoc, throw a party, exchange intelligence, or whatever else they want. Once the deed is done, the party over, the nomadic bands simply disappear back into the dense fabric of cyberspace. While decidedly romantic, the TAZ idea is attractive to many hackers and cyberspace residents who daily feel the fluidity of movement and the potential for invisibility offered on "the nets."

Of course, let's not kid ourselves, pirates were mainly concerned with stealing things. In cyberspace, piracy becomes a more ambiguous and contested can of worms. Are you really taking something if you're simply looking at it or making a copy of it? If you copy copyrighted material — let's say an image — and then alter it significantly, to the point that it is almost unrecognizable, have you violated the copyright? What if you're using it as raw materials in a piece of art, like collage? What does stealing mean when what is stolen is nothing more than a particular assemblage of electrical impulses? I regularly download recognizable audio bytes from networks, process them in a sound editor, and then use them in various audio art projects. Am I stealing? If I publish the work commercially, THEN is it plagiarism? All of these questions about sampling, copying, cutting, pasting, re-purposing, and altering have become the thorny legal and ethical issues of our cybernetic age. Hackerdom is one of the domains that is rapidly fueling the fire.

The Hacker as
Biblical David

When liberal and fringe media want to feel good about hacking and cracking they start invoking images of the hacker as a do-gooder David against a military/industrial Goliath. This myth of the hacker, based on the "parity of power" theme discussed above can bring comfort to those of us who are paranoid about megacorporate and government big brothers. However over-romanticized this myth is, there is comfort to be found in the knowledge that individuals can penetrate even the

most behemoth systems. If big brother gets too big for his britches, "Davidian" (?) hackers are standing by to do some necessary tailoring.

The Hacker as
Security Informant

Another do-gooder myth revolves around the hacker as an either self-appointed or hired security checker. Many hackers, true to their ethos of simply wanting to push the limits of their ability and not to cause harm, will report holes in security after they've breached them. To the hacker who is interested in the gamesmanship and challenge of penetrating a system, tipping off the system's administrators means a new level of challenge should they ever return. Hackers who are hired for purposes of testing system security, called "tiger teams," also work to compromise the security of a system to find weaknesses. Often times, these hired guns are convicted computer criminals who "go straight." Several members of the legendary Legion of Doom, caught in the Operation Sundevil busts, formed COMSEC, a computer security team for hire. While many hackers bristle at such turncoat maneuvers, other more politically neutral hackers point out that it doesn't really matter to them who they're working for as long as they get to hack.

The Hacker as
U.S. Cavalry

Just as Hollywood movies raised the lowly dirt-lickin' cowboy to mythic status, it is now presenting hackers as a tech-mounted U.S. Cavalry, a cyberpunk version of Mighty Mouse, here to save the day — and save the movie — in the final seconds. Movies such as *WarGames*, *Sneakers*, *Jurassic Park*, and TV shows such as *Max Headroom* glamorize hackers, often portraying them as misguided geniuses who finally see the light and prevent calamities they're often responsible for initiating. At the same time that the mainstream media has demonized hackers, Hollywood has romanticized them. John Badham's 1983 film *WarGames* probably did more to stimulate interest in hacking and phone phreaking among young people than anything before or since. Numerous legendary hackers have credited that film as their chief inspiration and raison d'etre. All these films have also played into the myth of the evil government and megacorps who deserve the harassment that the hacker protagonists dish out. As this introduction is being written, rumors are flying fast and furious that a number of near-future hacker/cyberpunk TV shows are in the works. It will be very interesting to see how Hollywood continues to re-invent the hacker.

The Hacker as Cyborg

Ultimately computer hacking and net navigating, and the images and fantasies surrounding them, represent something greater than the sum of the parts outlined here. It is this writer's opinion that hackers represent the scouts to a new territory that is just now beginning to be mapped out by others. Hackers were the first cybernauts, the first group of people to understand that we as a species are about to disappear into a cyberspace at least similar in function to that posited by William Gibson in his 80's fiction. As Manuel De Landa explains in his book *War in the Age of Intelligent Machines* (MIT, 1991), we are forging a new symbiotic relationship with machines via computers. The nature of this relationship and the level of individual freedom afforded by it has a lot to do with how hackers, visionary scientists, and the first wave of cyber-settlers go about their business. While De Landa is very laudatory toward the "freedom of information" ethic and developmental ingenuity of hackerdom, he cautions those who wish to make too much trouble for individuals and organizations, leading to retaliation, escalation of tensions, and increased paranoia. He writes:

"...[S]ome elements of the hacker ethic which were once indispensable means to channel their energies into the quest for interactivity (system-crashing, physical and logical lock-busting) have changed character as the once innocent world of hackerism has become the multimillion-dollar business of computer crime. What used to be a healthy expression of the hacker maxim that information should flow freely is now in danger of becoming a new form of terrorism and

organized crime which could create a new era of unprecedented repression."

De Landa argues elsewhere in *Machines* that the U.S. government's, especially the military's, desire to centralize decision-making power has been seriously compromised by the personal computer revolution. He speculates that those outside the military-industrial machinery have only a few years to develop a new and truly decentralized system of networks before the military devises a new tactical doctrine that subsumes the distributed PC.

The images of hacking: coming in under the wire of mainstream society, cobbling together technology for individual and group purposes, overcoming limitations, and all the other real and imagined dimensions of hacking, have become part of a new academic trend that uses the sci-fi image of the cyborg as a model of late twentieth century humanity. These academics have embraced cyberpunk sci-fi, the politicized image of the hacker, and postmodern ideas about posthumanism (a future of human/machine hybridization). Anyone who spends most of their waking hours patched into a PC and the Internet or in hacking code has felt the margins between themselves and their machines getting very leaky. Hackers were the first to experience this, many others are now following in their digital footsteps. Hacking has become trendy and chic among people who, if pressed, couldn't even define an operating system. The "idea" of hacking has migrated far from the actual act of hacking. It has become a cultural icon about decentralized power for the turn of the millennium.

The Knightmare's Vision

Behind all these lofty notions lies the tedious and compelling act of the hack itself. Hacker-monikered "The Knightmare" presents his complex view of hacking in *Secrets of a Super Hacker*. In this classic hacker cookbook, the author has gone to great pains to explain the massive width and breadth of hacking, cracking, and computer security. With Sherlock Holmes-like compulsion and attention to detail, he presents the history of hacking, the how-tos of hacking, the legal and ethical issues surrounding hacking, and his own personal reasons for hacking. Numerous examples and "amazing hacker tales" take the reader inside each level of the hack. Reading *Secrets* will change the way you look at computers and computer security. It has already been very valuable to me. I am a smarter computer/net user now and much more attuned to computer security.

When Patrick McGoohan conceived of *The Prisoner* he wanted to create a show that would demand thinking. He wanted controversy, arguments, fights, discussions, people waving fists in his face. You might love the show, you might hate the show (or both), but you would HAVE to talk about it. Computer hacking and the wooly frontiers of cyberspace are similar domains of controversy. In the true spirit of freedom of information, *Secrets of a Super Hacker* is being made available to anyone who cares to read it. It is my hope that it will help keep the debate alive and that those who make use of its privileged information will do so responsibly and without malice.

Be Seeing You,
Gareth Branwyn
August 29, 1993
Nantucket Island, Mass.

Part One
Before Hack

"Given that more and more information about individuals is now being stored on computers, often without our knowledge or consent, is it not reassuring that some citizens are able to penetrate these databases to find out what is going on? Thus it could be argued that hackers represent one way in which we can help avoid the creation of a more centralized, even totalitarian government. This is one scenario that hackers openly entertain."
— Tom Forrester and Perry Morrison in *Computer Ethics*

Chapter One:
The Basics

Reading vs. Doing

There are two ways to write a book about computer hacking.

The first is to write an encyclopedic account of every known system and its dialup numbers, passwords, loopholes, and how to increase one's access once inside. There is nothing particularly wrong with this approach except that by publication time much of the contents will likely be outdated. And surely, after word leaks to the computer sites of the world the remaining information will be rendered non-functional. Such a specific approach, while exciting, is best left to periodicals, which can keep readers updated on the constantly changing security frontier. Indeed, there are both print and on-line publications which attempt to do just that.

The second way to write a book about computer hacking is to write an encyclopedic account of the *methods* by which security is breached and systems penetrated. This is a much more agreeable solution to the problem of how to distribute changing information. The readers of such a book can then follow those methods, those *algorithms*, add some of their own creativity, and will never end up facing a situation drastically different from

the ones the text has prepared the hacker to encounter. Naturally, way-to-write-a-book Number Two is the way this book has been written.

At some points during the course of writing this book I've found that to talk about certain information requires knowledge of another aspect of hacking entirely. I tried to keep this book flowing in a logical order, conducive to understanding, but occasionally you will find ripples in the flow.

If you come across a term or situation that the book hasn't yet prepared you for, forget about it. You'll learn soon enough. Or look in the glossary — you might find the answer you seek there. Computer hacking is a subject which contains a voluminous amount of information. Repeatedly, as I prepared the manuscript, I had to decide whether or not to go into great detail in a particular area, or allow you to discover certain inside tricks on your own. Sometimes I compromised, sometimes I didn't. Some things I left out because they were too scary. When all is said and done, the important part isn't the writing of the book, it's the reading of it, and the actions that result from the reading. Hacking is about *doing something*, for yourself and on your own. It's not about *reading* about doing something. I will gladly point you in the right direction, but I won't be your guide once you're on your way.

Speaking of books being read, it is often a wonder that they ever *do* get to that readable finished state at all. Thank you R.S. and J for critiquing selections from this book; thanks to the people at Loompanics for recognizing that the Constitution does, after all, allow freedom of the press; and to the many hackers and crackers who offered suggestions: Morris, Janet, Sex Pack, Carl Fox and the happy Gang Of Demon Street.

Opening Remarks

This book will show you various methods you can use to break into computer systems.

In some ways this is harder to do than it used to be. Nowadays people are more strict, more cautious about security. That's how it seems, anyway. But there are plenty of holes still left in any system's armor. System managers can tighten up computer security as much as they want but there will always be ways to get around their efforts. Remember the first rule of hacking: Whatever a human mind can achieve, another can also achieve. Whatever one mind can hide, another can discover. People tend to think and act alike, and it is this sameness of thought that you, the hacker, will exploit.

What is a hacker? I'm going to give a definition now, and if you don't fit the description I give, you can just close this book and throw it away:

A hacker is a person with an intense love of something, be it computers, writing, nature or sports. A hacker is a person who, because he or she has this love, also has a deep curiosity about the subject in question. If a hacker loves computers, then he or she is curious about every aspect of computers. That curiosity extends also to the ways other people use their computers. Hackers have respect for their subject. For a computer hacker that means he respects the ability of computers to put him in contact with a universe of information and other people, and it means he respects those other people and does not intentionally use this knowledge of computers to be mischievous or destructive. That sort of thing is for social-outcast junior high school kids. The serious computer hacker simply wants to know everything there is about the world, and the world of computers. The True Computer Hacker is a computer enthusiast and more importantly, a Universe enthusiast.

You should already be enthused. Are you ready to learn?

Equipment

There is only one piece of equipment you need to be a successful computer hacker... a brain.

That's right — you don't even need a computer. In fact, you might be better off not having one as you will see later on. However, to start out you will want to have a computer, a modem, and a telephone line close by so you can connect to the outside.

It's inconsequential what kind of computer it is. What's more important are the modem and the communications software you use with it.

Modems And Speed

Remember the old puzzler, "Which weighs more: a pound of feathers or a pound of lead?" Well, here's the same puzzler with a modern twist: "Which transmits data faster: a 600 baud modem, or a 600 bits-per-second modem?"

The answer, of course, is "Both transmit data at the same rate!"

But the real answer gets a little more complicated. Let me explain.

"Baud" is the measure of the rate at which a modem sends and receives information. Below speeds of 600 baud, the baud rate is equal to bits-per-second. Due to the restrictions of telephone equipment, high speed modems may transmit far fewer bits-per-second than their baud rate. For example, a 2400 baud modem may only be sending 1200 bits-per-second.

For traditional reasons, modem speed is still stated in baud. While a hacker should be aware of the difference between baud rate and bits-per-second, the important thing to remember about modem speed is: the faster, the better. Just don't expect a 9600 baud modem to be four times as fast as a 2400 baud modem.

Five years ago, 300 baud modems were quite popular. Today, 9600 baud modems are fairly common. Higher speed modems, such as 14,400 baud and 19,900 baud, are now available in fairly inexpensive models. Many of the services you connect to will not be able to accomodate these higher speeds; however, a high-speed modem can always "step down" and connect at a slower speed when necessary.

Hacking is a hobby that requires little equipment; when it is necessary to buy something, you should try to buy the best available. This doesn't mean you should get what the salesperson or a magazine review says is best. It means, get what is best suited to your needs. You will want your modem to be fast. When I got my first modem, I thought of 140 baud as being the slowpoke. Now I look at the 300 baud crawler I used to use and wonder how I ever managed to stay interested when the words dribble across the screen at such an agonizingly slow pace.

Realize that whatever speed modem you get, it will usually run even slower than advertised. When there is static on the line, the modem is forced to resend data over and over until it has been sent or received correctly. Modems may run at half their listed speed, or even slower if they're in a particularly bad mood. They get even more snailish when you're calling long distance, or you're calling one computer through another through another (to make your call harder to trace back to its source), or if the remote computers are getting heavy usage.

For all of these reasons it's crazy not to get a fast modem. It will make every bit of electronic communication much more enjoyable.

Communications Software

It's hard to find truly splendid communications software, and yet it is the software (in conjunction with a fast, high-quality modem) which will determine how much enjoyment or frustration you get from your on-line interactions.

There are lots of communications software ("terminal emulators" or "term programs") out there. Just because a particular package comes with your modem doesn't mean you should feel obligated to use it. A good piece of telecommunications software will have many of the following features. For the hacker, it is necessary to have *all* these features. Well, maybe it's not necessary, but it will

sure make your hacking experience more pleasurable.

Handy Features

The monitor on your computer was probably specially designed for your computer. When you dial who-knows-where over the phone, you can easily be talking to some computer with a completely different screen design than your own. Consequently, certain standards (rules of behavior for monitors to follow) have been devised. If you call up a hundred different computers, there will be many differences between the characters each can display, the control codes used to perform various screen functions, and so on. Your communications program, or "comm program," should be able to adjust to a wide range of these codes and characters. This feature is known as *terminal emulation*. Software that can't do that will often represent data from the remote computer in peculiar ways, or as garbage characters. Your comm program must be able to emulate a good number of terminals, such as ANSI, VT52 and VT100. It is also handy for the software to have a translation table — the ability to translate incoming and outgoing characters to other characters.

The terminal program you choose should be able to send and receive files using the Xmodem, Ymodem, Zmodem, and Kermit protocols. A protocol is a set of rules. You see, if you're trying to move files between two completely dissimilar computers, those machines need to know how to talk to each other. These *file transfer protocols* set up specific guidelines for the two computers to follow regarding how the file should be sent and received. Each protocol has its own set of advantages and applications. The Zmodem protocol transfers files fast, and with good error recovery, but it isn't as prevalent as the original Xmodem. Ymodem is another improvement on Xmodem, but its error detection isn't as keen — only use it on clean phone lines. Kermit is used on many university mainframes for speedy, efficient file transfer. Make sure your terminal software has at least these four protocols.

Choose software that allows you to enter "AT" commands. ATtention commands were developed by Hayes to allow the user to control the modem. They have been adopted for most makes of modem. AT commands allow you to program the modem to dial, go on line, go off line, and perform various other functions.

You should also be able to shell to your computer's operating system while maintaining the connection — sometimes you will want to run another program while on-line.

The software should allow you to be able to store many phone numbers, names, and comments for a large number of dialups. You should be able to store more than just the ten digit phone number — extensions and special codes should be programmable, as well as sign-on macros for faster connections. It is also helpful to have auto-dial capacity, which repeatedly calls a busy phone number until the line is free.

Overall, the program you use must be pleasant and easy to use. If one program doesn't suit all your needs keep several on hand and use whichever you need when you need its special services. Generally I tend to stick with the PC Tools Desktop comm program. It doesn't have too many advanced features, but its ease of use more than makes up for that. ProComm Plus for the IBM and Macintosh is the Lotus 1-2-3 of communications software. It's a huge package that includes every conceivable feature you'll ever need. There are also many low price (free) alternatives in the world of shareware and public domain software. QModem is one good shareware communication program for IBM computers.

There is one final necessity for the hacker:

Data Capture

Your terminal program should have a data capture feature. This means that as information gets sent through your modem and put onto the screen, you should be able to capture it in a disk file.

It's important for you to keep the data capture feature on whenever you're using your modem. You do this for several reasons. When I'm logged in somewhere, I like to poke into all the text files I can find, but I don't like to waste my time on the system by actually reading them while on-line. Instead, I turn on my data capture, store what can be hundreds of pages of text in separate files, then sort through the data later, offline, at my leisure. (At other times it is more appropriate to simply trans-

fer the files; what one does depends on circumstances.)

Data capture is also handy to pick up control codes and text that scrolls off the screen too fast for you to read. And sometimes text is immediately erased after it's put on the screen, either for security reasons or due to faulty software. With data capture you retain a permanent record of that text. In any event, it's nice to have an official record of your hacking activities that you can use for reference and research.

One time I called up a bulletin board (BBS) that was run by a local company, mostly for the purpose of advertising its products. The modems connected, I pressed Enter a couple times, and I got the usual random characters on the screen, then the login prompt came on. It took a little longer than usual to get to the login prompt, and I was wondering about that, but nothing seemed really unusual so I went about my business.

Later, I was going over the print outs I made of the break-in and I took a second look at what at the time seemed to be just normal login garbage. In the middle of the nonsense symbols was this: "d-b". And on the next line, sandwiched between two plus signs, this: "ye!". On the surface this doesn't look too interesting, but think about it: put "d-b" and "ye!" together and you get "d-bye!". What I was looking at was the last half of the word "good-bye!".

From using the BBS I knew that "good-bye!" was the last thing one sees before logging off. In other words, I had called the system just after someone else had logged off, and I had gotten the tail end of their log-off message. This meant there was something wrong with the way the remote software handled disconnections. This meant there was a *bug* that could be *exploited*.

I logged onto the system again, and the first thing I did was go to the "User Log" to find the record of my last login to the system. The person who had been using the BBS before me was a regular user of the system and, sure enough, according to the log she had logged off just seconds before I was recorded as having logged in.

Later I was able to incorporate my knowledge of this flaw to make myself a system operator by calling up and connecting soon after the real system operator had finished a scheduled maintenance check. I wrote a letter explaining to him what

I had done, and how. Over the next few days we corrected the problem.

So you see, sometimes weird things happen while you're logging on or off, but anomalies can occur at any time. The moral of this story is be prepared to capture this weirdness, and be prepared to analyze it when you find it.

You never know when something out-of-the-ordinary is going to happen, like the system operator (sysop) coming on and doing system maintenance while you watch. I've had that happen to me more than once. In fact, there was one week in which it happened twice.

When I was in high school there was one day near the end of September that I was sick, so I was staying home from school. Instead of rushing off to the bus stop, I was on my computer, dialing BBSs. The first day I was sick, I had just finished logging onto a system and was about to read my e-mail when the sysop interrupted. "I have to do something real fast," he typed, "and I'm late for school." Then he went about doing whatever it was he had to do. He went into the back screens of the bulletin board system program, then shelled out to his hard drive, and came back in again. He was doing everything so fast I couldn't keep track of what was going on, but later, after I'd logged off, I was able to go through the file I'd made of the event, and analyze it thoroughly. The information I learned from watching that sysop fix his system did not help me break in anywhere, but it taught me more about how telecommunication systems work. And that's the whole purpose of hacking.

A few mornings later, I was on another system and almost the same thing happened. Another sysop was late to an appointment, but before he went he just had to do some last minute rearranging. This time I was able to understand as I watched what was going on: one of the things the sysop did was to validate a new user's password (a dumb thing to do in front of somebody, but maybe he didn't realize I could see what he was typing). Since I was capturing the event in a text file as I watched it, there was no need for me to scramble for a pen to write down the passwords as I saw them scroll across my screen.

An alternative to data capture is to have your printer running continuously. There are people who do this, but it's always seemed to me to be a complete waste of ink, paper, time (especially if you have a slow printer) and electricity. Also, a printer won't be as efficient as your communications program at capturing strange control codes and foreign symbols. You're better off capturing data in files, then using a word processor to sort through those files, erase what you don't need, and then perhaps print out the rest.

Past and Future

As you read about the many facets of hacking, you will be introduced to more equipment, tools, software and hardware that will be of interest to hackers who wish to try their expertise in more specialized areas of interest. For now though, all you need is the understanding that...

Days Of Yore Live On

When you start reading through the literature of data security, you begin to get worried.

Gone, it seems, are the days of "Joshua doors" as in the movie *WarGames*. Gone are the system bugs and loopholes, the naively entered "PASSWORD" used as a password. Gone, *it seems*, is the reverent awe people once held for the lone hacker, cracking secret government databases in the middle of the night. Gone are the *lone* hackers.

It seems.

But all of this really isn't true! As recently as just a few years ago, Robert Morris, Jr., was hacking into computers using system bugs that he himself had discovered. These weren't even new bugs — they were old ones that no one had ever noticed or bothered to correct before! Who knows how many more similar bugs like it are out there, waiting to be manipulated? And the trap doors will always be there as well: it is the programmer's vanity that leads him to stylize otherwise joint or corporate software by inserting covert code, either for benign, "jokey," Easter Eggs purposes — or to wreak havoc later on.[1]

And don't forget all the stupidity: the test accounts and demo modes, the default security

---

[1] An Easter Egg in the computing sense is some unexpected, secret thing you can do with a piece of software that the programmer put in but doesn't tell anyone about.

measures that nobody bothers to delete or change. In July 1987, a bunch of Chaos Computer Club members hacked their way through the network, from an entry in Europe, to NASA's SPAN system (Space Physics Analysis Network). These crackers exploited a flaw in the VMS infrastructure which DEC Corporation had announced was remedied three months earlier. There must be hundreds of VAX computers still out there, still running the faulty parts of the operating system. Even with the patch in place, the Chaos members reportedly were laughing themselves silly over the often trivial passwords used to "protect" the system. Some of the passwords were taken straight from the manufacturer's manuals! On the one hand we have a top secret VAX 11/785 computer with the full power of NASA to protect it; but on the other hand there are approximately four thousand users of that computer. *Never* can you get 4,000 people together and still keep secrets hushed up.

Hacking may seem harder than ever before, but it really is not. The *culture* may have gotten more security-aware, but the individual user still lives in a world of benign indifference, vanity, user-friendliness and friendly-userness. Users who are in-the-know will always want to help the less fortunate ones who are not. Those who aren't will seek the advice of the gurus. And so Social Engineering and Reverse Social Engineering live on, as you shall discover within these pages.

Ease of use will always rule. The "dumb" password will be a good guess for a long time to come. After all, people just don't choose "6Fk%8l0(@vbM-34trwX51" for their passwords!

Add to this milieu the immense number of computer systems operating today, and the staggering multitudes of inept users who run them. In the past, computers were only used by the techno-literate few. Now they are bought, installed, used, managed, and even programmed by folks who have a hard time getting their bread to toast light brown. I'm not downgrading them — I applaud their willingness to step into unfamiliar waters. I just wish (sort of) that they would *realize* what danger they put themselves in every time they act without security in mind.

It is a simple and observable fact that most computer systems aren't secure. If this isn't clear now, it certainly will be once you've read a few chapters of this book. Ironically, many of the peo-ple who operate computer installations *understand* that there is a problem with system security; they just don't do anything about it. It seems incredibly naive, but it's true.

There are lots of reasons why companies don't increase computer security. Publicly or privately, they say things like:

- Extra security decreases the sense of openness and trust which we've strived to develop.
- Security is too much of a nuisance.
- Extra security just invites hackers who love a challenge.
- It would be too costly or difficult to patch existing security loopholes.
- The reprogramming could open up new security problems.
- We've never had a security problem before!
- The information we have here is not important to anyone but ourselves; who would try to break in here?
- But we just *had* a security breach; surely they won't come back!
- Didn't all those computer hackers grow up and go on to better things?

There are different reasons why each of these statements is either wholly or partially incorrect. The last one is certainly false as any reader of this book should be quick to point out. Computer hacking (as well as the misuse of computers) will always be a contemporary issue because of the great value computers have in our daily lives.

Some of these sayings also have their validity. In any case, the people who run computer installations (call them sysops, system managers, computer operators or whatever) very often believe in these things, and so the window of opportunity is left open. With a little work we can often ride the breeze inside.

Computer Crime

I would love to honestly be able to say that computer crime does not exist in the world — but I can't, because it does. When you're talking about the bad stuff that people do with computers, hacking truly is at the bottom of the list, and it certainly is the farthest removed from traditional crimes — things like murder and burglary which we feel in our hearts are wrong. True hacking is victimless, so it is in my way of thinking only vaguely a crime. Perhaps it is immoral or wrong, but there is much worse that can be done.

Computer crimes come in seven basic categories, all of which are related to the concept of "hacking" in some way. The seven categories are financial theft, sabotage, hardware theft, software theft, information theft, and electronic espionage. The seventh "crime" is computer hacking.

Stealing Money

Financial theft occurs when computer records are altered to misappropriate money. This is often done by programming the computer to route money into a particular bank account, usually by the use of a salami technique.

A salami technique is a method used to steal small sums of money over a long period of time, with the assumption that such small sums won't be missed. The criminal reprograms the computer at a bank or some other financial institution so that fractions of pennies will be given to a dummy account.

For instance an account might hold $713.14863, where the "863" occurs because of the multiplication involved to figure interest rates. Normally the computers would say this person has $713.15 in the bank, rounding up the 4 to a 5. However, a computer programmed with salami in mind would slice off those extra digits and put them into a separate account. Now the person may only have $713.14 in the account, but who's going to notice or complain about a missing penny?

The computer is not generating new money, it's only shifting valid money to an invalid account. This can make salami thefts hard to detect. Once the criminal's account has grown big enough on those fractions of pennies, he or she can withdraw the money and most likely will get away with the crime. Many thieves have tried this form of bank robbery, and many have been caught, but dozens or hundreds of such operations could be going on today without anyone's knowledge (or so the "experts" claim).

The way investigators check to see if a salami technique is being used is to have the computer make a list of all accounts, and how many times per day over a period of days a transaction has occurred with that account. Next, any account that is accessed an exorbitant number of times per day is checked to see how much money each of these transactions represent. If it's tiny sums, someone's up to something!

While I don't condone such thievery, I feel obligated to point out where computer criminals have gone wrong in the past and how to avoid future mishaps. Instead of reprogramming the computer to immediately transfer those fractions of pennies to an account, they would have been wiser to simply subtract the amounts and keep track of how much money is collected in an area separate from the account files. Then, the portions of code which print out total bank holdings should be altered to include that hidden figure in its summation, so those minuscule amounts aren't missed. Once the figure reaches a certain point (for instance, some random value over one hundred or two hundred dollars) only *then* should it be transferred to the thief's account. I say some "random" value so every transaction on the thief's account won't be exactly the same and thus suspicious.

Such thievery requires access to a computer; usually these crimes are committed by employees of the institution at which the crime occurred, and so true hacking is not necessary. However, when an employee with limited computer access or a complete outsider pulls off a financial theft, computer hacking will surely be involved.

Sabotage

Computer sabotage is the physical destruction of computer hardware or firmware, or the tampering or erasure of information stored on a computer. The point of sabotage may be to force a competitor out of business, or, as is sometimes done with arson, to get the insurance money. Computer hacking has only limited involvement with sabotage, since it is the goal of most hackers to keep computers secure, not to destroy them. Still, sometimes sabotage does creep into hacking in limited ways. Reverse social engineering uses what is called sabotage, but it is actually just a bit of tomfoolery used to get a computer to temporarily misbehave. You will read about reverse social engineering later on.

Computer vandals frequently sabotage the information stored on computers after first using hacker's methods to gain entry to them. Vandals should not be confused with hackers, however.

Neither should those folks who introduce incorrect or misleading data into a computer system, or otherwise sabotage the data stored therein. An illustration of such data tampering is given by Thomas Whiteside in his book *Computer Capers* (Crowell, 1978). Between 1968 and 1972 the FBI planted false adverse information on radicals and other people who had wild political views into the computers of credit reporting agencies, "the idea being to harass those citizens by making it difficult, if not impossible, for them to obtain loans or other forms of credit." For all we know various agencies may be continuing this practice. Want your own file verified for accuracy? Hacker to the rescue!

Various Thieveries

Hardware theft is either the stealing of the actual computer or its peripherals, but it can also include the piracy of a computer's internal design. It is related to hacking in that stolen or "borrowed" hardware may be used to procure access codes. In the case of design piracy, a hacker might clandestinely monitor the private e-mail and other computer files of a hardware designer in an effort to steal innovative ideas.

Software theft or piracy is the unauthorized copying of programs protected by copyright. Often hackers will make personal copies of software they find on a computer system, so they can learn how it was programmed and how it works. As with hardware piracy, there is also the aspect of wanting to get an edge on a competitor's new line of software, and so there is the hacking connection.

Information theft may include stolen credit card numbers, TRW reports, new product specs, lab results, patient or client data, or any other data that might be potentially valuable. Electronic espionage occurs when that information is sold to a third party, making the hacker a spy for either another country or company. In both cases hacker techniques are used to steal the information, and possibly even to make contact with the spy agency in the first place.

The Seventh Crime

Finally, there is hacking. Hackers have the ability to do any of the above, but they choose not to.

Read that again carefully, and see if you can detect the paradox.

The person who perpetrates the seventh of seven computer crimes — hacking — has just been described as a person who chooses *not to commit any crimes* at all.

Of course, there is that small matter of illegally breaking into other people's computers *before* that choice is made. But we conveniently disregard that because we don't see any harm in the simple act of "breaking in."

Where other computer crimes are concerned, motivations are obvious. It is obvious why a person would steal a computer, or engage in a financial crime, or a crime of vengeance.

But with pure hacking, essentially a peaceful, harmless act, motivations might not be as apparent.

The traditional motivation for a hacker was the quest for knowledge. But nowadays that quest may be ruled by higher motives — like money. There are hackers who see their talent not as a hobby, but as a trade. In fact, there are a number of both moral and immoral reasons one would provide one's hacking services for a fee. Before we get further into the How's of hacking, let's take a brief look at the Why's.

Hacker Motivations

The IRS has a bad reputation — and it *deserves* it. Sure, they pretend to play fair (I have a friend who received a refund check from the IRS for one cent; so apparently they can be honest at times), they pretend to do things in our interest, but underneath it all they do a lot of cheating, conniving things.

For instance, the IRS has a computer selection program called the Discriminate Function System. DFS is a system used by the IRS to select over 80 percent of the income tax returns which will be audited. When the DFS selects a return for audit, it is because the program believes there is a high probability the citizen made improper deductions, or hasn't reported all income, or for some other reason believes the filer has lied.

Now, as citizens of the United States, we are entitled to know all the laws and regulations of our country, right? Not so, according to the IRS. The decision-making formula (algorithm) used by the

DFS to select which returns will be audited is kept secret from us (so we can never really know to what extent an action of ours breaks the IRS's return-selection laws).

It seems logical and fitting for the IRS to not reveal this secret, because doing so prevents a lot of fraud. But it also restricts our rights, and several years ago, two outraged citizens sued the IRS to reveal their selection formula. The citizens won and the IRS was ordered to reveal the formula. The IRS was not ready to reveal their secrets, and they appealed their way up to the Supreme Court and *still* lost in favor of the Freedom of Information Act.

But since the IRS is a crying, whining, wily baby, they refused to obey the court orders, and ran to Congress for help. Congress, of course, immediately enacted a statute which made the IRS's audit selection algorithm immune to the Freedom of Information Act.

Now, I ask you: Can you think of a better reason to hack than to get back at the IRS? I'm sure that someday some hacker will surreptitiously stroll into the IRS's computers and make off with their Discriminate Function System, and publicize it widely for all to see and file by.[2]

Even if that doesn't happen, and even if that's not a hacker's main goal (which I wouldn't expect it to be), there are plenty of motivations from which to choose.

Dissemination of information is always an honorable incentive to hack. According to Tom Forester and Perry Morrison in their book on computer ethics (listed in the bibliography), following the Chernobyl nuclear disaster, hackers in the Chaos Computer Club "released more information to the public about developments than did the West German government itself. All of this information was gained by illegal break-ins carried out in government computer installations." Certainly that was a noble and just act on their part, from our point of view.

---

[2] This has already happened in Australia. A computer professional working for the Australian Taxation Commission wrote up a guide to the confidential computer program which the commission used to determine the legitimacy of a taxpayer's income tax form. Taxpayers could use his guide to safely overstate the amount of deductions they claimed.

Hackers also see themselves as preventers of disasters — computer disasters that is. There have been several recent examples of computer security companies from all over the world putting their security products to the test. They did this by publicizing a phone number hackers could call to try to beat the system. Sure this is done for advertising hype, but it is also a good idea, and it gives hackers a chance to do some computer cracking in a benign setting.

Hackers who maintain a high degree of virtue will use their illegal hacking to prevent disasters. Once they have discovered (and misused) a security loophole in a system, they will warn the system operator of that fact. Hackers are thus beneficial to the world in that they act to keep the world informed and secured.

But we can only be assured of these traits if the hackers themselves conform to ethical behavior. Unfortunately, due to the exciting/risky/devilish nature of hacking, the people involved are often immature and play around in juvenile activities such as vandalism and carding (mail ordering stuff on other people's credit cards). These are the sorts of activities that True Hackers should strive NOT to be associated with, as they degrade the word "hacker."

Many hackers, even some very good hackers, have done their part to give hacking a bad name by having skewed motivations. There have been plenty of destructive hackers, and those who just did not know when to quit.

There are also hackers-for-hire. Private citizens are willing to pay hackers to change computerized information for them — grades, ratings, bills, access levels. Or there are the people who want information about themselves deleted from the record, because they are in hiding. Private investigators can always use the skills of the hacker to find addresses and phone numbers, credit ratings, and other private concerns of clients and suspects which are contained on computers. Office workers have hired hackers to scope out the personal electronic mail and files of coworkers and competitors, to gain an edge when making a proposal or a bid. There is not only industrial, but governmental espionage. All of the above has been done and is being done RIGHT NOW, by hackers who hack for money.

Hackers tend to look down on other hackers who fall into this line of work. Maybe a once-in-a-while job is okay, but to do it extensively and exclusively is to sell out one's integrity.

I like to think that all people reading this book, and all hackers, will use their talents to good ends: to promote public awareness, prevent tragedy, and to learn new technologies and new innovations for one's own self-growth.

Chapter Two:
The History of Hacking

First Came Hardware

Where does one begin a history of hacking?

Do we start with the creation of the computer, by J. Presper Eckert and John Mauchly? During World War II this pair of engineer and physicist approached the US Army with a proposal for an electronic device that would speedily calculate gunnery coordinates — a job that was then tediously being done by hand. With the government backing their way, the Electronic Numerical Integrator And Calculator (ENIAC) was born in 1946. It was a year after the war's end — the machine's designed function was now superfluous — but the dream behind its imagined future uses lived on.

Of course, the origin of the computer — the *computer* for god's sake — the most revolutionary invention since the telephone, can not be so easily summed up in a tidy paragraph of wartime patriotic stupor. The real story goes back further, to Konrad Zuse, whose patent for a general-purpose electromechanical relay computer in 1938 was turned down by the Patent Office as being not spe-

cific enough. It may have been ENIAC that spawned the next generation of computers, but ENIAC was a one-task machine. Zuse's contraption had the feel of modernity to it: a machine that would do... *anything*.

But is that where hacking began? Certainly not. The longing to do... *anything* has been in the human psyche for ages. Perhaps we should begin with the revolutionary creation of the telephone, culminating with Alexander Graham Bell's historic "accident" on March 10, 1876. The telephone was not an immediate best seller. After all, you couldn't simply buy one and place it in your house and use it. Lines had to be installed. Networks had to be created to link home to home, business to business, and finally, state to neighboring state. Almost thirty years of growth for the phone to spread throughout the country.

YIPL and *TAP*

So, there was the telephone, there was the computer, and there was an undaunted inquisitiveness in the collective human subconscious. It took another war to shake that curious imagination loose onto the world, and on May Day, 1971, the *Youth International Party Line* became the newsletter of the fun-seeking, disenfranchised riffraff of New York City's Greenwich Village. Abbie Hoffman and a phone phreak who went by the handle Al Bell used *YIPL* to disburse information about cracking the phone network. It was the first instance of subversive information of its kind finding a wide audience. Subscriptions to the journal spread the word of this arm of the underground far away from Bleecker Street to people of all walks of life. Today this distribution would be done by computer, and indeed, a great deal of hacker/phreaker/anarchist material surfs around the world on the invisible waves of cyberspace.

A few years after *YIPL's* inception, it became *TAP — Technological Assistance Program —* when the goals of the phreaks collided with the more politically-minded members of *YIPL*. *TAP* was more technical than partisan, and more suited for hackers and their kin.

Computer Crime

The first recorded computer abuse, according to Donn B. Parker, a frequent writer on computer crime, occurred in 1958. The first federally prosecuted crime identified specifically as a *computer* crime involved an alteration of bank records by computer in Minneapolis in 1966. Computers were not so widespread then as they are now, and the stakes weren't quite so high. It's one thing to have money controlled and kept track of via computer; it's quite another to have *power* controlled in this way. In 1970, many criminology researchers were stating that the problem of computer crime was merely a result of a new technology and not a topic worth a great deal of thought. Even in the mid-1970s, as crimes by computer were becoming more frequent and more costly, the feeling was that the machines themselves were just a part of the environment, and so they naturally would become a component of crime in some instances. It doesn't matter if a burglar carries his loot in a pillow case or a plastic bag — why should the props of the crime determine the way in which criminologists think about the case?

This was an unfortunate mode of thought for those charged with preventing computer crimes, because while research stagnated, the criminals, crackers and hackers were actively racking their brains to come up with more ingenious methods of doing things with computers they were not supposed to be able to do. The criminologists could not have realized then that the computer really was an integral part of the crime, and that the existence of these machines — and the systems built around them — led to whole new areas of crime and thinking about crime that had never before been explored.

Lawmakers and enforcers, however, finally did sit up and take notice. In 1976 two important developments occurred. The FBI established a 4-week training course for its agents in the investigation of computer crime (and followed it up with a second course for other agencies in 1978). Also in 1976, Senator Abraham Ribicoff and his U.S. Senate Government Affairs Committee realized that something big was going on, and it was important for the government to get in on it. The committee produced two research reports and Ribicoff introduced the first Federal Systems Protection Act Bill in June, 1977. These reports eventually became the Computer Fraud and Abuse Act of 1986. Florida, Michigan, Colorado, Rhode Island, and Arizona were some of the first states to have computer crime legislation, based on the Ribicoff bills that had developed into the 1986 Act.

A year before, a major breakthrough was announced at the Securicom Conference in Cannes by a group of Swedish scientists who had invented a method of silently eavesdropping on a computer screen from a far-off distance. But let's save this story for later. Much later.

2600

Tom Edison and Cheshire Catalyst, two phone phreaks who had been interested in the nether side of technology for ages, took over *TAP* in the late '70s. The journal came to an end before its time in 1983 when Tom Edison's New Jersey condominium burned to the ground, the victim of a professional burglary and an amateurish arson. The burglars had gotten all of Tom's computer equipment, the stuff from which *TAP* was born. The arson, perhaps an attempt to cover the burglary, did not succeed. It was a sloppy fire, one which Tom and Cheshire hypothesized had been engineered by some irate phone company officer. A few months later, the original *TAP* printed its final issue. The following year, in 1984, hacker Eric Corley (aka Emmanuel Goldstein) filled the void with a new publication: *2600 Magazine*. Ironically, Goldstein is more a rhetorician than a hacker, and the magazine is less technical and more political (like the original *YIPL*).

Networks were being formed all over, enabling hackers to not only hack more sites but to exchange information among themselves quicker and more easily. Who needs published magazines? The City University of New York and Yale University joined together as the first BITNET (Because It's Time NETwork) link in May 1981. Now there are networks of networks (such as Internet) connecting the globe, putting all hackers and common folk in direct communication with one another.

WarGames and *Phrack*

A hacker named Bill Landreth was indicted for computer fraud in 1983, and convicted in 1984 of entering such computer systems as GTE Tele-mail's electronic mail network, and reading the NASA and Department of Defense correspondence within. Naughty boy! His name will come up again. 1983 also saw the release of *WarGames*, and all hell broke loose. Certainly there had been plenty of hacker activity before the movie came out, but previous to *WarGames* those hackers were few in number and less visible. The exciting story of David Lightman (played by Matthew Broderick), a school-age whiz kid who nearly starts World War III, became the basis for many modems for Christmas presents that year. Suddenly there was a proliferation of people on the hacking scene who were not really hackers in expertise or spirit. Bulletin board systems flourished, and a large number of boards catering to hackers, phreaks, warez d00ds (software pirates), anarchists, and all manner of restless youth sprung up.

The online publication *Phrack* was founded on November 17, 1985, on the Metal Shop Private BBS in St. Louis, Missouri, operated by Taran King and Knight Lightning. The term "online" referred to the fact that this magazine was distributed, not at newsstands and through the mails, but on the "news racks" of electronic bulletin board systems, where collections of files are available for the taking. Later, when the journal's founders went off to college and received Internet access, the publication was distributed through list servers which can automatically e-mail hundreds of copies of the publication throughout the world. *Phrack* is still distributed in this way. As the name implies, *Phrack* deals with PHReaking and hACKing, but it also is pleased to present articles on any sort of mischief-making. Annual conventions, hosted by *Phrack*, called SummerCons, are now held in St. Louis.

Shadow Hawk

Bill Landreth, who had been arrested in 1983, was let out on parole and there are reports of his mysterious disappearance following publication of his guide to computer security called *Out of the Inner Circle*. He left a note stating that he would commit suicide "sometime around my 22nd birthday..." There was much discussion about all this. Was it a publicity stunt, or for real? Eventually Landreth reappeared in Seattle, Washington, in July, 1987, and he was hastily carted back to jail for breaking probation.

The month before — on the anniversary of D-Day — a cracker named Shadow Hawk (also identified by some press reports as Shadow Hawk 1) had been discovered by an AT&T security agent to be bragging on a Texas BBS called Phreak Class-2600 about how he had hacked AT&T's computer system. Shadow Hawk (really Herbert Zinn of Chicago) was an 18-year-old high school dropout when he was arrested. He'd managed to get the FBI, the Secret Service, the Defense Criminal Investigative Service and the Chicago U.S. attorney on his tail for not only the above mentioned hack, but also for invading computers belonging to NATO and the US Air Force, and stealing a bit over $1 million worth of software. Shadow Hawk's case is important because in 1989 he became the first person to be prosecuted under the Computer Fraud and Abuse Act of 1986.

Shadow Hawk is just one example of how this hobby has gotten people in trouble with the law. Around this time there were a lot of hackers being brought down by all manner of cops: security officers for the telephone companies and other organizations, the FBI, local police and concerned citizens. This was the time when the investigators got smart. Not that they suddenly knew more about computers and hacking, but now they understood that to catch a lion, one must step into its den. These police agents started logging onto hacker BBSs and amassed huge dossiers on the people who normally used those boards. Many warnings were issued, and many arrests were made.

In August, 1986, Cliff Stoll first set out to find out why there was a 75¢ imbalance in the computer accounts at the Lawrence Berkeley Laboratory in California. Stoll's efforts led to the discovery of a group of German hackers who had broken into the computer system. In October, 1989, a book about Stoll's exploits called *The Cuckoo's Egg* was published and became an instant best seller.

Organized and independent hacker activity continued for the next few years with little public interest. There were threats in early 1988 by the West Berlin Chaos Computer Club that they would trigger Trojan horses they had implanted into NASA's Space Physics Analysis Network, thus causing the chaos of their name. The threats never materialized but minor havoc was wrought anyway, as many computers were temporarily pulled from the net until the threat could be analyzed.

The end of 1988 — November 2, to be exact — marked the beginning of a new surge in anti-hacker sentiment. It was then that Robert Morris Jr.'s computer worm began its race through the Internet. Exploiting an undocumented bug in the **sendmail** program and utilizing its own internal arsenal of tricks, the worm would infiltrate a system and quickly eat up most or all of the system's processing capabilities and memory space as it squiggled around from machine to machine, net to net.

The Electronic Frontier Foundation

The birth of the Electronic Frontier Foundation was announced July 10, 1990. EFF is a group dedicated to protecting our constitutional rights; it was created as a response to a series of rude and uninformed blunderings by the Secret Service in the witch hunt known as Operation Sundevil. By May, 1989, this "hacker hunt" had led 150 Secret Service agents to serve 28 search warrants in 14 cities. They seized 23,000 disks and 42 computers, often for inappropriate reasons. E-mail was left undelivered. Public postings never made it to the screens of the computer community. Many innocent bystanders (as well as criminals) were arrested.

John Perry Barlow (author, retired cattle rancher, and a lyricist for the Grateful Dead), and computer guru Mitch Kapor, best known for writing Lotus 1-2-3, were outraged by these events (and by their own run-ins with the FBI over stolen source code that was being distributed by the NuPrometheus League). They teamed up with attorney Harvey Silverglate who was known for taking on offbeat causes. Some yellow journalism by the *Washington Post* provided the publicity needed to attract Steve Wozniak (co-founder of Apple) and John Gilmore (of Sun Microsystems) who offered monetary support for the enterprise.

It was at this point that the Steve Jackson incident made the headlines. An Austin, Texas, publisher of role-playing games, Jackson's business was raided by the Secret Service because one of his games, called *GURPS Cyberpunk*, had to do with a kind of futuristic computer hacking. The Secret Service called Jackson's game "a handbook for computer crime." This was ludicrous, akin to arresting Milton Bradley because they sell Chess, which teaches kids how to wage war.

Jackson's office equipment was confiscated, he was forced to lay off half his staff, and he very nearly went into bankruptcy. "Eventually," Jackson later wrote, "we got most of our property back (though some of it was damaged or destroyed). The Secret Service admitted that we'd never been a target of their investigation." Jackson sued the U.S. government (the Secret Service, two of its agents, and a Bellcore official were named in the suit) on charges that the Secret Service had violated his right to free speech during the office raid. Justice prevailed and the SS was held guilty. Jackson has since made a role-playing game about the incident.

The summer of 1990 was filled with all sorts of similar surprises. There are the famous stories, the infamous ones, and the ones that barely made the back page. In the middle of August, thirteen New York young adults and minors were charged with felonies involving computer tampering, computer trespassing, and theft of services. They had broken into the Pentagon's computers, among others, and got a whole load of law enforcers on their tail. $50,000 worth of computing equipment was seized, said to have been used by the hackers to do the break-ins. Dozens of stories like this were reported then quickly faded. Other tales and other hackers held more interest, like Acid Phreak and Phiber Optik, who became "celebrity hackers," speaking on behalf of the hacker community for various media. Phiber Optik was eventually arrested and sentenced to thirty-five hours of community service in February, 1991.

And the Craig M. Neidorf story made headlines. We have already mentioned Neidorf (Knight Lightning) as one of the co-founders of *Phrack*. Neidorf published an (edited) internal BellSouth paper in *Phrack* and was quickly charged with interstate transport of stolen property, with a possible sentence of 60 years in jail and $122,000 in fines. What was particularly absurd was that the document was easily and legally available (though BellSouth declared it to be full of company secrets), and it talked about the BellSouth bureaucracy as it pertained to 911 lines. Sixty years in jail for copyright infringement?

The EFF helped Neidorf through these troubled times (as they'd helped Steve Jackson, and would come to aid many hackers and crackers who'd been treated unfairly or with ignorance by the law). The U.S. dropped its case against Neidorf at the end of July, 1990.

There are dozens or hundreds of stories about hackers every year, and there have been for quite some time. Some are quickly forgotten; others provoke controversy. Such was the case on November 6, 1992, when a group of hackers, peacefully convening in the food court of the Pentagon City Mall outside Washington, D.C., were bullied and manhandled by mall security personnel, Secret Service and FBI agents.

Hacking has had a long past and will continue to enjoy a prosperous and successful future because of people like us who enjoy seeing what secrets are out in the world, waiting to be unearthed.

Chapter Three:
Researching The Hack

Any serious hack will involve some preparatory research long before the hacker sets foot near a computer. This is simply because to hack intelligently, one must have knowledge of certain facts and ideas.

With computer hacking, you should obviously have some knowledge about computers and telecommunications (ideas) but to actually carry out a hack requires just one fact: a phone number. Or if not a phone number, at least one way of accessing a computer. Either case requires some research. Once you've called the computer for the first time, some *on-line* research is required to tell you how you should proceed with the hack. And finally, there is the ongoing research you will do once you've gained access to a system, to help you make full use of the facilities you've conquered. The "after research" is discussed in the chapter "What To Do When Inside." For now, let us discuss what to do to get started.

Targeting

By targeting, I'm referring to the process by which a hacker will decide which of all possible computer installations to attempt to breach. This may seem like a trivial topic for many reasons, but in fact it is a topic well worth discussing.

Let's suppose you are a rookie at this game. You have gotten — through research of some kind, or just plain luck — a piece of information you feel will be helpful in entering a specific system. For example, suppose you've discovered through the computer crime grapevine the phone number of a large governmental espionage database. Naturally, it seems reasonable to call the number and see if it actually is what you've heard it to be. On the other hand, it might be better to first research your target to see if it's worth the time and the risk, and the phone bill. Look up the number in a criss-cross telephone directory for that region. Criss-cross directories, which are available at many libraries, are books (usually non-licensed by the phone company) which list the names and addresses that go with phone numbers. Unlike regular phone books, criss-cross directories are sorted by *number* rather than name. If you can't get this sort of directory, call the operator and ask who the number belongs to. Naturally it is preferable to use a directory on your own, eliminating extraneous interaction with phone company employees ("witnesses"). If the phone number is publicly available, it probably isn't a computer line after all, let alone a secret one.

It may seem crazy to you to go out of your way to look up a number before dialing it, but remember, it is important to get as much information as you can about a system before you make the first call. If it really is a top-secret database, it's reasonable to assume that your call will be traced, or at the very least, will arouse suspicion. As a novice one tends to get excited with one's first big break — and tends to do stupid, dangerous things. You may not yet have the expertise to alter phone company data, or call from a pay phone, or in some other way make it seem like you are not the person placing the call. The rookie who calls a number of this kind after doing a bit of research might be taking a stupid risk, but that's a few steps higher on the professional hacker's scale than the one who calls without any preparation at all. That's just being stupid, period.

So, as far as targeting is concerned, you may not want to follow up that first big lead right away. It may be preferable to wait awhile, until you have the expertise to do it properly. If you know something about a system no one else knows, it's very likely going to remain a secret unless you spill the beans. If you try to act on your inside knowledge and fail, you are ruining your chances of getting in later, as the system managers might see their mistakes and correct them.

My word of caution is this: Don't get in over your head. Get familiar with floating on your back before trying to scuba dive for sunken treasure or else you may end up being the one who's sunk.

Targeting also involves other research. What if you do have some exciting secret that will let you get in somewhere? Perhaps you should think about the best way of reaching that system in the first place. For instance, if the system you're stalking is on the Internet, you would have to determine a way to access the Internet disguised as someone else before you could proceed to your main goal.

If you are enrolled at a college, or live near one and have access to your own Internet computer account, it is a trifling matter to log in as yourself and, from there, attempt to connect to other systems. It's not only trifling — it's dumb! Regardless of whether you have mischief in mind,

it's irresponsible and lazy to do hacking logged in as yourself. Before you can move out of the few directories allowed by your minimal access level, you will have to figure out a way to disassociate yourself with what you do. That is — and I can't repeat it enough — you will have to find a way to connect as somebody else, and through that connection go on to bigger things.

Breaking into major league computer systems is very often a matter of, first, personal hacking, and second, institutional hacking. That is, first you hack a person (figure out a way of masquerading as that person), and then you hack the institution (figure out a way of disguising that person as a legitimate user of the protected system).

Time, money and effort can be spent needlessly on attempts to access systems that ultimately turn out to be dead ends. Maybe your target is a school's computer, because you want to change your grade from an F to A. You may think your target individual would be the dean or some other school head, but as it turns out, in many instances you would be wrong. School heads often have little or no access to the computers which hold grades, unless they themselves teach classes. In this case you would want to target a professor or more likely, a teaching assistant (T.A.). They're the ones who have to do the actual inputting of grades. Consequently you would want to research the professor or T.A. to get a handle on what their passwords might be.

Then there's the matter of the computer. Which computer should you target for your hack? Teachers, especially in math and computer science courses, will usually tell you their computer address so you can send them e-mail. But that isn't necessarily where you need to go to change your grade. More likely there is some hush-hush administrative computer which carries out those functions, and it is that computer you would want to hack.

It seems logical to assume that the president of a university has the highest level of computer access. But does he or she really? Does the president actually have a computer account AT ALL? You're probably better off targeting individual professors. One English teacher I had mentioned Kojak a couple times in class, and on several occasions made references to things that could be interpreted as having some relation to that television show (sometimes he would use phrases that Kojak used in the series). Obviously, Kojak is the place to start if one is interested in forcing one's way into this guy's account (especially since he's an English professor, and therefore less likely to understand the value of non-real-word passwords). And trying Kojak-related words like "Telly Savalas," "lollipop," "bald," for passwords is the obvious way of personally targeting that English teacher's account.

But is he REALLY the one you want to use in the first place? If I had been failing that class and wanted to get into his account to change my grade, Kojak wouldn't have helped me; as far as I was ever able to determine, it was the teaching assistants who had control over the grading, not the professors! This is why it's necessary to target in order to achieve your intended purposes. If you have goals in mind, do the necessary research to find out if you are targeting the right PEOPLE, as well as the right computers.

Potential targets can often be found by reading publicly available documents about a site. Documents pertaining to "ethical use" of the system, and articles encouraging "preventative security" are often particularly enlightening. For instance, here's a little quote I picked up from an outdated memorandum about security policies. This is one suggestion taken from a list of what was felt to be necessary improvements in security. By the time I read the article the improvements had already taken place, but thoughts of needing security were long gone from the minds of those who had written the memorandum, and so security was lax. Here's the one suggestion from the list that stuck out:

Net 19 must be isolated completely by gateways from PCs and from the broadband. Terminal server logins must be strictly enforced on all machines. PCs should be implemented which will run software that will monitor the network for signs of misuse and/or unethical usage.

Look at the goldmine of information that is given here. We have these suggestions for improvement, so now it should be a simple task to determine which software was purchased to implement the suggestions. From there we can see what the software will and will not do, find out about bugs or loopholes, and use other means to discover ways around that software. But most interesting of all (and the point that is related to this discussion of

targeting) is the mention of "Net 19." What is Net 19? Obviously it is something that the administration wants to go out of their way to protect. Clearly it's something well worth hacking. If you had been the hacker to first read these words, clearly Net 19 would be the target of your hack.

Keep in mind that I read this document from a public terminal, without having to log in as anybody. It was accessed from a public information system. It is information available to anybody, and look at the wonderful clue it holds for all who see it! Now, when I read this I didn't know what Net 19 was, but I knew immediately to target all efforts to finding that system and penetrating its security. This is an example of accidentally found knowledge being put to good use. But don't forget — I was reading through every publicly available document for the SOLE PURPOSE of breaking into the system. The specific bit of information I found was accidental, but my finding it wasn't.

In a way, doing this kind of on-line research — exploring every inch of the system available to you before going after the private regions — is a kind of targeting. If your goal is a specific private computer system, target all public systems related to it before you begin. This can only help you in the long run. It might lead to helpful hints, such as the mention of Net 19, or it might at least familiarize you with various aspects of the system.

Things you should be looking for when you target a public system in this way, with the intent of going after a correlated private system, are: how it handles input and output; if any bugs are present and how the system reacts to them; what the command format is (three letters? control sequence?) and what kinds of commands are available; and machine specifications and hardware. Of course, there are numerous other things you should either be looking for, or will unconsciously be picking up anyway as you look around, like what the visual display is like and how long it takes the computer to process commands. These are things that will be helpful later on, because when you actually are trespassing, you won't want to spend hours trying to find the help command or how to log off.

Targeting may seem not just trivial, but distracting as well. After all, a scientist can analyze a rainbow using specific technical terms that explain what a rainbow is, how it is formed, and why it displays its colors as it does. But in a way, this complicated description of a rainbow is completely unrelated to the rainbow being described. The explanation ignores the beauty of it. The techno-jargon shuns the poetic connotations that we associate with the rainbow we are so interested in describing.

You may use similar arguments to complain that targeting and pre-thought and planning of hacking attacks distract from the pleasure of the hack itself. If you are a hired hacker you will need to get the job done if you expect to get paid. But otherwise, why should we bother to discipline ourselves with such nonsense as targeting? You're right! Certainly you're correct! There is no reason to feel obligated to apply these suggestions that I present. There is no pressing *need* to think carefully about what you do before you do it, but you should be aware of these things as you start. At least, if you break the rules, you should understand how following them might have helped.

Targeting specific computers that hold interest to you, and that you are sure hold the information you seek, and targeting people who have specific access levels and abilities — all of this is like analyzing a rainbow and ending up with nothing but gobbledygook. But in the long run, if you really want to end up at a position further from where you started, if you want to hack for the enjoyment of it and maintain high pleasure levels throughout the endeavor, I suggest you do these things. They will help lessen the amount of frivolous searching and brute-force monotony needed to get in, and will help you stay out of trouble. So, set up a general plan of action. Make sure the goals you've outlined are really the ones that apply to your case. That way you'll know that what you are hacking won't turn out to be a series of blind alleys.

I keep bringing up the point of "intentions," and "goals," but unless you're a private investigator or some sort of muckraker, you're probably willing and happy to break into any computer available — any and all opportunities that present themselves. This is fine too, and many hackers are so devoted (fanatical?) in their pursuits that even if they know a computer system will offer them nothing exciting once they get inside, they persevere because it is the thrill of the break-in itself that drives them.

But as you can well imagine, it is much more interesting to break into a system that holds secrets, than one whose contents are worthless to you. Is it worth it to spend months trying to get into a sys-

tem that contains statistics on the copulation patterns of lab rats? (Not unless you happen to have an interest in that sort of thing.) Choose your targets carefully. Getting into the system is half the fun; once you're inside, the other half can be more exciting.

Collecting Information

Before you begin researching you should know what kind of information you should be trying to find out. There are three topics a hacker should be concerned with: Telecommunications in general, computer systems in general, and specific systems.

There is a certain level of understanding you should have about computers, modems, the telephone and human nature. Hopefully this book will prepare you with most of the information in these categories that you will make use of. If not — and I readily admit this is not an all inclusive Bible of the Universe — then go around to some local or special libraries and find out what you need to know.

Maybe there isn't anything you specifically need to know. You will still want to keep up with the latest developments in technology as well as the organizations who run the computers you intend to hack. Even if you think you know everything there is to know, it can be most helpful to do a bit of reading to make sure you really are an expert in your field, especially when dealing with such rapidly changing fields as computer hardware, software and telecommunications

So go to your local library. Go to the shelves with the computer books, and the shelves with the criminal justice books, and the shelves with the business management books. That's where you'll find the "legit" books about hacking and computer crime. Every once in a while, take out some books on telecommunications and look through them. You want to start getting familiar with the various situations you'll be encountering, so look through books on the different information services, on-line databases, computer crime, operating systems, BBSs, and anything else that pertains to what you can do with a computer and a modem. Look up "telecommunications" in the card catalog. Also, "security," "computers," "hacking," "telephones," "modems," and anything else you can think of that's relevant. Also, remember to look through the books in the reference section; you will find the most useful materials there. Hacking is best learned by doing, but many good tricks and leads can be found in the literature.

By the way, do you know who the biggest book publisher in the world is? The United States government. If your library is a government depository, read through all the relevant government publications that interest you. You'll learn a lot from that stuff.

I'm not saying you should read every book in the library, and I'm certainly not saying you should read all this before you begin your hacking exploits. What I am saying is that very often people don't realize the wealth of information that is available to them free for the asking — no need to hack. And by reading these things you will get familiar with what different computer systems look like when you log onto them. You will get to know the kinds of commands that are available to you, and what formats the systems use for names and passwords. Also, you will often find toll free numbers listed in these books — lines you can call to test out various systems, or to get information on the systems. All this information will be helpful to you as you proceed.

While you're at the library go to the periodicals section and take out some computer magazines and newspapers. Borrow some that you don't normally read, or that you've never heard of before. It is useful to write away for information from the magazines, and to send in the Reader Service postcards to get free information. It's amazing what companies will send you, and it's further amazing to think about all the great tips this information offers to the hacker. I'm now on several perpetual mailing lists from various computer security companies. I know everything I need to know about all their products, their upgrades, what businesses use their software — and from that information, I can hack my way around their products. Knowing how they go about catching hackers, I know how to avoid getting caught.

Another, sometimes more practical way to use the library is to find out about donated books. Many libraries get donations of books, either for an annual book sale or for their shelves. A lot of those books are old technical and company manuals for computers, software, and operating system procedures. The librarians who deal with donated mate-

rials will probably look at this sort of thing and throw it out as useless. If you make friends with them, surely they would prefer giving such "useless" items to you, rather than discarding them. I've gotten many valuable guidebooks, reference guides, operating systems manuals, and disks this way. I even have a very nice and very current set of AT&T security books.

Sometimes the books you pick up have notes scribbled in the margins or on the cover. My favorite note was the one that gave a phone number and group ID access code. The access code had since been deleted, but the phone number still worked — and so did the sample visitor's password listed in that manual.

Some Unusual Research Methods

They aren't really all that unusual, because after all, anything that works — works! Any time you get an idea for a new way of discovering more about an online system or the people who run it you should do your best to act on that idea. In the long run every bit of data is potentially useful. Anything you manage to find will either help you get in your present target computer, or get in another one some time in the future.

Besides, it's always a delight to find confidential data or insider secrets about a system. Share that knowledge with other hackers and you will be rewarded with interesting tips that will be beneficial to you.

Here are five further research methods: online computer simulators and tutorials; sorting through trash; found disk analysis; examining screenshots; and snooping. Remember — these research methods *work*. Use them to your advantage.

Online Computer Simulators And Tutorials

Computer-based simulators and tutorials are often employed in teaching the ways of the company computer system. These programs mimic the computer screens users would see if they were to log in to the actual network. Tutorials and simulators differ from the actual network in that they talk the user through a typical use of the system, perhaps showing off special features available to the user. If the user isn't given a guided tour, there is often a workbook that is to be used with a scaled-down version of the actual system, often one with extensive help facilities to teach the new user the ropes.

Tutorials and simulators give new users hands-on experience with the problems and policies of software they will encounter. They are very often used for training purposes instead of the actual system, or as a supplement to it. There are several reasons for this. What if the system is still being installed, or undergoing a renovation? Or perhaps not enough terminals are connected yet for all employees to access the actual system. Using simulators eliminates these problems since they can be set up on any computer.

Temporary employment agencies may use software from a specific company to pretrain their workers, especially if the agency gets a lot of jobs from a specific company. Or regular employees may want the convenience of being able to borrow a tutorial disk from the company library to practice on at home. Finally, a good tutorial program or simulation can ensure that everyone receives the same quality instructions, without leaving out important details which a human instructor might forget to teach.

How to get them? Simulation programs may be available from corporate, special or even academic libraries. You may also get hold of one from the publisher. Write to a software publisher, saying you're interested in making a large purchase and ask if a demonstration disk is available. And you may be able to procure one from a friendly member of the company's computer department (do some social engineering[1] — pretend you're a company manager or supervisor).

Simulators and tutorials are great things for a hacker to come across; the usefulness of them should be self-evident. They will help you learn the systems, and perhaps reveal default entry-words, and might even come with descriptions of system bugs.

Sometimes you have to use your imagination to find other ways in which online simulators can help. I was waiting in an office one day to see someone. The receptionist stepped out for a moment and I stepped behind her desk and borrowed a computer disk I'd noticed stuck in a book. The disk held a program called ARRSIM (ARRangement SIMulator) which was actually a copy of a program they used on-line, only with a minuscule database of names. The program was used to teach employees how to use the computers to arrange and schedule meetings between customers and potential contractors.

When I got home I booted it up and started playing around. At one point I tried changing an address and the computer responded, "Supervisor Approval Required" and put a cursor on the screen. Apparently it wanted a password. I tried the one that was used to log into the simulator (which was scribbled on the disk label) but that didn't work. I scanned through the disk with a file maintenance utility, but could find no text (i.e., hidden password) that I had not already seen.

Now, it occurred to me that address changes were probably something that everyone had to do every once in a while. So why had it asked for a password when I tried to change an address? Obviously the program had been designed by your usual paranoid manager who did not trust a receptionist to change a name or address by herself.

So I called my favorite receptionist at the company, and after some suave insider gossip about company matters ("So Sheila's a grandma! Was it a boy or a girl?" I had heard her discussing this with a coworker the day I was there), I popped the question: "Gaye, do you know what to type when it says 'Supervisor App'—"

"Oh isn't that silly!" she laughed. "It's really horrible. Type 'morris.' I don't know why they have that there. Nobody's supposed to know about it but we use it every day!" I thanked her and — you know what? — 'morris' didn't work as a password on the simulator (I don't think anything did). But it *was* the password used to get into the actual network. Apparently only supervisors were supposed to be able to log on the terminals scattered throughout the offices.

---

[1] Social engineering is the act of talking to a system user, pretending that you are also a legal user of the system, and in the course of the conversation, manipulating the discussion so that the user reveals passwords or other good stuff.

Sorting Through Trash

It isn't really a dirty job, and nobody *has got* to do it, but serious investigators will. By "investigators" I refer to hackers who are researching a company or computer. It really isn't all that messy going through the garbage of most places. Often you'll find a separate bin for white paper. Some may be shredded, but mostly not. Try to plan your trips to the trash on days following a few days of sunny weather. You want your garbage to be in tip-top shape.

While I'm inside the dumpster I like to make stacks of the papers I find and load them into garbage bags. Then I bring it home to examine what I've collected. You'll find internal phone directories, names of public and private individuals, training manuals, outdated files, letters, information about projects being worked on, and sometimes even mention of the computer system. Much of it is helpful, and most is interesting too.

Even the regular trash is usually a pretty clean place to be (somewhat). Rummaging around in the garbage bins of various companies, office centers and other institutions, I have come across: microfiche, computer cards, entire boxes of business cards, books, a dead cat (really gross), broken electronic junk, and lots and lots of, well, garbage. Of course most of it isn't helpful for the hack, but often there is knowledge to be gained. You can find out a lot about how an organization functions by its trash, and the way in which that trash is organized.

The first time I did this, I took a single green trash bag from the bin behind a bank. Bank bags, by the way, are stapled shut with a paper receipt that tells the name of the bank, and the time and date of disposal of the bag. The trash within is of two types. There are smaller bags containing refuse from each individual's office in the bank, and then there is the cytoplasm of crumpled forms and discarded paper tapes from behind the counter. The interesting parts are the bags from individual offices. In my first garbage heist, one banker was Japanese — he was throwing out a Japanese newspaper and a Japanese candy wrapper in addition to his bank-related stuff. There was also the woman on the diet, the struggling-to-make-ends-meet single mother, and the assistant bank director. Now the bank director

— her garbage was very interesting. It contained a discarded lock from the vault, a box of orange "key hole signals (style 'c')," some vault-key envelopes, a slip of paper with the combination to a safe scrawled across it like a clue in a parlor mystery (12R-32L-14R in case you care), and a memorandum to "Branch Managers" from the woman in charge of "Branch Automation," which apparently had accompanied a disk. From that letter I was able to get the name, address, and room number of the bank's Branch Automation Department and from there evolved a social engineer through the mails (see chapter on Social Engineering) which resulted in myself getting a copy of the disk in question as well as some other very useful information.

If you were caught hacking a trash bin, you used to be able to say that you were "just looking for cans to recycle." Now offices pretty much recycle everything, so that won't do for an excuse. The old "school" or "community project" ploy is always a good bet: Say you are rummaging around in there doing research for a report on government or business waste.

Before you even step out of your house the first time, do a bit of phone work to find out what the garbage situation will be like. Call up the Solid Waste Department and ask when garbage collection is for the street you have in mind to plunder. If pickup is Monday morning, that's good, since you'll be able to go at night over the weekend, when no one is around. You don't want to end up going the day *after* collection, so make that call before you hop in your car.

As for recycled white paper, if there aren't any outside bins devoted specifically to it, you might want to go to the office during the day (if it has a publicly-accessible area) and take a casual look at the level of white paper in the recycling cans inside. Do this at different times of day for a few days, and you'll get their recycling schedule. Again, you'll want to nab white office paper when the bins are at their fullest.

GIRK

Of course, you can go out scavenging unarmed through the trash bins of the world, but to facilitate and quicken results, you will most likely want to

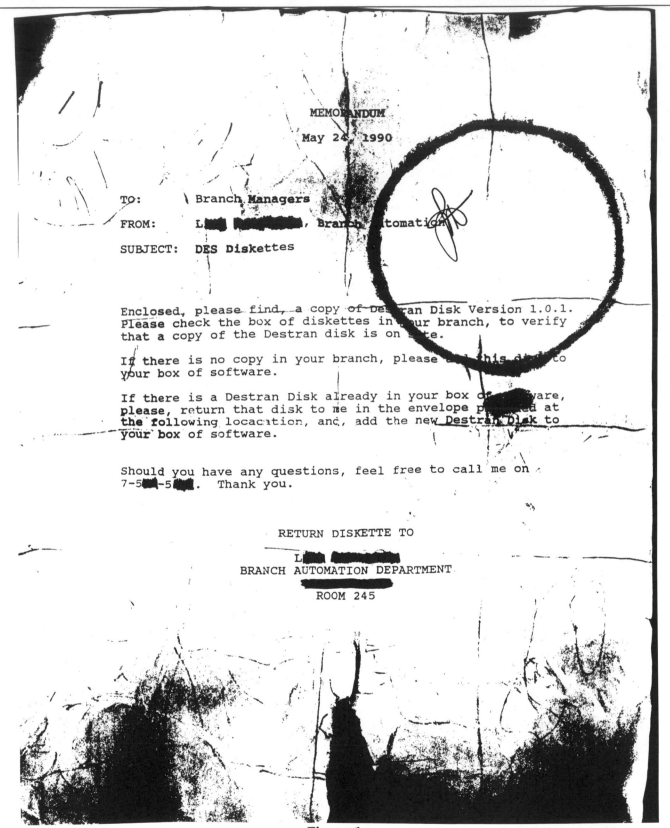

Figure 1

A memo retrieved from the garbage contains valuable information.

prepare beforehand for your excursion into the trash of white collar America!

Here are the things you should consider including in your GIRK — Garbaged Information Retrieval Kit:

Rubber gloves. Either surgical gloves, or the kind you use while washing dishes. Though most garbage you'll be rummaging through is "clean" (white paper bins for recycling) it's a good idea to wear some sort of thin gloves anyway. You'll also want to wear gloves when you're at home sorting through the bags you lifted.

Ladder. I'm not talking about real ladders here, although you may want to use one. Some dumpsters are very high, or are vertically-oriented, and so climbing out of them may be difficult. Find yourself an old chair or hassock somebody's throwing away, and take it in the trunk of your car. Then you can either put it into the bin from outside if it looks like you'll have trouble climbing out, or you can use it to climb into the bin in the first place. Either way, if you have to leave in a hurry for some reason you can safely leave it behind — after all, it was garbage to begin with, right?

Flashlight. Take a piece of rope or a strip of denim or something and fashion a strap. Make the strap just big enough so you can easily slip the flashlight on and off your hand. Especially if you'll be rummaging at night, you will need a powerful flashlight to guide you through the garbage. Make sure the batteries are okay — best thing is to use rechargeables.

Garbage bags. Not the clear kind. You must use black, brown, or similarly colored bags for this. After all, you don't want people to see what you've got in them. If you're just pulling manuals, memos, etc., out of the trash and are not bringing home whole, intact bags, you should bring along at least one of your own dark-colored garbage bags, to put everything in. You might want to take two bags, placing one inside the other, to insure against breakage.

Appropriate clothing. Don't go rummaging through garbage bins in your Sunday finery! Wear shoes you'll be able to climb and jump with. Wear clothes that won't snag, old clothes, clothes that you don't care if they get destroyed.

You might want to wear a custodial type outfit, if you have it. If you know the company maintenance staff tends to wear baseball caps, or a certain color shirt or jacket, then by all means dress similarly. Wear dark colors, not bright pinks, reds, or yellows that everyone's going to be staring at.

Empty soda cans. Some hackers tell security guards or other onlookers that they're searching for aluminum cans to recycle. You might want to fill up the bottom third of one of your garbage bags with cans, or maybe leave an open bag of cans outside the bin so bypassers will be able to figure out for themselves that you're collecting cans for charity.

One time I told a stodgy old guard, "The science classes at my school are competing to see how many cans we can recycle. For every pound of cans we bring in, our school gets three dollars. The class that brings in the most cans wins a prize. Right now we're in second place, so I want to bring us up to first!" He walked away and came back with a handful of empty beer cans and bottles. "Are you doing glass too?" he asked.

Remember: don't carry unnecessary things in your pockets, or things like watches that are going to fall off your wrist. You don't want to lose money, wallets, credit cards, notebooks or anything else to the hungry stomach of a garbage bin, so leave all that at home. Before you leave the house, do a pocket check. Make sure you have nothing that could identify you and nothing you can't afford to lose. This seems like obvious advice but I can recall at least four different messages posted by hackers on private BBSs where they said things like, "Jeez! I just came back from the CompuPhone dump and I forgot to put my ring back on after I climbed out of the can! Now I'll have to go back there tomorrow!"

On the other hand, you might want to take along a cheap watch or something that didn't cost much but looks expensive. Then if some curious person comes along you can jump up and say, "Here's that stupid watch! I knew that idiot janitor threw it out with the trash!"

Also, another good idea: Take a shower when you get home!

Found Disk Analysis

When you hack you begin to find disks everywhere. Some have been discarded, mangled, warped, bent; some have been carelessly lost, in the drive of a public computer, under a keyboard, behind a desk; and others you will find in their natural place — lying around on people's desks, in disk boxes, in library reference books, in file cabinets. You will want to be able to read data files off these disks and rerun any programs on them.

I am not going to suggest that you actively steal disks that you find in an office or wherever, but if you can manage to sneak one away for a few days or overnight without it being missed, then the best of luck to you!

Before I go into what should be done with found disks, let's get our terminology straight. Here I will be talking about microcomputer disks, which come in two varieties: 5¼" and 3½" disks. A disk is composed of two parts. There is the square plastic outside, which I will refer to as the *envelope*, and the circular mylar *disk* inside. The square envelope is simply a means of protecting the flimsy and fragile disk within, and can be horribly mutilated without damaging data on the disk itself. 3½" disks have a small plastic or metal door that slides open to reveal the disk inside. 5¼" disks are unprotected in this way; their disks are exposed through an oval hole.

WARNING!

Never put a disk of unknown origin, especially a physically damaged one, into a good disk drive. Before examining found or damaged disks, you should get ahold of a cheap, second-hand drive and use *that* for found disk analysis.

Examining bad disks can easily damage your disk drive. Never use bad, damaged or found disks on a good quality drive!

Check Up

Begin a found disk analysis by removing the disk from its paper sleeve if there is one, and eye-balling both sides for any distinct problems such as grooves, coffee stains or wrinkles. It is amazing what disasters disks can live through. During the early '80s when home computers first hit the marketplace, there were warnings everywhere: "Don't put disks by magnets, by your monitor, on your printer, or near your telephone. Don't bend disks, don't let your fingers stray from the label..." And on and on. Certainly you should treat disks carefully, but as we've learned since floppy drives became inexpensive enough for anyone to afford, disks just aren't as fragile as they were once thought to be. And certainly the plastic and Teflon they are made of are cheap enough to throw away, meaning discards are common. So if you are rummaging through a company's trash bin and you see a mangled disk, *take it* — you might be able to get something interesting off it.

If there is nothing visibly wrong with the (5¼") disk, but you're still wary (because you found it in a garbage can or in a dusty place or something) you should carefully hold the envelope with one hand while rotating the disk with the other hand (using the hub ring). Look at the disk through the oval window as you do the rotation. Then turn the disk over and inspect the other side the same way. For 3½" disks, you will have to hold open the sliding door with a finger as you rotate the disk using the hub ring.

If you suspect that a 5¼" disk is filthy, or if there is any dirt at all inside, rotating the disk may scratch it. Instead of rotating it, do this: Push the disk to the bottom of the envelope with your finger. Take a pair of sharp scissors or a knife and cut off a very thin strip of plastic from the top (label) edge of the envelope. With thumb and fingers, puff out the envelope, and ease out the disk. Don't wipe dirt off the disk — you don't want to scratch it. Try to blow away dust and dirt, or use a hair dryer set on low heat, or a can of compressed air.

Now look inside the plastic envelope. You will see a lining of a white gauze-like material. If that's dirty, throw away the envelope. Take a different disk (that contains data you don't need any more), slit the envelope open the same way, remove the disk and replace it with the other round floppy. Make sure the reinforced hub ring (if it has one) faces *front*. Now you can try using this disk on your cheap second-hand disk drive.

For 3½" disks, you can first carefully remove the door, then gently pry open the plastic envelope case with a knife. Don't jam the knife into the envelope; rather work around the edges and corners where the two halves are snapped together. Remove the floppy disk. Blow away any dirt, then put the disk into a clean envelope, using tape to keep the pieces together. Replace the sliding door if you can, but don't worry about that aspect if you have trouble doing so — most drives will not miss it.

5¼" disks sometimes get folded or bent. They are still usable but the bending can misalign your drive head. Not only will this ruin your disk drive, but subsequent disks inserted may be irreversibly damaged. Therefore, *never* use bent disks on a good drive, or good disks in your bad drive.

If you find a bent disk in the trash, first flatten it out as best you can. Put it on a hard, smooth, flat surface. Cover it with a few sheets of paper, then take a heavy book and press it down. Do NOT try to straighten disks by bending them the other way. If the outside envelope still seems in pretty bad shape, remove the inner disk and insert it in a good, flat envelope as described earlier.

Let's look at some of other ways a disk can be damaged but still remain salvageable.

Damage To One Side

If the damage to a disk is limited to a single side, you will still be able to read data from the other side. There are two ways to do it.

The first way is to use a superzap program to selectively read tracks, piecing together data as you find it. Superzap programs, such as DOS's DEBUG utility, allow you to alter the data on a disk one bit at a time. If you can get your hands on an old single-sided drive it will make your work a bit

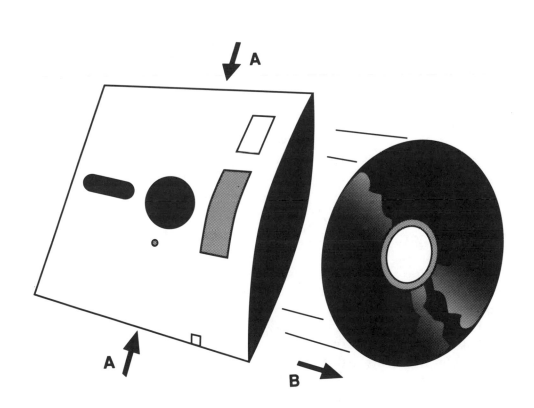

Figure 2

Don't try this with your store bought disks! After slicing open the top, apply pressure to the sides (A). Then (B) slide out the disk. Now you can repair the disk, clean it, and slide it into a fresh envelope.

easier: simply insert the disk bad-side-up, and read away. (In single-sided disks, data is normally read from and written to the *back* of the disk — the underside, if you hold the disk label-side up.)

A second option is to use a cosmetic disguise to hide the damaged side of the disk. For example, suppose you have found a 5¼" disk with unremovable blemishes on one side only and your drive simply refuses to read the disk. Here's what you do. Take another 5¼" disk, format it, then cut it open. Remove it from its envelope, and tape the new disk over the blemished disk. The tape should be between the two disks (thin double-sided tape works best). Make sure you line up the two disks precisely. Insert the taped disks back into a clean envelope, and see what you can make happen!

Rips And Tears

You can very carefully tape a ripped disk back together with thin transparent tape. Make sure to only put tape on one side at a time. Once you've gotten all the data you can off one side, you can remove the tape and repair the other side. As before, it is imperative that you don't let the tape get onto the side of the disk which the drive will be reading, or you could throw off your drive's read/write head, and may get sticky stuff on it, too.

Imperfections

If a disk looks okay, but will only give you "Read Errors," it is probably physically damaged on a microscopic level. It may have little holes or dents in it, imperfections that are too small for the naked eye to see. You can push past bad spots on a disk by manually rotating the disk inside. If the damage is limited to a small area of the disk, it may be that the damaged segment is the part the drive tries to read first. If you manually rotate the disk a little to the left or right, the new section of disk which you reveal may not have that damage and may therefore be readable. Keep rotating the disk, a little at a time, until you've found a spot that is readable.

If you never find a readable spot, perhaps you've been duped! Maybe the disk is blank, or it isn't suitable for your computer. Or maybe it's single sided and you've inserted it with the wrong side facing the drive's read/write head.

A disk that you find in the trash bin may hold corporate data, proprietary software, maybe even a tutorial or simulation like we discussed earlier.

You never knew there was an archaeology side to computer hacking, did you? But that's exactly what all of this is; we are looking into people's lives to see what they think about, to find out what's important to them, and to learn from their experiences. Hacking a damaged disk that you have unearthed from a trash bin will lead you to details you would otherwise never have imagined existed. I highly recommend the exercise for the thrill value, and for the intellectual workout to be gained from this pursuit.

Examining Screenshots

The photographs of computers you see in books, magazines, system documentation, promotional literature such as posters and pamphlets, government publications and booklets, as well as the pictures of computers available on television documentaries, news shows and commercials — can all contain valuable hacking information.

Computer photos might show just the screen (or monitor), or the entire computer, including keyboard, CPU and accessories. Or the picture might depict an actual computer in its natural environment, with perhaps an operator visible.

The first group, essentially "screenshots," can be helpful in showing you what it looks like to be inside a particular system that you have never really accessed. This can clue you in on what accessing style the system uses, if the password is displayed on-screen as it is typed, username and password styles, what features are available, and much more, depending on what the photographs are attempting to illustrate. Similarly, in user manuals and other instructional aids, drawings of screens are often found containing the same information, also default login codes, text specifics, error messages, and other handy stuff.

Knowing error messages and knowing the layout of the screen will make you a more believable system administrator or low-level user when you attempt some of the social engineering tricks mentioned later in this book, especially if the computer system in question is one that is closed to outsiders. Seeing examples of logins will give you ideas on how to go about a brute force attack. If a user name is shown or illustrated, it may be a valid one. Even if lower down on the screen all you get for password information is a row of asterisks ("password: *******") it will still help you in determining the length passwords are required to be. If in separate photos taken from separate sources, both passwords are shown being covered by eight asterisks, that is a good indication that either there is a default eight-character password used to demonstrate the system, or that passwords are a maximum length of eight-characters.

Style of username is important too, and will usually be visible. Seeing examples of usernames lets you know if first *and* last names are required, if uppercase letters are needed, whether abbreviations or company names or group names are used for usernames.

Photographs that include more than just the screen often show the keyboard being used (look for misplaced or special keys), keyboard overlays, the kind of computer setup, and possibly messages taped to the CPU or monitor. A more generalized shot may show the computer's surroundings. Is it in a closed office, or are many terminal operators working together in close proximity? What books are there on the shelves? You may be able to see things of interest hanging on a wall, or lying around on the desk. A user might be in the picture; is he or she wearing a name tag? Are pictures of a family present, or items suggesting a hobby, such as a mounted baseball or a fishing rod? *All* available data can be put to use by a hacker.

When I refer to the computing environment, I am, of course, only referring to pictures of computers in their natural environments, as opposed to staged photos in advertisements, like the kind showing a Macintosh in your typical teenager's room. Newspaper and magazine articles are often accompanied by the kind of computer photo you will want to analyze.

Seeing these things — signs of family life, books and hobbies, a typical user and what he or she is wearing — gives clues to passwords. The specific kind of computer may suggest ways of breaking in using known bugs or loopholes. The computing environment also will allow the social engineer to pretend familiarity with an otherwise private room or office inside a building.

An additional way computer photographs can help is by looking to the bottom, usually in the caption, to where the *source* of the photo is listed. The source may give a photographer's name, in which case that photographer may be discreetly pumped for information, or it may give clues as to a relevant city, business or organization. This can help in determining phone numbers, means of access, and also passwords.

These are just some of the ways in which close magnifying glass work will help you find out more about your intended target system. You can see why it is a good idea to videotape as many computer-related TV shows as you can; you can always fast-forward through the boring parts. Freeze framing a specific scene may help give insight into the hidden side of a system and the people who run it.

If you get a lot of static on your television when you freeze a frame, try cleaning the VCR. If that doesn't clear up the problem, it may be the audio component of the tape that is interfering with the video picture. Try taping just the video part of the tape you want to freeze. One way to do this is to connect two VCRs together using just the Video In/Video Out cable, ignoring the audio link. Copy the relevant portion of the tape, and you will have a picture without accompanying sound to muddy the screen.

You should only have an audio problem like this if there's a lot of background sound to begin with, like loud narration or loud music going on.

Here's an example of how this kind of photographic detective work pays off:

A hacker named Bellee was watching a behind-the-scenes-at-the-police-station show on her local cable channel. A close-up on a computer screen revealed the last three digits of a phone number that was being dialed by modem. The rest of the number was invisible due to glare on the screen. Bellee knew the police databank being called was headquartered in a specific town in Maryland, because the officer giving the tour had mentioned it. Some of the access codes being typed to get into the databank were easily visible or inferable by all who watched the show, but some weren't. A bit of library research got Bellee the three-digit exchanges that were local to the township the cop had mentioned. Bellee then dialed each of those exchanges until she found the correct phone number. (Because she had the last three digits from the television show, she only had to call each exchange 10 times to fill in the missing digit.)

Once she got through, she was able to use the login information she knew (a precinct number, municipality and state were needed) and hack the part she didn't (she knew she needed an eight-letter password from the TV show). So watching television paid off for Bellee.

Even widely syndicated shows can mess up by inadvertently revealing important clues to an observant audience. Anyone who happened to be watching a certain episode of Geraldo Rivera's *Now It Can Be Told* news show in late 1991 would have seen a story on a group of hackers and how they broke into a military computer. Several times during the course of the story the camera came close to the computer's screen, where the electronic address of the computer they had hacked was visible. The story also reported that the hackers had added an account to the system under the name "dquayle," with no password. As you can imagine, soon after the segment aired the account was closed up. As of this writing there is definitely no "dquayle" account on the system (I just called and checked), and some of the more common ways of gaining access to the system have been noticeably shut down. For example, it is no longer possible to call up anonymously and retrieve files from that system.

Snooping

You can go on tours of a lot of places, either officially or unofficially. A tour might be one that is regularly run for wide-eyed kiddies and their parents, or it may be one specially set up for you because you say you are a journalist who wants to do an article on the company. While taking your tour you will be gleaning valuable information about the computer rooms, and about the person conducting the tour. That's all good information that can be put to use in guessing passwords. If you're suave enough, you can talk a proud computer owner into showing off the power of his machine or the new game he's gotten. This can only help you when you go home that night and hack the place.

Just seeing the computers can be a boon, and seeing the screen setup is helpful as I've outlined above.

Now here's a hint I like to make use of, though I get to do so only irregularly. We are all familiar with the phenomenon of phosphorus burnout. That is, when one image is displayed for an extended period of time, the image gets burnt into the screen. Very often menus get burnt into the screen, and so occasionally I've been in places where there is an old terminal that used to be for employees only, but has been moved into a publicly accessible spot. Many of the functions available for staff use only are visible on the screen and can be put to use or hacked. (You might have to fiddle with the brightness controls to see what it all says.) Other times I've snuck a peek at the computer behind the counter, and although an innocuous screen was being displayed at the time, there was worthwhile stuff barely visible, burnt into the screen.

Many businesses, institutes and organizations run what are called special libraries. These generally concern themselves only with the product or service which is the group's field of interest, but also include valuable details on the group itself. For instance, a company library might have manuals in it to the company's unique computer system. Often there is a helpful listing of what programs are available on the mainframes. Such a program listing might include mention of what security products are enabled, and you can write to the maker of those security products for details.

Snooping around buildings undergoing reconstruction can be worthwhile, as can snooping around buildings whose occupants are moving to a new building.

In such cases, doors are found wide open, with computers and manuals laying around all over the place. I remember one building I went to that was temporarily vacated due to construction, which had tons of cartons, desks and workstations out in the corridors (they were repainting offices). I found masses of passwords stuck to keyboards by Post-It Notes, and passwords scribbled on desk blotters, and taped to the underside of drawers. It was amazing that people could leave their secrets laying out in the open like that, and yet it happens all the time.

From snooping around the lounge in a school building, I came up with handy reference manuals,

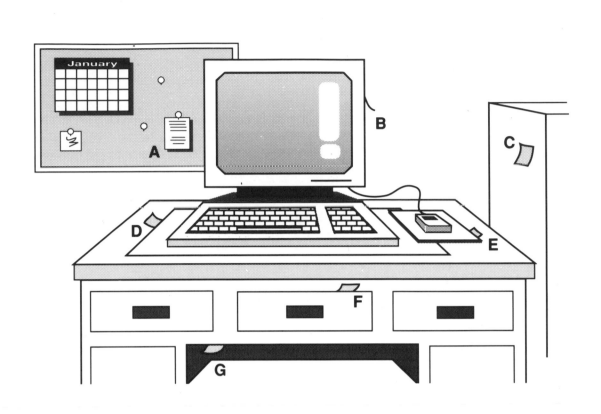

Figure 3

Secret information that must be used every day (such as access codes) is often found hiding on little scraps of paper: (A) on a cork board, (B) attached to the side or top of the monitor, (C) on nearby file cabinets or other furniture, (D) under blotter, (E) under mouse pad, (F) in desk drawer, or (G) underneath the the desk.

decade-old literature from a defunct computer users group, programmers' guides, and other stuff. This wasn't all necessarily useful for hacking purposes, but it was interesting to read. And it was interesting to rescue it from its dusty box on the top shelf of a closet.

In that same building I found a little room whose door was closed and had four signs attached to it. The first, formal and engraved said, "Computer Room." The rest were menacing, either hand lettered or printed by computer: "Keep this door locked at all times!" "For authorized persons ONLY!" And lastly, another stern reminder, "ALWAYS lock this door when you leave!"

Needless to say, the door was unlocked.

Inside there was a huge and informative operating system reference manual and two PCs, each of which had modems. From surfing the hard disks on one of those computers, I found that the terminal program was set up with script files[2] that contained phone numbers, passwords and other login procedures. Always look for such things when you snoop.

Snooping can bring to you those tutorial and simulation disks, as well as damaged disks, trash

_____

[2] A "script" is a file that you use with a terminal program. You set up the terminal program so that when you log onto a system, the contents of the script file are sent to that system. So if you have to go through some long and convoluted login procedures, you can put the commands into a script and have the computer automatically log in for you. This is handy, both for legitimate users, and for hackers who happen to gain access to those script files.

and insider literature which one can only get from either being employed by a company, or by snooping around. It adds a bit of physical excitement to the usually passive art of hacking, and it gets you away from the eyestrain of computer screens for a while.

It is not always necessary to research before a hack, but it is always helpful. Research in any form doesn't have to be undertaken with a particular hack in mind. Like my random snoopings of the torn-apart building and the university lounge, general explorations can lead to fruitful information. In other words, all hacking doesn't have to be done on computers. There is also such a thing as the person who hacks — joyously — *life*.

Chapter Four:
Passwords And Access Control

Three dominant classes of access control have developed to protect computer installations. They are:

- knowledge-based controls (passwords)
- possession-based controls (keys)
- controls based on personal characteristics (biometric devices)

Possession-based controls have to do with things the user owns, like a physical key or magnetic card. Sometimes there is a metal clip of a peculiar shape that must fit into a hole in the computer before the computer will operate. A "key" could also be an identification badge, or a signed letter from a person of high status in the company, granting permission to access a site.

Biometric devices are those which look at some trait of a potential user and compare it to traits previously recorded, such as fingerprints, signature, or geometry of the hand.

These two forms of computer security may be designed for remote access control, although usually they are implemented at the site where the computers are located to limit access to either the computer room or the computer itself. Thus, descriptions of biometric and physical keys will be further developed in the on-site hacking section of this book.

The first class of access control — also the most common — is knowledge-based. That is, control is limited to those persons who can prove they have knowledge of something secret, usually a password. Discovering that password constitutes a large portion of hacking. Here, then, is everything you need to know about passwords: how they work, how they are stored, and how they are broken.

Passwords

The cheapest and easiest way to protect any kind of computer system is with that old standby: the password. Even computers that under normal circumstances have no need for security features often come equipped with password protection simply because it feels good to use and doesn't cost much in terms of time, effort or storage space to implement. Furthermore, systems which are protected by other means — by magnetic cards or by software alternatives such as encryption — will double or triple the security of their assets through the use of a password system. Thus, on practically all computer setups you are likely to encounter passwords of one form or another.

Passwords are usually thought of as the entrance keys to a computer system, but they are also used for other purposes: to enable write access to drives, as encryption keys, to allow decompression of files, and in other instances where it is important to either ensure that it is the legitimate owner or user who is attempting an action.

There are seven main classifications of passwords. They are:

- User supplied passwords
- System generated random passwords
- System generated random passcodes
- Half and halves
- Pass phrases
- Interactive question-and-answer sequences
- Predetermined by code-indicating coordinates

If you intend to hack a computer installation you will first have to figure out which of these seven password types are used by that system. The first type is the most common; generally users are asked to think up a personal password for themselves.

System generated random passwords and codes may be of several kinds. The system software may supply a completely random sequence of characters — random to the point of cases, digits, punctuation symbols and length all being determined on the fly — or restraints may be used in the generating procedures, such that each passcode conforms to a prearranged constitution (like "abc-12345-efgh" where letters and numbers are randomly generated). Or, computer-produced passwords may be taken randomly from a list of words or nonsense syllables supplied by the program authors, thus creating passwords like "nah.foop" or "car-back-tree".

Half and halves are partially user-supplied, while the rest is composed by some random process. This means that even if a user supplies the easily-guessed password "secret," the computer will tack on some abstruse gibberish at the end, forming a more secure password such as "secret/5rh11".

Pass phrases are good in that they are long and hard to guess, but easily remembered. Phrases may be coherent, such as "we were troubled by that," or they may be nonsensical: "fished up our nose." Pass phrases are used when the manager of a site is par-

ticularly security-conscious. Usually you don't see pass phrases *required* by a system, although the programming required to enforce a pass phrase rule is trivial.

Related to the pass phrase concept is the phrase acronym, which security experts have been applauding as a short but equally safe form of password. In a phrase acronym, the user takes an easily remembered sentence, phrase, line from a song or poem or other such thing, and uses the first letter of each word as the password. For example, the acronyms for the two pass phrases above would be "wwtbt" and "fuon." You can see that innovations in password theory such as this will greatly increase the difficulty hackers will encounter in future electronic espionage.

The sixth password type, question-and-answer sequences, requires the user to supply answers to several (usually personal) questions: "Spouse's maiden name?", "Favorite color?", etc. The computer will have stored the answers to many such questions, and upon login will prompt for the answer to two or three of them. These question/answer sessions can be delicious to the hacker who is intimately familiar with the user whom he or she is attempting to impersonate. Systems which use question-and-answer sequences also tend to be programmed to interrupt users while online every X minutes, and require them to answer a question to reaffirm their validity. This can get pretty annoying, especially if someone's in the middle of an exciting online game when it happens. Q&A is used only rarely nowadays. When it was first proposed it seemed like a good idea, but the bothersome factor has resulted in this method being pretty much phased out.

Passwords which are predetermined by code-indicating coordinates usually rely on some external device, such as the code wheels used to deter software piracy. In any case, a set of key prompts are offered by the computer, and the user is required to return the appropriate responses to them. You'll often see this type of password being used on a system with once-only codes.

Once-only codes are passwords valid for only one access. Sometimes they are used as temporary guest accounts to demonstrate a system to potential clients. Once-only codes may also be employed by the system to allow actual users to log in for the first time; the users will then be expected to change their password from the one provided to a more secure, personal code. In situations where groups of people must log in, but security must be maintained, a list of once-only codes may be provided. Users then extract one code at a time, depending on external factors such as time, date or day. Maybe you can find a list of codes by going through the garbage of a place? The codes won't work anymore, but you'll get a sense of what the system expects from you.

Passwords Supplied By The User

Most passwords are of the choose-it-yourself variety, and due to security awareness most contemporary programs which ask for a password to be supplied will not accept words of a certain short length which the program deems to be too easily "hackable." Most passwords will be more than four or five characters long. Other measures to protect users from their own lack of password creativity might be taken as well. For example, systems may force passwords to contain a mixture of upper and lower case, numbers, and perhaps disallow obvious passwords (such as "computer").

Software is available for most operating systems which looks through the computer's password files, analyzes user passwords and decides how secure they are. Unsecure passwords will be changed, or prevented in the first place. This is one area where your prior research should help you. Generally you will know which of these programs your target has installed, and what passwords the software will not allow.

Regardless of how clumsy-brained or brilliant a person is, all people tend to think alike. It is only through learning that they begin to think in creative ways. Even then, initial assumptions and first conclusions are similar for a given peer group. What this means is that when a person logs onto a computer for the first time, and is prompted for a password — especially if that person is under stress of time or place — that password is likely going to be a variation on some common themes.

Imagine some of the situations people are in when they are asked to create a secret password for themselves. They may be calling a remote computer over a long distance phone line, or surrounded by a group of technicians who are there to teach them to use the system. In any case, the prompt is there on the screen and with it, a sense of urgency is brought to mind. People type the first thing they think of, the first thing they see, or hear, or are hoping to do once they get past the login procedure. The password is entered quickly, and rarely is it changed to a better, more secure one.

Thus, many passwords relate to top-of-the-mind thoughts, such as job, family, possibly current events, possessions, environment, hobbies or interests. If you can either find out or guess any of these traits of a valid system user, the number of potential passwords you will have to guess will decrease significantly.

Get catalogs from the companies that make wall posters, humorous mugs and other novelty items one finds around offices. How many times have you seen that tired phrase, "You don't have to be crazy to work here... But it helps!"? I guarantee the word "crazy" gets picked off that mug every day as a password. Think about the age and lifestyles of the average user whose account you are attempting to breach. An office in a corporate setting probably wouldn't have a nudie poster hanging up — but a college dorm would, and so you may get passwords such as "playmate," "victoria," "body," or "month."

The easiest way to get a password is to enter it yourself for the user, or to supply the password to the user who is logging on for the first time. You might be acting the role of computer tutor to a novice, and while showing him or her the ropes, downplay the security aspects and allow him or her to tell you the password as they type it, either because they spell it out loud, or because you watch the person's eyes light up as his or her gaze falls upon the wall poster with the word "surfboard" written across the top. (Or they say, "Gee, what's a good secret password? Oh, I know — " and proceed to spell it out to you as they hunt and peck at the keyboard.)

Most often you will be hacking away at user accounts that have been long-established. On these you will have to use some kind of either brute force method, observation, social or technical method of password retrieval.

Most passwords are dictionary words, like "subway," "table," "chocolate" or "hotdog." Honestly, can you imagine any computer novice sitting down and entering "fMm6Pe#" as a password? Of course not!

Scrabble rules do not apply here: proper names are allowed in password creation, as are misspellings, abbreviations, non-words and foreign terms. Thus a person who likes watching Star Trek may have the password "enterprize" instead of the correct "Enterprise." Whether that's due to bad spelling habits or because he or she simply likes it better that way is unimportant. What *is* important is that you have to be aware that misspelled words exist in passwordland. You are going to find the letter "k" used in place of hard "c," as in "koka kola." You will find "x" for "ks" (thanx), and other phonetic substitutions, like "lether," "fone" and "stryker."

Some hackers will go through every word in the English language until they find something that works as a password. If the password they seek *is* a real word, but isn't spelled correctly, they are going to be wasting vast amounts of time. *Complete* brute force dictionary attacks are often fruitless, useless, adolescent ways of doing things.

Many words recur frequently as passwords, and examples are given in the appendices. However, there are many words that you would almost never expect to find as a password on a system. Is it reasonable to suspect a person will enter an *adverb* for a password? Words of this sort would be the last ones to try. Real-word passwords will generally be nouns, ("eyeball," "drums," "kitchen"), verbs, (usually obscene ones), and perhaps adjectives ("purple," "great," "happy").

Girl friends, boy friends, and the cute pet names they give each other are popular passwords; these you would have found out from prior research. Also semi-popular are passwords with the word "sure" embedded inside them, as in "forsure" or "fursure," "surething" or "asb" (short for "a sure bet"). Besides dictionary words, you can expect to find names of relations, streets, pets, sports teams and foods; important dates and ID numbers, such as social security numbers, anniversaries, or birthdays; and keyboard patterns. Examples of keyboard patterns include "jkjkjkjk," "7u7u7u," "WXYZ," "ccccccc," "0987654321," "asdfgh" or "qazwsx." Look at the location of these letters on a keyboard if you are confused about these last two examples. Keyboard patterns will usually be simple repetitions of characters, portions of columns or rows or every-other-letter designs. Keyboard pat-

terns may be wholly unguessable and yet fully logical when you know what's going on at the other end of the phone line. For example, "05AF" may seem a funny thing to pick up from a keyboard, but when you know the computer in question has a special hexadecimal keypad attached, the whole thing starts to make sense.

Figure 4

A hexadecimal keypad, used by some computer programmers to allow fast entry of numbers in base 16. The keypad illustrates a principle smart hackers will follow: That what you see on your side may be different from what they see on theirs.

Some keyboard patterns I've actually seen being used on systems: "abcdef," "qwerty," "12345," "xxxxxx," "opopopopp." If you know the minimum password length is six characters, don't expect patterned passwords to go much beyond that minimum. On the other hand, you can't reasonably try out every possible pattern: there's an infinite number. Beyond a certain point, guessing keyboard patterns is strictly reserved for amateur hour.

Possible Password Investigation

One of the sources I used to research this book was an unofficial manual for a popular fee-based information service. Throughout that book, the author continuously made references to her pet cat, her love of Philadelphia soft pretzels, her favorite football team, her husband and children, and her newly acquired interest in computers. Not only did references to these aspects of her life abound in the text, they also appeared in illustrations of the service's "Find" command, sample messages and sample letters.

I knew the author's name, of course. I knew she had a membership on this system, and I knew about her life. It was insanely simple to get her personal ID number on the system and, yes, within two dozen password guesses, to access the service under her account. She has since taken my advice and changed her password.

This isn't an isolated example! Every day you and I read newspaper articles, magazine columns, and books — in which the authors give away their computer addresses so readers can respond. Yesterday I heard a radio talk show host give out his CompuServe address for the large listening audience who didn't get the chance to speak out on the air! We know enough about many of these authors and others to be able to make educated guesses of their passwords. Even if an author doesn't mention personal details in the book, there's usually an "About the Author" section to turn to for facts. Many computer books are written by college professors; naturally you'll know what college they're at, and so you have a lead to an account. If the sample program segments they list entail baseball trivia, you've got a good idea where to begin a brute force siege.

With all of this said, I want you to realize this is *for informational purposes only*. I made the above remarks only to point out some of the lax security around anyone in the public eye. Don't get any funny ideas about breaking *my* passwords!

Another trick is to look in *Who's Who* books. Almost all industries have a yearly *Who's Who* published. Many of these are vanity affairs: people pay to get a write-up about themselves listed. You can get good data from these, and if you can't get enough good data, print up your own official-looking *Who's Who* form and mail it to the person you have in mind at the company. Make sure the accompanying letter states that once they fill out the form, their entry will be included free of charge in the eventual book, and they will receive one copy of the book, free. This will help ensure that they mail you back the form. It also ensures you get good data to help you crack their passwords.

One more helpful subterfuge, this one involving socializing with cronies at the company. Call up an office and talk to a receptionist or anyone who knows everyone's gossip. Say you're from a new trade magazine specializing in that business's field of endeavor. Ask for the names of all the major department heads, and their secretaries, so you can send them a free trial subscription. Then call back and talk to each of their secretaries. Have them fill out "market research" cards, again for some prize, like a free subscription or a clock radio or something. Typical marketing questions for trade magazine subscribers include inquiries about schooling, degrees held, industry awards, trade association memberships, military service, salary range, and length of service at the company. As the conversation continues, start asking about hobbies and outside interests, favorite sports, names of kids and spouse, and home address. These too are acceptable questions for a market research surveyor to ask; they are also valuable possible password leads.

The short version of this is to call up, say you're one of the assistant editors for a trade magazine, and you're trying to find interesting people in the field. "Do you know of anyone there who has done anything at all spectacular, or has any particularly unusual hobbies?" You might get a "no," but keep pressing: "Anyone with special talent? Musical talent, for instance?" Keep going like this; eventually you'll hit upon something, and you can use the above tricks to find out more about that person than you ever thought you could.

Uncovering a subject's interests is called making up a personality profile or, for hackers, a password profile. The technique is done whenever the hacker has a specific individual in mind, whose computers the hacker wants to crack. If you wanted to read the e-mail and other private files of some head honcho at a corporation, you would go find reports of said honcho in the media, see what he or she likes, and go from there. One popular stratagem, mentioned by Hugo Cornwall in his *Hacker's Handbook*, recognizes the fact that often a chief person in an organization is given an account to demonstrate the new computer system, under the assumption that setting up a new account is too difficult or time consuming for the busy leader to do on his or her own. This account will of course have a natural English password, something of either the easily-guessed variety, or something from the boss's list of interests. ("Say, Mr. Larsen likes fishing, doesn't he? Put in 'FISH' as the password!")

So let's suppose you know a person's hobbies or interests: From there, how do you proceed?

To start, you could go to a library and get all the books you can on that subject. Then make up word banks from the glossaries and indices. People like to use big and (they think) obscure names/words from their coveted subject which they think no one else would ever think of. So you get students of literature using names for passwords, like "Euripides," "Aeschylus," and in general, a mess of lengthy technical terms.

Make up word lists, try them out, and if all else fails you can go on to a new password type. Just because someone's a doctor doesn't mean his password will be "pericardiocentesis." People's lives are composed of many subjects, their occupation being just one.

Password Studies

If you think all of this talk about easily guessed passwords is balderdash, think again. A good number of formal and informal studies have been done to see just how good people are at picking safe passwords.

One such experiment found that out of 3,289 passwords:
- 15 were a single ASCII character,
- 72 were two characters,
- 464 were three characters,
- 477 were four characters long,
- 706 were five letters, all of the same case, and
- 605 were six letters, all lower case.

The point being this: That hackers can simply sit down and guess passwords is FACT *not* FICTION. It can be done, and sometimes quite easily.

Another example of the ease with which passwords can be hacked is the Internet worm which squirmed through the net, disabling much of it, in 1988. The worm had two tactics it used to spread itself, one of which was attempting to crack user passwords. It would first try inputting the typical passwords, like login name, a user's first and/or last names, and other variations of these. If that didn't work, the worm had an internal dictionary of 432 common passwords to try. Finally, both of these methods failing, the worm went to the UNIX system dictionary, attempting each word in turn, until something hopefully worked. As we know, the worm's method worked superbly.

By the way, if you're ever on a UNIX system and need to do a brute force attack to gain higher access, the system dictionary is very helpful. You can find it in a subdirectory called "/usr/dict." The file is called "words." You can also download this file or capture it to another computer, if you need a plaintext dictionary file for use on other machines.[1]

Password Restraints

Most operating systems weren't developed with security as top priority. Indeed, password-based accounts should be all the security required on a time sharing system. As we have seen, however, too frequently passwords are chosen that are easy to guess. The UNIX operating system does restrain password selection by suggesting that passwords contain no less than five lower case characters, or only four characters if at least one of those is nonalphabetic or uppercase. However, if a user insists on a shorter password, disregarding the plea that security be maintained, that shorter password will be allowed.

Sysops know that most passwords aren't secure, so many have installed programs which disallow obvious passwords from being generated.

---

[1] One problem with using the UNIX dictionary "straight from the box" is that the words it contains do not genuinely reflect words in common English usage. There is a high preponderance of scientific words, due to the manner in which the dictionary was constructed.

Passwords are then forced to conform to certain characteristics, such as:

- Passwords must be of a certain length.
- Passwords must include a mixture of upper and lower cases.
- Passwords must include one or more numerals.
- Passwords must include a non-alphanumeric symbol.

One or more of these constraints might be enforced. The program may also test the user's password against a list of known "bad" passwords, which are not allowed to be used.

Not allowing single-case passwords or strictly alphabetical passwords does add some difficulty to a guess-attack, but not much. One time I had someone in mind who I felt certain had "popeye" for a password, due to his large collection of classic comic books and the big deal he always made about Popeye. The system software required a mixture of cases (which helpfully informs you, by the way, that upper and lower case are distinguished by the system), so instead of just trying "popeye", I tried:

Popeye	PoPeYe	popeyE
PopEye	popEYE	popEyE
PopeyE	PopEYE	PoPeye

and also tried each of these with cases reversed, such that PopeyE became pOPEYe (in case the user thought of capital letters as normal for computer keyboards, and lower case the exception). It was highly unlikely that this particular Popeye lover would try anything so bizarre as capitalizing in the middle of a syllable, or without some pattern to it. Indeed, when forced to capitalize, who in their right mind *would*?

As it turned out, his password was "OliveOyl."

If not capital letters, *numbers* might be forced into one's password upon first login. Again, you can hardly expect Joe User to break up syllables with a number, and the numbers that are used you should expect to be not more than one or two digits. After all, the user thinks of it as a pass*word*. The number will generally be slapped on as a necessary afterthought.

Thus, what you will normally find are passwords in the following forms:

password #
pass # word
password

Numbers will be those which are easy to remember, or easy to type, like 1 or 0. Numbers from one through 31 should be most common, along with numbers either repeating, ending in zero or nine, such as "888," "500" or "1999." It is reasonable to expect typists to use the numeral "1" substituted in for the letter "l" (lowercase "L"), in passwords which contain that letter. Cyberspace devotees might do likewise, as well as using zero for their required number, putting it in place of the letter "O." This means that if you ever suspect a word that contains the letters "L" or "O," instead of finding something like "cool," "computer," "lucifer," "lemon," or "colts," you may find "c001," "c0mputer," "1ucifer," "1em0n," and "c01ts," where the digits 1 and 0 have replaced the appropriate letters. (Actually, "c001" is usually spelled "k001.")

Computer Generated Passwords: Fakery and Analysis of Machine-Generated Passwords

Many passwords that the computer generates on its own will have some flavor of randomness to them. For instance, look at this bit of imaginary program segment:

```
5     Randomize Timer
100     For i = 1 to 6
110       Char = Int (Rnd * 91)
120       If Char < 65 Then Goto 110
130       Password = Password + Chr$ (Char)
140     Next i
200     Print "Your new password is: "; Password
```

Here, six uppercase letters are selected independently and concatenated to form the password. The way the letters are selected is that a random number between 65 and 90 is chosen — this correlates with the ASCII code for the letters of the uppercase alphabet. The *randomness* of the numbers chosen is based upon the randomizer function being used. In this case, pseudo-random numbers are generated based upon the exact time of the computer's internal clock, although randomization could also have been based on a practically infinite, hardware-dependent range of inputs. I said "pseudo" random numbers because no matter how random these numbers may appear to us, to the computer they are just values plugged into a formula.

If the password-making program could be altered in the right way, then all randomly-generated passwords after the time of

A more logical choice is to have the program generate a random-looking password based on some information about the user that you can easily determine from publicly available sources, such as the user's birth date or Social Security number.

Username Inputted: halbfish

Username letter	ASCII code	Sine of ASCII	Selected Values	Convert to Range	New ASCII
h	104	0.9702957	95	114	r
a	97	0.9925461	46	117	u
l	108	0.9510565	56	101	e
b	98	0. 990268	26	97	a
f	102	0.9781476	47	118	v
i	105	0.9659258	25	122	z
s	115	0.9063077	07	104	h
h	104	0.9702957	95	114	r

If Selected Value < 26 Then ASCII = Selected + 97
   else
       If Selected Value < 52 Then ASCII = Selected + 71
          else
              If Selected Value < 78 Then ASCII = Selected + 45
             else
                 ASCII = Selected + 19

Resulting password: rueavzhr
Cut to six characters: rueavz

Figure 5

A sample username is encoded into an obscure password using the method outlined in the text. On inspection the password seems random and secure, but a hacker can determine a user's password using publicly available information about that user (in this case, the user's last name).

---

alteration may be yours for the taking (or deducing). If you have the ability to change the program and save the changes to disk, or the ability to reroute the password-making subroutine, then here are some further items to consider.

The easiest thing to do would be to change the program by getting rid of the randomization factor entirely and simply inserting a "Let Password$ = "EVBDCL8"" statement. Then every new user would be given the same seemingly random password. The problem is this is not going to go unnoticed by the system administrators (although you might be able to restore the original program before your change is noticed).

Then you can simply plug that piece of information into your copy of the code on your home computer and reproduce the new user's password. One encoding algorithm that works well is to take the sine of the ASCII value of the first six or eight characters of the user's name, then take the second-to-last two values of the sine, convert them to fall within a suitable range, then concatenate the corresponding ASCII characters to form a "word." Thus you have a random-seeming password that can be easily constructed, even by hand. If the username is less than six characters, the remainder could be filled in by a predetermined set. (See Figure 5.)

This is just a simple example; your password would have to comply with case mingling, length, or digit sprinkling requirements where appropriate.

Forcing a password in this way can help if you run an electronic messaging or bulletin board system: users may get so comfortable with their new, secure passwords (wouldn't *you* think "rueavz" was secure?) that they transfer them over to other accounts elsewhere.

Another possibility, again requiring the ability to covertly change the password generator, is to alter the randomizer's *seed* to a constant value, thus causing the program to produce the same series of random numbers each time it is run (as long as the computer stays on and the program is not reset). This is risky though, and unwanted side effects may result.

One method utilizing the flaws in pseudo-random number generators was actually accomplished, and reported on by UNIX co-creator Dennis M. Ritchie in a 1986 security bulletin entitled "On the Security of UNIX." To increase security at a computer installation, the administrators decided to provide safe, computer generated passwords. Each password would be a string of lower case letters and digits, eight characters long. This calculates to 2,821,109,900,000 passwords which, according to Ritchie, on a PDP-11/70 would take 112 years to brute force through all those combinations. But the hacker knew that the random number generator could only take 32,768 seeds, and so only that many possible outcomes needed to be looked at. "The bad guy did, in fact, generate and test each of these strings and found every one of the system-generated passwords using a total of only about *one minute* of machine time." [Emphasis added.]

Clearly, sixty seconds plus some programming time is worth spending to have access to every account on a system!

If you can't insert code to generate machine-made passwords, you might be able to analyze them after they've been produced. This requires having access to a minimum of one password, preferably two or more, from a given system. If you have a legitimate account, there's your first password. If it's a local BBS you're hacking, or some other sort of system where multiple anonymous logons are possible, try calling back a few more times and collect new passwords under different names. Or get ahold of the BBS software or the password-generating routine, and work that to collect various passwords.

Once I was going through some new BBSs that had started up and I came across an ad for a system that was a couple states over but still seemed worth a try. I called up, logged in as a new user, and found it wasn't all that interesting after all — run by a factory supervisor mainly to let site agents order inventory stock. I used the made-up name and address Roger Eichner, 13 Stem Court, North Coast, WA 64203 to log on. The password that was generated was "roghner24." I was astounded! Obviously the program had simply taken the first three letters from my first name, the last four letters of my last name, and stuck a number at the end!

Or *had* it? I called back a second time, logging in as a new user with a different name. This time there seemed to be no correlation at all with any of the personal information I had given. Now I was not only astounded, but confused as well! Had the first password been simply a fluke? Was the second a fluke? Was it *programmed* to only sometimes use parts of the username? I called back a third time and again logged on as a new user. Again the password was unrelated to anything I had entered. Now I was pretty positive the first password had just been an unbelievable coincidence. I wrote a message to the system operator, saying he could delete these three new users of his (I supplied their personal info so he would not think I was playing a joke) and I didn't call back until a few weeks later.

Even though my second two passwords were unrelated to both each other and my personal data, I thought that perhaps I had missed something that first encounter, since some of the characters were repeated from one password to the next. Could these characters refer to my baud rate or computer type, or some other parameter that had stayed the same from one login to the next? Or was it possible that what was random about the passwords was which pieces of data it selected to insert into the password? This would account for my name in the first case, and one of the items (which I didn't recognize as relating to me) being repeated in the third call password.

Logging on with the same name, address, terminal characteristics and everything else as I had originally done, I received, to my disappointment, not a computer-generated password but the following astonishing message:

Dear Member:

Sorry about having to go through this again but we've had a problem the last few days. I will have to ask that you be patient with the low access level you will receive until I get a chance to validate you. Please note, when asked to supply a password do not give the one you were previously assigned. Make up a new and totally unconnected password.

See General Posting #1 for explanation.
StRaPmAsTeR === wIlLiE ===> (sysop)

Input Password ==>?

General Posting #1 said that a certain (relatively new) user of the BBS, whose handle was Mr. Joke, had kicked into action a "feature" of the BBS software that produced less-than-secure passwords. The previous year the system had "crashed, apparently as a result of a rogue program that was uploaded to file section by Mr. Joke." No further details were given on the cause or nature of the crash, because apparently regular callers of the system already knew the story.

Anyway, you can see how it's possible to occasionally get some good information by analyzing "random" passwords. Even if there doesn't seem to be any discernible pattern, that doesn't mean there isn't one hidden somewhere. There might be some subtlety to the pattern or, if not a pattern, a bug or strangeness that you might be able to spot. For example, in the first version of one BBS program — a program that was so godawful the board folded after about a month — the random password generator would *never* produce a password with the letter A or the digit 0 in it. Knowing this does help a little: for a seven character password of the form WXYZ123, where WXYZ are letters of one case and 123 are numbers, there are *only* 284,765,630 possible combinations of letters and numbers, instead of 456,976,000 — a difference of 172,210,370 passwords! This software was riddled with bugs, many of which have become famous as

the worst blunders in the history of horrible programming.

Non-Random Machine-Generated Passwords

Finally, let's consider random*less* machine-made passwords. Often users are entered into a computer system before their first logon. Then, unless the sysops can relay information to users off-line, the password must temporarily be something that the user already knows, such as their Social Security number (SSN), date of birth, or other personal data. Users are *supposed* to change this easy-to-guess password to a more secure one, but unless they're specifically shown how or required to do so, it is unlikely they will follow through.

Here's a non-computer example which demonstrates this weakness. In April of 1992, students at a New Jersey university received a memo, informing them of new over-the-telephone class registration procedures. The memo stated that the Personal Access Code (PAC) assigned to authenticate one's registration was the first four digits of one's birthdate (month and day), entered in conjunction with one's nine digit student ID number (essentially, one's social security number).

What got me was that first of all, they told students that their top secret PAC was their birth date. This violates all the security precautions they're trying to maintain. After all, how difficult is it to find out someone's birthday? But the PAC is only half of the "password" — the other part is a student ID. Again, it's a piece of cake to find out someone's ID. IDs are publicly or semi-publicly available at the student health centers, on computer room sign-up sheets, on identification cards, class rosters, housing lists and elsewhere! The memo does say that those concerned with security can come into the registrar's office to change their PAC, but who's going to go out of their way to do that?

Anyway, changing just those four numbers doesn't do much to stymie the determined hacker. Following a change of PAC there are 10,000 minus one possibilities to try. This is as opposed to the mere 366 possible PACs before that security-aware person changed his or her number. Sure, ten thousand is a lot of numbers to try, but it's certainly not impossible. A touch-tone auto-dialer can phone through all of those in about seven minutes, given unlimited PAC-entry retries per phone call. In any case, I'm using this story to illustrate the principle of least resistance: Users are not going to go out of their way to change access codes if they don't have to. And even if they do, it doesn't matter much. After all, we are *hackers*.

Let's move back to our discussion of non-random passwords which are generated by computer; or rather, passwords decided upon by the programmer or administrator and selected from data files by the computer.

Computers will select passwords any time a large number of passwords must be assigned at once. During the first week of a college semester, thousands of new accounts must be created for students enrolled in computer classes. For the most part, these accounts are going to be set up with username equal to some truncation or bastardized form of one's real name, and the password will be either one's Social Security number (SSN) or student ID number.

So if you want to hack a college system, start early in the semester — before those passwords get changed by the user to something more secure. Social Security numbers may be easily hacked by brute force, especially when you know how they are distributed.

Social Security (or other ID numbers) may also be obtained through social means (see the chapter on Social Engineering) or by other forms of chicanery. I've sat in on college classes where the instructor hands around a sheet of paper, on which the students are asked to write their name and ID number. This sheet is then handed to the teaching assistant, who enters this information as accounts into the computer system. If you happen to find some classes that operate like this, make sure you sit in the back of the class, where nobody will notice you copying other people's private data. A hand-held scanner/copier makes life easier at times like these.

You can also get names and SSNs from attendance sheets, or class rosters, which usually list both pieces of information for every individual in the class. If the professor doesn't make the roster available for student perusal, make up some excuse to swipe a look at it. For instance, say the registrar had your name incorrectly spelled on your last transcript, and you want to make sure they've cor-

rected the problem. Professors will love any excuse that points out slip-ups in the bureaucracy of the school system. Use their mindset against them!

Several court battles have ruled that use of one's Social Security number in conjunction with one's name in a public environment is unconstitutional, as it is an invasion of personal privacy. Therefore, we may see a trend starting, with SSNs getting used less and less for identification purposes, and an organization-defined ID number being used in its place. If that's the case, you will have to rely more on brute force to access the array of ID numbers assigned to a person.

Pre-usage passwords won't always be Social Security numbers or other ID numbers. If some non-computer communication is possible between the sysadmin and the user, other words may be assigned as temporary passwords (to be changed when the user logs on).

There might be a generic "new user" password which is given to all accounts, which shouldn't be very hard to crack. Or the password might be something very obscure and security-conscious, like some long string of random characters. It may be necessary to intercept the new user's physical mailbox for that envelope which contains the assigned password.

Programs Are People Too

Sometimes computer systems are set up with programs that have usernames and passwords, just like any other user of the system. Thus if you login as that program, the program is executed. Programs might be a tutorial on how to use the network, information system, database, messaging system or just about any sort of application program. Some sites also have accounts whose username is that of an elementary command, such as "time," "date" or "who" (which tells you who is logged on). This allows people to carry out certain quickie functions without having to go through the hassle of logging on to the machine. Often these command accounts don't have passwords associated with them, which is ironic since many are given superuser access permissions.

It's possible that you may get in to one of these program-users with a name/password combination chosen from words such as these:

guest	demo	help
info	tutorial	tut
menu	data	base
intro	anonymous	database
visit	welcome	hello

"Visit" or "visitor" might be the username, and "tut" the password, for example. Other possibilities are trying to get in with usernames "calendar," "cal," "sched," "schedule," "whois," "ftp," "who," "lpq," "archie," or other common command names. Many installations will have a general-usage or even public information system set up. Access may be gotten by logging in as "info," as suggested above, but other variations are possible. The fictional Wakka Doo University may require logging in as "wdu," "wduinfo," "hellowdu," "wdunews," "wdumail," "welcomewdu," or some other variation on the University's initials.

If you do manage to get in this way, first of all you are to be congratulated for a very successful hack — but *then* what? If you are interested in gaining higher access levels or in escaping out of the program entirely, you could have a lot of difficulty ahead of you. An upcoming section will offer suggestions for getting beyond limited access restrictions.

Brute Force Methods

Brute force means manual labor for your computer and, usually, lots of it. It isn't too difficult to do, but it is time consuming. What brute force methods entail is the inputting of one password after another until finally — *maybe* — something hopefully works. Or just until you give up and move on to a better method.

Brute force methods are usually the first and last thing a hacker does when trying to break into a system. The first time he does it, it's a half-hearted attempt. If he can guess the password right away, or after the first seventy-five or hundred attempts or so, then that's fine. After that fails it's on to trying out other angles for a while. If none of those more sophisticated ways work, then it's back to brute force for the big finish.

Brute force, after all, *must* work eventually. The "must" is what draws hackers to it; the "eventually"

is what drives them crazy. Brute force takes a lot of time, but not much else. That time is spent in research, trial and error, and in writing special programs to hurl one password after another at the system.

Brute force is the least graceful way to fly, but since it eventually must be effective, eventually all hackers will resort to using it at one time or another.

You may find yourself in a situation where you know nothing about the people who use a particular system; where common names and passwords have failed; and where no trick seems to work. In these cases, you will have to try the most brutal of all brute force approaches: you will have to write a little program that will repeatedly dial the computer system, enter a new name/password combination, and keep repeating this until something works.

This could take forever.

Some hackers use a dictionary file they get from their word processing programs or off a bulletin board. This is a good idea, but only if you use it properly. Edit the dictionary file so it includes common names, each letter of the alphabet, musicians, names of cars and presidents, numbers, celebrity nicknames and other common password material. Get rid of the words like "perspectives" that just seem too weird for anyone to use as passwords.

Speaking of making things go faster for yourself, the same holds true when brute forcing non-language passwords. If you live in New York, you should begin your attack by brute forcing New York SSNs only. There are many ways to bring down the number of potential codes you have to check. The military uses what is called the TAC Access Control System (TACACS) to ensure legitimacy of usership of its network computers. The access codes that TACACS looks at are strings of alphanumeric characters — but the strings will never contain the numerals zero and one, nor the letters Q and Z. The theory behind this decision is that a user reading his or her access code off a code card can easily confuse 1s, 0s, Qs and Zs with other letters or numbers.

Once you have edited your dictionary of possible passwords to best suit your needs, or once you have determined which codes are the ones most likely to occur, you write yourself a little program in whatever language you know, to dial the modem, enter one word at a time as a password, and try, try again. And again. And again. This is a simple program to write, but if you don't have the expertise to do so, plenty of programs like this are available on BBSs.

There are some things to consider when writing the program. How many times will the computer system allow you to enter bad name/password combinations before it logs you off? Three? Eight? If it gives you three chances before saying bye-bye, make sure your program outputs exactly three name/password combos before redialing the number.

Often remote computers will accept characters as input even before the input prompt is put on the screen. If this isn't the case with the system you're trying to get into, you'll have to put a delay loop in your program to make sure passwords are not being entered before the cursor is on the screen.

Finally, what happens when your program does manage to ferret out a workable username and password? Unless you're sitting there, monitoring the computer as it does its thing, you need some way of knowing when a brute force attempt has been successful. Otherwise your program will continue to spit out passwords, and the system operators — who by now almost certainly have noticed what is going on — will be absolutely furious! Have the program monitor text as it is sent from the remote computer. When something other than the login prompts are received, have the program flash the screen and ring the loud bell on your printer. Either that, or have it input the logoff command, and print the usable username/password on the screen for you to see when you wake up the next morning.

If you know Joe User works for Company X, then you can have the program run through every combination of password with usernames Joe, User, JUser, and Joe User — not to mention other varieties like joe, JOE, and joeuse. (But from your research and experimenting you should have some idea what format the username will be in, so you shouldn't have to try too many variations.)

If, on the other hand, you don't know the name of anyone who works there, you'll have to either find out (i.e., look in company directories, call up and ask, look in annual reports, newspaper articles,

or any of a hundred other places to find names) or try every combination of possible first names. If you must resort to trying every first name, make sure you try female and foreign names. You might want to take a trip to the library and find out what the most popular first and last names are. But remember, you don't need the current popular names — you need names that were popular and common twenty or thirty years ago, when parents were naming the people who work in the company you're trying to break into.

Certainly, it is not absolutely essential to write a program to spit out passwords. If you have the time and patience, you can sit down and enter passwords yourself. But remember that this will take even longer than the already immense amount of time it takes a computer to brute force its way in. I must emphasize that no matter how many precautions you take to eliminate excess work, brute force will almost always take an extremely long time to bring results. Therefore, it's important to do what you can to speed up the entry of passwords. If you have to redial the modem after every three passwords, make sure you're running your attack off a phone line with Touch Tone capabilities.

Also, before you begin a brute force approach, set yourself up with the highest baud modem you can possibly acquire, even if you need to borrow one from a friend. Moving just a few notches up the baud ladder makes a big difference in speed.

Foiling The Brute Force Assault

As a youngster I remember going out to dinner with my family one night, where they had an all-you-can-eat special. Naturally I decided to do my part to see that I ate my fair share, but by the third reorder, we were getting increasingly frustrated with the long waits and smaller portions. My dad explained it: "You see, that's what they do so you won't eat as much. They keep taking longer and longer to come out with the food, and they give you less of it." I don't know how true that was, but after a while it certainly was not worth waiting around forty minutes just to shovel down another plateful of food.

The techniques used to thwart brute force attacks work on the same principle as that all-you-can-eat restaurant. As mentioned earlier, if one is persistent enough then it is really only a matter of time before a legal username/password is hacked by guesswork or by chance. Therefore, the way to prevent such an attack from succeeding is to structure the system prompts to frustrate the hacker into quitting early.

The most common defense is allowing only a few login attempts before disconnecting. The computer may then refuse to allow a reconnection within a certain period of time. The drawback to this is that a legitimate user might be inconvenienced — though having to wait a few minutes is much less of an inconvenience than logging on to find one's files have been tampered with by some cracker.

Another method is to increasingly slow the response time to each successive login attempt. A prospective hacker might find himself waiting thirty seconds for a response from the remote computer... Then a minute... Then two minutes... The long waiting periods wouldn't start until the first three or four login attempts were tried and found unsuccessful. Then the computer would say to itself, "Gosh, no real user would spell his name wrong that many times. Must be a hacker!"

Another trick is the dummy login prompt. After a certain number of unsuccessful login attempts the system continues asking for login information, but returns an error message no matter what the input is.

The moral of this story is, if you write a password-cracking program, be sure you monitor its progress. Don't just set it to run overnight and leave it unless you've first determined that such security measures are not in place. When you wake up the next morning you may find it's been taking forty minutes for the computer to respond to your inputs. Or you may find that every possible combination has been tried to no avail, and so you know that you've been wasting time responding to dummy login prompts.

Conclusion

Much of this chapter has focused on different "likely" passwords to try when initializing an educated brute force attack. We can go on forever list-ing common passwords — names of pets, historical dates, room numbers, book titles — not to mention all of the above with vowels removed, backwards, and in various anagram forms. There comes a time when you have to forget about trying to limit the number of possible passwords to a select few, because your "limited" number will be as infinite as before you put the restrictions in place.

Besides, a password may be "easily guessable" and yet be secure enough to thwart your attempts to guess it. The password "Smith" is not secure, and "Jones" is not secure, but "Smith@#Jones" is as obscure as anything. Outsiders see password guessing as a valiant pastime for the hacker, but in essence it is only the beginning of the hack. Brute force is best carried out by computers, and should really only be used when a computer is necessary to gain access (I'm thinking about Robert Morris Jr.'s worm program as an example).

The thing is, the whole business of hacking has to do with skill and knowledge. Brute forcing passwords requires little of either. But no one's going to look down on a hacker who does some *educated* brute force work, especially if that hacker has a good reason for doing so. But don't rely on the computer's brawn to do your dirty work: Use the ingenious computing power of your brain. And that is the topic of the following two chapters.

"Computer crimes deal with people to a far greater degree than they deal with technology."
— Donn B. Parker

Chapter Five:
Social Engineering

It is somehow shocking the first time one hears about "social engineering." At least it was shocking for me. Hacking is thought of as an activity pursued solely, nocturnally, *relentlessly*, for hour after midnight hour, by some dazed and nerdish character banging away at a computer keyboard in feverish pursuit of that single golden word which will grant access to the technological secrets of the universe.

That *is* how it *was* at some point in the past, until it became impractical. Those brute force methods are certainly valid, and they are the bread and butter of any well-stocked hacker's arsenal. But there are other ways to learn passwords; social engineering is one of them.

"Social engineering" is the attempt to talk a lawful user of the system into revealing all that is necessary to break through the security barriers. The alternate term for this is "bullshitting the operator."

Social Engineering (SE) appears in a variety of forms and disguises. Here I will list many of them. As you will surely discover for yourself, there is a cornucopia of clever twists and variations to be made on each of these examples.

Some twists I will examine, others will be left for you to creatively imagine.

The Noble Form

To those hackers whose sense of ethics does not allow them to use trickery in an attempt to ascertain passwords, one form of social engineering still might be used without straying from one's sense of morality: the gentle art of asking, "*Please...?*"

I think I've never heard of a verifiable instance where this has worked, though there are rumors that hackers have simply requested — and received — passwords from system users. Usually, the story goes, the system operator is either asked over the telephone, or e-mailed a letter which says something like: "I am a hacker. Give me a low access account and I will use my skills to show you what your system's weaknesses are. That way you can correct them and won't be troubled by *malicious* crackers in the future."

The other way to do this is to call up some-one — *anyone* — a secretary in an office for in-stance — and just ask, "What do you type in to start the computer in the morning?"

Will this work? Well, you would have to be lucky enough to call someone who's fed up with his or her job, and who doesn't know any better about security procedures.

Social engineering minus the deceit is not likely to work, and could make it harder for you to get in, in the future. More likely you will want to bone up on your acting skills and try some telephone shenanigans.

Hacker As Neophyte

Here you play the role of a new user. Let's say you're trying to get into a company's com-puter system. The time is 8:55 in the morning. You call up the computer department (from your home or wherever) and this is the conver-sation that follows:

PERSON ON OTHER END: *"Hello; Jack Chipper, Computing Department."*

YOU: *"Hello, Jack, this is Gary Harris from the Researching Department. Maybe you could help me with a problem?"*

JACK: *"Maybe... What is it?"*

YOU: *"Well I'm the first one here, and I can't seem to get things started up. Will you talk me through it?"*

JACK: *"Sure. You by your computer?"*

YOU: *"Yes."*

JACK: *"Okay. Turn on the red switch on the floor. You see it there?"*

YOU: *"Yes, okay. I see it... Okay."*

JACK: *"It'll take a few minutes for everything to boot up."*

YOU: *"To what?"*

JACK: *"Uh, boot up. I mean, it'll take a minute or two for the computer to set itself, to get ready to use."*

YOU: *"Okay, it stopped."*

JACK: *"What do you see?"*

YOU: *"Just what you always see. It worked up to here fine before, but after this, it didn't work. What do I do when it doesn't work here?"*

JACK: *"What do you usually type?"*

YOU: *"I don't know. This is my first day here. I'm just a temp — they said someone would tell me!"*

JACK: *"Okay, press Enter."*

YOU: *"Enter... Okay."*

JACK: *"Now type 'TEMP' spacebar 'PUPPY.'"*

YOU: *"Okay... Oh!"*

JACK: *"See?"*

YOU: *"Thank you, Jack — I don't know what went wrong before!"*

Now I want to run through this conversation again, this time pointing out some of the essen-tial components of all successful social engi-neers.

PERSON ON OTHER END: *"Hello; Jack Chipper, Computing Department."*

YOU: *"Hello, Jack, this is Gary Harris from the Researching Department.*

Notice here, how you begin your conversa-tion by mimicking the technician's words, intro-ducing yourself in a way similar to the way the technician introduced him or herself. This is done to make the person on the other end feel more comfortable talking to you, and to show that you're not afraid to reveal who you are or what business you do for the company.

If Jack had said he was from the Computer Room, then you would say you were from the Research Room. Unless you have a company directory as reference, you won't know the exact names insiders use for each of the various segments of the corporation. Thus, it's usually a safe bet to talk like the insider — in this case, the technician. Even if you say "department" when you should have said "committee" or "room," the fact that the technician used that term will make you sound, in his ears, like an employee.

YOU: *"Maybe you could help me with a problem?"*

This appeals to the technician's sense of computer godliness. Also piques his curiosity as to what could be wrong with *his* system, or your use of *his* system. Saying "maybe" will get the technician somewhat flustered — you should know better than to question his ability to handle computers. He will then go overboard to show you how smart he is. Knowledgeable users love to show off their computing skills (I know I do, don't you?), especially technicians whose job it is to help the multitude of non-experts get through the day.

Also, notice the mention of the word "problem." Computer people love solving problems. Mention in a vague way that there's a problem with his system, and he'll go crazy: just open your ears and let the passwords roll right in!

YOU: *"Well I'm the first one here..."*

Notice at the beginning I mentioned that the time was 8:55 in the morning. It won't always be possible to call before the workday begins, but it sure does help if you can. Doing so gives you a valid excuse to call a technician for help; after all, if you're the first one there, there's nobody else to ask. But technicians won't always be available before anyone else at the office, so this won't always work.

Consequently, you may want to try making a phone call at the end of the workday. Then you'll be able to say that the other people in the office shut off the computers and went home before you had a chance to finish your work.

YOU: *"...and I can't seem to get things started up. Will you talk me through it?"*

Now that he knows he's the superhero, you immediately identify the problem, while still being vague enough to not alert suspicion if your assumptions about the login procedures are wrong. After all, dialing into the company's computer system from your house could look very different from actually being there, using it in person. You're better off staying with general questions, and allowing the technician to mentally picture the specifics of your trouble. The "will you talk me through it?" request begs him to do something he does by rote every day.

Again, it is important to request that he do something specific (such as talk you through the setup procedures) but not so specific that you blow your cover by making yourself seem suspiciously knowledgeable. For example, if you had simply said, "Can you help me?" he might want to walk over to your office to help you out. Since you are not actually *in* an office, this will definitely tip him off to your deceit.

JACK: *"Okay. Turn on the red switch on the floor. You see it there?"*

YOU: *"Yes, okay. I see it... Okay."*

You have to pretend to be doing what the technician asks you to do, because remember you're not actually in the office, and perhaps the reason you are social engineering is because you don't even have a dial-in number. It's good to have an actual computer next to you, so he or she can hear the power being turned on and you clicking away at the keyboard.

JACK: *"It'll take a few minutes for everything to boot up."*

YOU: *"To what?"*

JACK: *"Uh, boot up. I mean, it'll take a minute or two for the computer to set itself, to get ready to use."*

YOU: *"Okay, it stopped."*

"To *what?*" shows your complete helplessness when it comes to computers. You don't want to pretend you've been living in a cave the last three decades, however. Saying, "What's a keyboard?" will only provoke utter disbelief, not sympathy for your naiveté.

Don't forget that the conversation has a plan to it — you're trying to steer the conversation to your benefit, so make sure you stay in control of where it's heading. "Okay, it stopped," reassures the technician that the computer is working fine, and that his or her ability to give instructions over the phone has not faltered. But above all, it keeps you on track so the conversation can continue toward its ultimate reward.

JACK: *"What do you see?"*

YOU: *"Just what you always see. It worked up to here fine before, but after this, it didn't work. What do I do when it doesn't work here?"*

JACK: *"What do you usually type?"*

YOU: *"I don't know. This is my first day here. I'm just a temp — they said someone would tell me!"*

Boy! This guy isn't letting up! You can either try for another generic answer ("Usually I type my password here..."), but what if you guess wrong? What if at this point an office worker is placed at the DOS prompt or Macintosh Desktop? You see, it could be that dial-in lines are password protected while in-house computers are not. In-house computers might be protected by trust, physical keys, or biometric devices.

In this instance, you've used the "new person" ploy. It's usually a good bet to pretend you're a new person, unless it's widely known that the company is actively firing employees, or is ready to go bankrupt. Saying you're from a temporary agency may or may not be a good idea. Temps will generally have a site contact or local supervisor to whom they report and ask questions. The technician might not know that, however, and in any case you can always say that your supervisor is in a meeting and told you to call the computer department for advice.

JACK: *"Okay, press Enter."*

YOU: *"Enter... Okay."*

JACK: *"Now type 'TEMP' spacebar 'PUPPY.'"*

YOU: *"Okay... Oh!"*

JACK: *"See?"*

YOU: *"Thank you, Jack — I don't know what went wrong before!"*

The "Okay..." is said as if you've tried this same thing a million times, but it's never worked. Thank the technician profusely for his help, and reassure him that you are a genuinely naive but responsible member of the company (in this case, by saying you don't understand what went wrong before).

I based this sample script on hundreds of real-life conversations that technicians have with legitimate users who have the similar problems. I can recall dozens of times when I personally have been asked how to do something that the user has already done before, without getting it to work. Usually all it takes is a run-through and everything works fine. My experience has been that these calls usually end with the person who has been helped grouchily saying, "But I tried that before! It didn't work before!" So make sure that *you* are nice to your technician — you may be needing help from him or her again and it will certainly boost his or her ego to know you appreciate the help you have received.

Here's another example of how a hacker can pretend to be helpless when it comes to computers, but still make off with vital information. When a new computer system has been installed in an office, there will often be business cards or phone numbers taped near the terminals which are used to contact someone from the technical department of the company which supplied the computers, to deal with bugs that haven't yet been worked out.

The business cards (or you may just find a phone number on a slip of paper) may also be taped to a section of wall devoted to important messages, or they may also be hidden someplace behind a clerk's desk or counter. Crane your neck if you must to get the name and number off the card (or simply ask the person, we don't always have to do everything on the sly!).

Let's say you managed to get Frank Smith's number at Corny Computing while you were doing some business at a branch of an insurance company. Call the number and say, "Hi, this is Lauren from Booboo Insurance. There was some weird stuff going on with the computers and I had to shut them off, and now I'm stuck...." And let them lead the way.

One time I saw such a business card taped to a public access terminal at a library. I copied off the information, then called up, saying, "This is Jack [a guy named Jack really worked at the library] from Whoopie Library. I'm having trouble getting into the circulation system from public access mode. The computer's behind the counter, so I don't know what it was doing in PA mode to begin with, but..."

Hacker In Power

If appealing to a technician's sense of godliness won't work in your situation, perhaps it's time to *become* a god. In a military setting, pretending to be a high ranking officer can put fear into the hearts of any lowly receptionist. Just call up, saying either that you *are* the general, or you're the general's personal secretary. In either case, both of you are pissed off that your computer isn't starting up the way it should. Demand to know why your account isn't being accepted as valid. Don't whine or complain — just make angry *demands*. You will get results.

In a corporate milieu, pretend to be the CEO or the president, or secretary of a CEO or president, especially in organizations where it is well known that the leader is a hothead. No one wants to get fired or demoted. The anger routine is useful because the person who picks up will want to be rid of you as fast as possible, and will do *anything* to get you off his or her back.

Presidents, leaders, military officers, CEOs and the like, don't have to be angry, however. Just the mention that you are whoever you say you are will work wonders for your credibility

(who else would possibly dare to proclaim themselves General So-And-So?). But if you act as a high-up without being angry, make sure you've done your research beforehand and know what your name is.

This is a sample encounter:

PERSON ON OTHER END: *"Good afternoo— "*

YOU: *"THIS IS GENERAL FROBBS. I AM APPALLED BY THE CAVALIER WAY IN WHICH THIS PLACE IS BEING RUN! I WENT AWAY FOR TWO DAYS AND WHEN I RETURN I FIND I HAVE BEEN ERASED FROM THE COMPUTER! WHO'S IN CHARGE OF THESE COMPUTERS? I'M APPALLED! I DEMAND YOU RESTORE MY ACCOUNT. I HAD MANY IMPORTANT DOCUMENTS SAVED THERE!"*

PERSON ON OTHER END: *"Did you try typing 'GROUP.1,' 'SEC'? That still works."*

YOU: *"THAT'S THE DAMNED GROUP CODES! I NEED MY OWN PERSONAL ACCOUNT BACK! I AM APPALLED!*

PERSON ON OTHER END: *"I'm sorry, I can't help you with your own codes. Would you like me to find someone who can?"*

Notice in this example conversation you have managed to procure a username/password combination which, while not too powerful, at least will gain you access. Even if the person on the other end never does manage to find the general's password, at least you've ended up with not just one, but several accesses to the system. After all, if there's a GROUP.1, there must be a GROUP.2 , right?

Hacker As Helper

This type of role playing is like *reverse* social engineering without the sabotage (see next chapter). Here you pretend that something has gone wrong with a place's computers, and you are the technician who is calling to fix it.

Let's say you want to break into the computers at the mayor's office. You call up his secretary, and you say something like this:

"Hello, this is Jake McConnel from Computers. We were wondering, have you been having any problems with the computer system?"

Of course she's been having some sort of problem with it — there's always some problem with computers!

The secretary answers: *"Why yes! First this was happening, then blah blah blah..."*

You say, *"Yes! That's exactly it! That wasn't your fault — there's something wrong with the computers, and we're having trouble fixing it. When you first turn on the computer, what do you type in to get it started? One of the other guys here was screwing things around last night and we think that has something to do with it."*

The secretary will not be suspicious; after all, you've identified yourself. Even if you hadn't, what harm could possibly come from telling someone a password over the phone? You see, the secretary, or any other underpaid, overworked, menial user of the system, is a very weak link in the chain of security. The secretary doesn't understand computers and doesn't want to. All she knows is something's going wrong and you're going to fix it for her. This is a very effective ploy.

Peak Hours

Don't use the above mentioned sort of ploy around lunch time or early in the morning. It'll be harder to work effectively. Let the pressures of the work day start to pile up before you call.

If the system you're breaking into is a place you have access to, such as a library, dentist's office, bank or school, you should do a little research and figure out when the best time is to make your call.

At one of the libraries I belong to, the computer system has a "3 o'clock slow down." At around 3 o'clock every afternoon, the computers suddenly slow down to half their usual speed. This leads to various other computer problems and, ultimately, very frustrated library workers. I don't know why the computers slow down; maybe the system gets the most use at 3 o' clock,

or maybe at that time information is forced to travel through an alternate route to get from the library's terminals to the mainframe located at a college on the other side of town. If I were to try some social engineering on the library, I would do it during the 3 o'clock slow down, when most problems occur.

I've noticed another thing: The library patrons who don't realize that there's nothing wrong with computers (who don't know that they always slow down around that time) call up the "computer room" at the college and ask why their computers are down. Don't you think it would be a pleasant surprise, if one day they got a call from the "computer room" (i.e., me or you), asking if there's anything we could do to help? Surely they'd be more than willing to tell you the logon procedures they use, if only you'd speed up the system for them!

Computers tend to be at their slowest toward the middle to end of the day, when the most people are on the network. Especially in university settings, this is true. Frequently students and faculty will log on in the morning, then stay connected throughout the day, regardless of whether they're using the system. On the other hand, some systems will actually get *faster* as the day proceeds, so research is always a must. For example, the Prodigy service is proud of the fact that toward the end of the day and into the night, as usage increases, system speed also increases. This is because data is stored on a dual-tier basis. There are the mainframes situated in Prodigy headquarters somewhere on the globe, and various minicomputers scattered about the country. Users connect to the semi-local minicomputers, called Local Site Controllers, and as they use the system, data is copied from the far away mainframes, to the local minis. By the end of the day, most of the data a user would request to view will have already been transferred to the closer computer, making for less waiting time.

It's good to be aware of pace trends in the places you intend to social engineer. If you can find a noticeable difference in pace (like a 3 o'clock slow down) naturally you will want to work your magic around that time. Good times don't have to just be when the *computer* changes pace; if the workload, noise-level, number of customers, or some other aggravating condition worsens during a particular time, that is generally a nice time to social engineer. To find these times, try to visit your target's office at various times throughout the day. Find out when the office is busiest. If it's something like a library or travel agency, go visit the building or make some phone calls. Ask a question about something, and if they seem to be having trouble when they look it up in the computer, call back as the guy from the computer department. Remember, offices will be at their most hectic after being closed one or two days, so Monday morning is always a good shot. Just make sure they're not *so* busy that they don't have time to schmooze on the phone with you.

Social engineering will work with any computer system, of course, but you will naturally find it a lot more difficult to fool a system administrator at the community college, than a teenage bank teller. Social engineering has been successfully used to gain access to corporate networks, schools, government offices, and other systems. Social engineering is a powerful tool, but you have to be a good actor to use it properly.

Other Hints

If it's possible to research the place, do so beforehand. Do as much as you can to find out about busy hours and what kinds of problems they might experience with the system. If it's a public place like a library, for example, then try to figure out which people working there know nothing about computers. Try to get those people on the phone. Also, make sure you identify yourself as so-and-so from the computer department (or computer division, or section; if the person answers the phone, "Hello, registration office," then use the same terminology — computer office). And when you do so, use a common, everyday first name, and also a familiar last. If you can't get the login information the first time, try again at a different time, on a different day. Don't speak to the same person, however.

A friend of mine, Bill, told me this story. One summer day he called up a mail order place to buy some electronics equipment. As the woman was taking his order, she casually mentioned that she was doing everything by hand because the computers were down. Bill asked if she knew why they were down. She said she didn't know, but she was pissed about it because computers in other parts of the building were working fine. Well, as soon as Bill got off the phone, he called back and hearing a different operator on the line, proceeded to have this conversation:

OPERATOR: *"Shark's Radio Supplies, Pam speaking. May I help you?"*

BILL: *"Yes but actually I called to help you. This is Bill Robinson, in the computer department. Are you still having problems with the computers?"*

OPERATOR: *"We sure are!"*

BILL: *"Oh, okay. What's the computer showing right now?"*

OPERATOR: *"Nothing, we have them all turned off."*

BILL: *"Oh I see. I thought you were having problems with it, but I guess you're in the part of the building where they're not working at all."*

OPERATOR: *"Yeah."*

BILL: *"Well, have you tried turning them on lately?"*

OPERATOR: *"No — oh, are they back on again?"*

BILL: *"I think they might be. Now would be a good time to try."*

OPERATOR: *"Okay.... Nothing came on the screen."*

BILL: *"Can you type in anything?"*

OPERATOR: *"Lemme see.... No."*

BILL: *"Sometimes, even if it doesn't look like the letters are going to the screen, they still go there. Try typing in all the stuff you usually type in when you first turn on the computer."*

OPERATOR: *"Okay."*

The operator went on to give Bill all the information he needed to know. When the operator was finished "logging on," Bill gave a resigned sigh and said, "Oh well, it was worth a shot. I'll go back and tinker around some more. Thanks anyway." Of course, he still didn't have a phone number to call. He didn't even know if the computer system was connected to outside lines — after all, this all happened on account of a freak accident, his finding out about the downed computers. But now he knew how to go about logging in to Shark Radio Supplies's computer system, and he had made a friend on the inside. The login information was important in case he did find a phone number, or if another hacker needed the information. Having an inside friend was important because now Bill could use her as a further information source, if the need ever arose.

Sample Social Engineering Situations

It's easy to get yourself into awkward situations, especially at the beginning of your social engineering career. You will speak to receptionists and other company insiders who know the lingo, know policies and screen setups, and know how to spot a fake. Whether intentional or not, you will be asked questions to which the answers are not readily apparent, due to the fact you are an impostor. Here are some samples, and possible solutions.

RECEPTIONIST: *"You're Charles Green? But there is no Mr. Green in our computing department."*

YOUR RESPONSE: *"I've just been here a few days."*

RECEPTIONIST: *"That's funny, I didn't see your picture hanging up on the New Staff bulletin board."*

YOUR RESPONSE: *"Yes, I know. What's-her-name hasn't had a chance to take my picture yet. Maybe later today."*

RECEPTIONIST: *"What do you mean, 'What's-HER-name'? Jack's the one who takes staff pictures."*

YOUR RESPONSE: *"Oh yeah, Jack — right!"*

RECEPTIONIST: *"I won't be able to help you until I have your staff ID. What is your employee ID number, please?"*

YOUR RESPONSE: *"Oh, I don't have one. I'm just a temp. I'm filling in for someone who went off to have a baby."*

RECEPTIONIST: *"Just read the number off your ID badge."*

YOUR RESPONSE: *"I didn't get my badge yet — there was some mix-up or something. My supervisor said she would give it to me tomorrow, maybe. You know how it is, no one knows what they're doing, and all that..."*

RECEPTIONIST: *"Who's your boss/supervisor/manager?"*

YOUR RESPONSE: *"M_ _____. Do you know anything about him/her?"*

(You should've done your research, so you should know the answer to this sort of question. If you don't know and it's a large company, or a large building, you can try either answering with a false but common name, or try the old, "Uhm... Something with an 'S' — Schindler? Schindling? Schiffer? Schifrin?")
  Here's a different situation:

RECEPTIONIST: *"But I don't have a computer!"*

YOUR RESPONSE: *"I'm sorry. I must've dialed wrong. Is M_ _____ available?"*

(M_ _____ is the name of the receptionist's boss.)

If you can manage to work in some company news or personal tidbits in an unobtrusive way, then do so — if the person you're speaking to seems friendly. This is just another way of gaining credibility points.

YOU: *"Sorry, I didn't hear that last thing you said. It's really loud here with that construction they're doing next door."*

YOU: *"By the way, does M_ _____ have a kid in the Little League? My son has a friend named _____."*

Note that for maximum benefit, credibility questions, should be worked in *before* asking about login procedures.

Miscellaneous Social Engineering Tips

To improve your chances of getting in with social engineering, here are some tips.

Notice how the person you speak to reacts to your questions. If you speak to a receptionist or other worker on the bottom of the pay ladder, he or she may not want to chit chat or fool around with computers if he or she's being monitored, or if calls are being screened by the boss.

Go to some public place where they have terminals hooked up, and look at the wall where the terminal is connected to the phone box. Write down the four digits that appear on the box (these are the last four digits of the phone line that the terminal is hooked to). Guess the first three digits of the number by looking at a directory for the "public place" in question. Call a couple times at different times of day to make sure the line is always busy. Keep some of these "leased line" phone numbers handy when you social engineer to give to people who want to call you back. This is especially true of sysops who suspect you're a hacker and want to see if you're brave enough to give them personal identification information about yourself. This is better than just making up a phone number out of thin air, because if they do call up, the busy signal will at least create some reassurance in their mind that you weren't a complete fake.

Just giving them a number will usually relax them enough so they feel you are one to be trusted.

Confront people in a lighthearted way when they give you a password. Say, "Are you sure that's *really* the one you use?" Secretaries may have two passwords. One is their own, which grants them access to a low-level group account. The other is their boss's password, a higher level one that they know about because, frankly, secretaries know *everything* about an organization.

Challenging someone in a non-accusatory way about the password you are given may also cause them to fess up if they had indeed given you an invalid password to get you off their backs. Second guessing them shows that you already knew the correct password, and that you caught them in a lie.

If they are bewildered when you ask for a higher password, just say, "Didn't they upgrade your access yet? They just bought this whole new system that's supposed to work fifty times faster and everyone's saying how wonderful it is...." Then quickly change the subject.

Have a background tape playing with office sounds or whatever is appropriate for the number you call. Before using this tape, try to take a tour of the company and listen to the real sounds made during the work day. Also, play the tape for a friend over the telephone, and similarly have a friend play the tape while you listen over the phone — trying to adjust the tape to a realistic sound level. Remember that if you're the "first one in the office" as with our naive user example, you don't want the tape to include background chatter or typing!

When you're talking to people, even if it's just over the telephone, keep a smile on your face and act in a jovial, friendly manner. Pretend you're that person's best friend. If the person picks up the phone with a, "Hello, General Widgit Corporation, Lulu speaking," you respond with, "Hi Lulu! This is..." and go on with your spiel. Now Lulu doesn't know if you two have met before, and as you continue with your friendly attitude, she will begin to treat you more like a friend. Try looking through some books on voice marketing, telephone selling, etc., to get more ideas.

The way in which your phone call is received can also affect your credibility. Often a company telephone will make a different sort of ring, depending on whether the caller is on an inside or outside line. Since you are pretending to be an inside caller, you will want your telephone ring to reflect that. To fix that, call a wrong office or department in the company, and have them transfer you to the number you're after. For instance:

PERSON ON OTHER END: *"Advertising. May I help you?"*

YOU: *"I'm sorry, I guess I dialed wrong. Would you mind transferring me to extension 4358?"*

Now you'll get that in-house ring, and with it, an air of authority (and maybe even a special inside caller light will flash on the telephone, too).

Another way to get that desirable inside caller ring/light is to dial, not the listed number, but one *next* to it. Any organization with more than one phone line almost certainly owns a *block* of phone numbers. So if the listed number to call is 123-4567, try calling 123-4568, or something a few digits higher or lower. Your call will usually go through, and it will take on the clout of having been placed by someone who is apparently a company insider — anyone else would have dialed the listed number.

Another thing to consider is if you're trying to reach a higher-up in the corporation, you may only end up contacting secretaries, receptionists and/or other underlings. A good trick is to call an office of higher or similar prestige as your goal office, and let the secretary transfer you over. For example, suppose I want to try social engineering Mr. Palooka — a middle manager who runs the shoe division. But I can't get through to speak with him personally. What I do is, I call up Mrs. Colt, who is either a same-level, or higher-level manager, and I ask her secretary to connect me with Colt personally. Colt's secretary asks what I wish to speak to Colt in reference to, and I say, "Shoes!" But Mrs. Colt handles only the rubber band accounts, not shoes. So Colt's secretary says, "Well, you'll have

to speak to Mr. Palooka about that one; would you like me to connect you?" She will then transfer your call to Mr. Palooka's secretary. Palooka's secretary comes on the line, and you say to her, "Hello. This is so-and-so. Mrs. Colt's office suggested I speak with Mr. Palooka about shoes." Here you have a recommendation from another company member! You're now much more likely to get in to bullshit Mr. Palooka. Happy engineering!

Other Roles

Social engineering in its most important sense refers to the obtaining of personal or group passwords by making up a story about yourself and role playing it, hoping that whoever you end up speaking to will play along. But the goal of social engineering doesn't just have to be passwords. And the method of engineering doesn't just have to be over the telephone. Conversations may take place in person or through the mail. The first requires strong nerves and greater acting ability. The second is more suited to those who find it difficult to ad lib telephone SE conversations.

In-Person Engineering

Any instance of impersonation is a form of social engineering. The impersonation may be of an individual person (the president of a company who demands to know why his password isn't working) or of a generic person (Jill Technician, calling to ask if any computer problems have come up). The telephone is normally used because it enables a hacker to reach distant businesses without travel, as well as creating a defensive barrier between the hacker and the people he or she calls. If the conversation starts to go sour, a telephone can be hung up; if a face-to-face talk gets out of hand, it could be difficult to get out of the building.

A good rule of thumb when doing in-person social engineering is to always wear a suit — a good suit, one that fits properly. Make yourself look like you just stepped out of a fashion magazine. At the very least, wear a shirt and tie. Females, wear suitable business attire.

Many kinds of SE that work over the phone, won't work in person. You can't pretend to have an office, or pretend to have a computer terminal. Because of this the information you get from bullshitting in person may be minimal or only peripheral. You will probably end up with more background material than immediately useful information.

Pretending to be interested in wanting a job at the firm, or going on a tour of the place, or simply squeezing in and wandering around on your own, provide lots of good data on how employees interact among themselves. Hackers and crackers have also impersonated maintenance workers, painters, and other workers to get inside a company. Being a security guard is also a nice ruse.

The prototypical in-person social engineer is the survey taker. You make up a survey, and stand in the lobby of the building with a pen and clipboard, and get people passing by to fill one out for you. The survey asks for name, spouse's name, hobbies, pets and pets' names, and similar info. Then you go home and try all that stuff as passwords. You might want to say there's some prize involved. For example, that completely filled out forms will be entered in a raffle; winners get tickets to a local show, or a free meal at a nearby restaurant. (Hint: Don't ask people to fill out surveys in the morning when they're late getting to work.)

Written Engineering

Social engineering may be done through the mail or through other forms of written contact with users of a system. For example, the survey method can be altered such that the human element is eliminated. If you don't want to wait around in a lobby all day, just leave out stacks of the forms with either a drop-box or an address to mail them to. Expect minimal response.

Other written ruses take the form of advertisements. Put up a notice in a computer room, saying that paid volunteers are needed for a special project. "Become a System Manager! Great Experience!" Have interested folks mail you a post card with their name, address, desired password, and possibly the machines they currently have access to on the net. While making the ads you'll say to yourself, "Sheesh! This is so obvious!" But you won't believe how many people fall for it. Have them address the postcards to something like "X University, Computer Science Department, Roger Hamm's Office" followed by your address. If your address is thirty miles away from the university, forget about it.

Two Manhattan hackers tried this stunt. They noticed there was a blank space at the bottom of a particular magazine advertisement for one of the popular pay-for-play information systems. They went to local area libraries and borrowed all magazines they could find that had this ad in it. Using a "sideways printing" utility, they fed the pages into their printer, which printed out, "Manhattan Area Residents, Call [phone number] For Free Six Month Membership." Then they returned the magazines to the library.

When people called them up, they would begin by playing a corny recorded message: "Welcome to X-Net's Free Six Month Membership Program! Listen to all these great things you can do with X-Net...!" When that was done, one of the hackers would come on and ask the caller a few questions: "Where did you hear about this program?" "Have you ever subscribed to X-Net in the past?" "What other fee-based bulletin boards, or other computer networks do you belong to?" "When you call up X-Net, what would you like your sign-in name to be?" "And your secret password?" "Are you sure you're going to remember that password? Perhaps you'd like to choose something else?"

In this way, they ended up with a dozen names, computers they visited, and one or two passwords to try out. You won't get as big a response if you don't live in a big city, but it's worth a shot. Advertising can also be done by slipping a printed card into the magazine, or by advertising on BBSs.

A similar ruse is to advertise your phone number as a local call switcher, especially in places where there isn't already a Telenet or Tymnet link. When users log on they will see what appears to be the usual opening screen, but is in reality a simulation which you programmed. From hacking, you should be familiar with which networks have which addresses, so your program can simulate appropriate login screens for each of them that a caller might try. (Otherwise, respond with a message like, "Line is busy" or "Connection can not be established." Look at actual call switchers to see not only what messages are displayed, but to get the timing down right.)

After "connecting" to a computer or network, the program continues its simulation, collects the user's name and password, then aborts due to erratic line noise or some other ghastly problem. If the user tries calling back immediately, a message can be put up that warns certain transmission routes are undergoing maintenance, or similar baloney.

Request For Information

And now, back to some pure social engineering through the mails...

Scan all the computer mags and journals furiously, even the bad ones, for warnings about product failures and security loopholes. Journalistic morality generally prevents dangerous secrets from making their way to the mass media, so the exact details of system security failings won't make it to print. You'll see things like, "Four hackers were caught yesterday, after exploiting a loophole in the V software on the W machine at X Military Base." Or you'll see things like, "Company Y has released a warning about its Component Z, which is supposed to keep unauthorized users from penetrating a system...."

What you do is, go print yourself up some official looking stationery, mail a concerned letter to the folks at the company, and wait for their speedy reply. You can try the annoyed approach:

Dear Mr. Abel Jones:

It has come to my attention that there are serious shortcomings in your product, Component Z.

My business operates under the assumption that our data is secure *because* of Component Z.

Seeing as how we have been misled for six years, I expect either: details on the flaws which inhibit Component Z, or reimbursement for six years of twelve non-functioning Component Zs, the cost of which amounts to $14,000.

I expect a quick reply.

Or the "Let's work together to make this world a better place to live in," approach:

Dear Mr. Abel Jones:

I was dismayed to read in Friday's edition of *Computer Magazine* that your Component Z is defective.

My business uses twelve of these devices, and I would regret very much if we experienced a data loss due to their not working.

Please send an explanation of the problem in the enclosed envelope, so that my technicians may remedy the problem as soon as possible.

Thank you for your help.

Sincerely,

I'm divided as to whether or not you should mention specific threats in your letter to the company or organization. On one hand, you don't want them to suspect your letter is phony. But on the other hand, they're going to be receiving many letters similar to yours, most of which are legitimate. You shouldn't have any problem as long as you type the letter on good quality paper, with either a real or imagined letterhead on top. For added effect, type the address on the envelope, and instead of stamping it, run it through a postage meter. You may also slip in a business card of your own design; they are cheap to obtain.

If the company refuses to help you without proof of purchase, well then, you're on your own. You can always try to social engineer the company technicians into revealing the security flaws. There are also plenty of computer security associations, organizations and other groups which will have the particulars of the loophole.

You might also make an attempt to get the juicy details by calling the publication in which you read about the security failing. Try to speak to the person who reported the story. People at magazines and newspapers are surprisingly easy to reach on the phone, but getting them to talk is a different matter!

Message From God

Dear User:

This is most embarrassing.

As the director of PinkyLink, America's largest on-line information service, I was shocked to discover that a theft of several backup tapes took place over the July 6th weekend.

Contained on one of those tapes was, among other things, the personal security data on a small percentage of our customers.

While your name was, luckily, not on that stolen tape, there is still some threat to you. As of now we are uncertain whether any users with programmer-level computer access were backed up on the stolen tape. Therefore, we request you fill out this application and mail it back immediately in the postage paid envelope provided.

Fill out the form and return it to us as soon as possible. Once received, we will update you to this new, secure ID.

Thank you for your cooperation, and to offset any trouble this may cause you, we will be subtracting 75% off your August bill.
Name_____

_____

Address_____

_____

Zip_____

Day Phone(_____)_____-_____

Night Phone(_____)_____-_____

Old (Invalid) Password _____

New (Updated) Password _____

PinkyLink, America's Largest On-Line Information Service, guarantees that the above personal data will be inputted no later than September 1, 19__, (following verification), and will be kept confidential before and after such time.

Please keep a copy of this for your records.

Imagine Joe User gets this letter in the mail. It *looks* authentic, having the logo and letterhead of the service, and arriving in a metered, typed envelope. But will Joe *believe* that PinkyLink actually sent this to him?

The whole situation is preposterous! Any real life computer service with a password problem would require that all password updating occur on-line. It's simply the cheapest and easiest way to update hundreds or thousands of pieces of user information. Still, when Joe User looks at this letter, he will notice that he isn't in immediate danger as some other users of the system are; unlike those other poor losers who got their passwords stolen, Joe doesn't have to be concerned that he'll start getting huge bills in the mail from the criminal charging system usage to Joe's account.

And what about that 75% deal at the bottom? That makes Joe twice as likely to respond to the letter. Not only does he have a responsibility to himself to make his account secure again, he has a responsibility to the database: if they were nice enough to warn him of this and pay him for it, the least he can do is comply with them. And the return envelope is postage paid!

Of course, PinkyLink probably has an on-line way for users to change their password, but you don't have to mention that when you write a letter like this. Remember, the style is more important than the wording of the letter. Before you send out something like this, be sure to look at real examples of PinkyLink's correspondence, to get an idea of the kind of paper and printing used, sizes of fonts, coloring, etc.

You should expect high returns from this swindle, especially if the people you send the letters to are absolute rookies. Later we'll talk more about how monitoring BBS activity can pay off.

Trouble In Paradise?

Impersonating a huge corporation, or inducing people to mail you their passwords under false pretenses, can get you into big trouble. The Post Office considers such activity postal fraud, even if you're just doing it for laughs. These ideas are provided to stimulate your imagination — not to encourage you to do anything illegal. Before you go and do something stupid, you might want to read Chapter Fourteen.

When you social engineer there are many factors that inhibit the person you speak with from giving out security data. Consider, when you social engineer someone, that person

- may have been warned about security leaks
- may be knowledgeable about social engineering tactics
- can not verify your claimed identity
- might know you are not who you claim to be
- has no reason to assist you, and can give you wrong or misleading information
- can report your call to a security manager.

For all these reasons, a person you try to social engineer may not want to or may not be able to tell you passwords and other information that you request. Considering the above list, would *you* divulge confidential information to someone asking you for it over the telephone?

That's the problem.

The solution?

See you in the next chapter!

Chapter Six
Reverse Social Engineering

Reverse social engineering, or simply reverse engineering (or the simpler RSE or simpl*est* RE) is a sometimes risky endeavor that varies in its effectiveness and in its applicability. However, results from RSE are so strong — and often so humorous — that it provides a flashy alternative to other methods of breaching system security.

You see, even though social engineering is an accepted and revered method of finding out what you shouldn't know, it has its faults. No system is perfect, and clearly the list of flaws from the previous chapter shows that there are deficiencies in the usefulness of social engineering.

In many respects RSE is better than SE. However, reverse SE can only be used in specific situations and after much preparation and research. In addition, the best reverse engineering can *only* be done by more sophisticated (and mobile) hackers. Don't expect this technique to be your bread and butter as you are first introduced to the world of computer-criminal culture. Reverse social engineering in its most consummate forms takes information you don't yet have, and skills you may not have acquired. Here is a comparison chart that shows some of the pros and cons of each form.

SOCIAL: You place call, are dependent upon them.
REVERSE: They place call, are dependent upon you.

SOCIAL: You feel indebted to them, or they believe and act as if you should be.
REVERSE: They appreciate your help and concern, will oblige you in the future if ever you need assistance.

SOCIAL: You need help from them.
REVERSE: They need help from you.

SOCIAL: Questions often remain unresolved to the victim.
REVERSE: All problems are corrected; no suspicious loose ends.

SOCIAL: You have less control.
REVERSE: You retain complete control of the direction and subject of conversation.

SOCIAL: Little or no preparation required.
REVERSE: Lots of pre-planning required; previous access to the site is needed.

SOCIAL: Can work anywhere.
REVERSE: Only can be used under certain circumstances.

Much of social engineering is based on the premise that you, an impostor, pretend to have difficulties and need assistance from another computer operator to solve your problems. The reverse to this is that a *legitimate* system user has difficulties, and he or she asks *you the hacker* for assistance. In the process of assisting the user with his or her problem, the hacker is able to (effortlessly) find out account names, passwords — the works.

An RSE attack consists of three parts:

• Sabotage
• Advertising
• Assisting

Sabotage is an initial brief contact with an on-site computer, during which the hacker causes a malfunction of some kind that will need correcting.

Advertising is letting the user know you are available to answer computer-related questions.

Assisting is the conversation in which you solve the user's problem, and the user unknowingly solves yours.

Before I explain how this is accomplished and what good it does, you should understand why it's better to have them call you than the other way around. Let's step through that list of bad stuff about social engineering that was given previously, this time demonstrating how *reverse* social engineering overcomes all of those problems.

Overcoming Social Engineering Drawbacks

May Have Been Warned About Security Leaks Or May Know About SE Tactics

Trying to social engineer someone who knows about social engineering, especially hip programmers and other hackers, won't get you anywhere. Even if the other party doesn't know about "SEing" per se, he or she may take "Don't reveal the password" warnings seriously enough to see through your bull. Social engineering is based on the premise that the person you contact is naive. You can't always guarantee that will happen.

In RSE, the legitimate user is calling *you* for advice. Consequently he or she believes you are trustworthy, a member of the company or approved by the company, and one who already knows passwords and protocols anyway. There is no reason *not* to divulge this kind of data to you. In fact, it won't even be thought of as "divulging" since the person you speak with will just matter-of-factly spill his or her guts to you without hesitation.

It should be noted that reverse social engineering is *not* social engineering. It takes a backwards approach to the problem of getting users to talk, and so it won't be recognized by a person familiar with conventional hacker tricks. Furthermore, even if the person is so sophisticated as to understand RSE, that person will probably be so wrapped up in his or her own problem that he or she won't notice what's going on. He or she *needs* your help to correct the problem; he or she realizes that if he or she doesn't cooperate, you won't be able to assist.

Cannot Verify Your Claimed Identity Or Might Know You Are Not Who You Say You Are

Social engineering suffers because to the person you call, you are an enigma — someone they do not know personally. Besides, you never know if the person on the other end of the line has been tipped off that you are lying about your identity — using cues such as Caller ID, a distinctive in-house telephone ring, or a knowledge of employees and protocol. In any case, magic passwords might not be readily given to "mystery technicians" and "perplexed users" with modem troubles.

BUT in reverse SE, those who know the words of passage have no reason to suspect you of deceit: you are the one *they* call for advice. You are the one who is going to help them out of *their* misery. In fact, when they call you, you can legitimately request that *they* identify who *they* are. It is a matter of security, after all.

Has No Reason To Assist You, Or Can Give You Wrong/Misleading Information

What does the social engineered person care whether you are helped or not? I know if I were a busy back-stabbing office worker or receptionist in the midst of a hectic day, I would be furious if some idiot on the phone asked me to give up a few moments of my time to tell him things he probably shouldn't know in the first place. I would probably just tell the caller anything to get rid of him.

On the other hand, reverse social engineers know that the people they are speaking with *require* their assistance. Even the grandest guru of power users will call you if he thinks you will be able to quickly and simply pinpoint the problem and fix it, rather than wasting his time trying to do so. That power user knows he will get the solution when you reveal it to him, so he can solve it himself the next time it occurs.

Might Report Your Call To A Security Manager

The trained user will know immediately when you're trying social engineering. She can then go off and tell others about your attempted pilfering of passwords. Those "others" include co-workers, bosses, computer managers, the person you tried to emulate, guards, or security officers. None of this will help you get in later on, even if it doesn't immediately get you caught or hurt your chances of penetration. Discovery is certainly not on your list of birthday wishes.

On the other hand, reverse SEing is sure to make you a friend on the inside. When you help people overcome obstacles, they will happily spread the word of your courteous, efficient manner of help to others — thus spawning more calls and more passwords.

The preceding explanations were motivated by three goals. I want you to comprehend the reasons why even such a powerful force as classic social engineering will fail on occasion, and how reverse social engineering can eliminate those failings. Yet my main concern is this: Social engineering can not remain as a mainstay of the modern hacker's bag of tricks without word getting out to ordinary computer users. Ordinary users are becoming increasingly aware of the need for discretion when it comes to such intimate topics as passwords and computer security. Ordinary users are reading more in the mainstream press about how we hackers break into systems. They are attending computer security lectures given by their companies, their community colleges, and their local law enforcement branches. The systems themselves contain warnings not to reveal anything to anyone; their employers tell them that, their conscience tells them that. I — yes, even *I* — tell them that some vile people are out there trying to rifle through their computer files.

I doubt strongly there will ever come a time when *all* computer users know enough not to blab. Perhaps in a few years, businesses will have output from their telephones on a time delay, and have them hooked up to voice monitors. Then, if a naughty word is spoken, it can be detected and eradicated before the electrons that compose it leave the confines of the building's wiring.

Even if such a thing does become commonplace, or even if 95% of the computer-using public decide not to be bullshitted any longer by social engineers, there will still be those five percent, the hundreds of other new and old hacking methods, and there will still be Reverse Social Engineering to get the hacker through his day.

Reverse Social Engineering Sabotage Methods

The first step of RSEing is to disable the target computer or the user's ability to use that computer. Generally this means you will be disabling a user's workstation, terminal or computer so that he or she can not access the system properly. You want to do something that is hard to detect yet easy to correct. Here is a list of five *general* ideas, ranging in the amount of setup time and system familiarity required:

- Alter a parameter, the kind of parameter that novices don't know about or think about. Examples: default printer port, screen colors, macros, obscure printer codes, technical peripheral settings.
- Set files to read-only, or rename them, or make them invisible in their directories. Example: if

WP.EXE is the word processor used, change the name to WP.A.

- Hardware tampering. Examples: switch a color monitor to monochrome mode; reverse disk drives; disconnect or loosen the keyboard, or unplug the computer or surge protector.
- Install memory-clogging TSR programs. User won't know why program fails to run.
- Run a simulation program, such as an operating system simulation, which gives lots of ugly error messages.

WARNING!

Sabotage should not be permanently harmful to the user or the computer! Do NOT delete files or directories: they may become unrecoverable. Do NOT install viruses: they can easily get out of hand. Do NOT sabotage in a way such that the operating system refuses to boot: they may not have a bootable DOS disk handy when they call you later!

RSE Case Study: The Translation Table

A hacker and phone phreak nicknamed Phlash — because of the speed with which he'd managed a number of great hacks — was once almost resigned to the fact that he couldn't get any information about the computers at a particular embassy. "They were really tight-lipped," he told me. "I tried bull-shitting them, but they wouldn't have any of it. And line connections were hard to establish. And once on, they only gave you two chances before disconnecting you. So I needed some other way of getting in."

From scavenging around in the trash bins he found evidence that at least one computer there used a particular cheapo-brand modem. Since it was his only clue, Phlash got some literature from the modem manufacturer, and found that all their modems came with a home-brew terminal emulator, which featured, among other technical details, the ability to define character translation tables for both incoming and outgoing data.

Sometimes people want to be able to press a certain key on their keyboard, but have it come out as a different key on the computer they're connected to. For example, a lot of times editing keys such as Backspace don't work the way they should when you connect to a different computer, because when you press Backspace, the remote computer ignores it. To *really* send a Backspace to the remote computer, you might have to type Control-Backspace.

If your terminal program allows it, you can set up a translation table to press Control-Backspace for you. A translation table is a file that contains each key you can type, and the character that is to be sent through the phone lines when you type that key. If you had this Backspace problem, you would set up your table so that any time you pressed Backspace, the computer would translate that to Control-Backspace, and send *that* to the computer on the other end of the line.

Translation tables also work the other way. They take incoming data from the remote computer, and translate the characters into other characters. If you want to get rid of annoying linefeeds in a file, for instance, you can set up the table so anytime it sees a Control-J, it translates it to a null, or to a tap of the spacebar.

Phlash realized that a translation table could be used to his advantage. He took a copy of the terminal program and composed both an incoming and outgoing translation table, both of which were made to jumble characters. If someone were to connect with a computer using these translation tables, nothing they typed on the keyboard would match its on-screen output. Any data they received would be totally garbled gibberish.

He typed up a short INSTALL program and saved it to a floppy disk. His INSTALL program looked in the directory for the already-installed terminal program, moved any existing translation tables to the floppy disk, and copied his newfangled tables over.

Phlash then printed up a convincing letter from the desk of "Technology Office, Second Branch, Director" which said,

> To comply with new regulations governing cryptography, and the exchange of com-

munications between ourselves and others in any foreign nation, we ask that you install this new, more secure version of communications software which includes functions to ensure the confidentiality of all state matters.

He gave explicit instructions for the installation, then concluded with, "Any questions or comments should be directed toward Sr. Benjamin Marcques, at telephone number 9-212-WXY-WXYZ." And he mailed it to a top person at the embassy.

Weeks later he got his phone call. "Actually, they had tried calling before but I had been away," Phlash told me later. "That poor woman went almost a week without being able to use her modem because I did that sneaky thing to her! When she called me, I went through the whole engineering bit, asking her to try logging on like she usually did. Of course it didn't work. I asked her if there was anyplace else she usually called, and there was. So we tried that. Didn't work either. Finally I decided it was in her best interest to try going through the reinstallation again. Naturally that reversed the four translation tables, so everything was peachy again. Of course now I also had all I needed to get into two important government accounts!"

Phlash said that he was getting so caught up in his pretend role that he almost forgot to get the passwords and phone numbers. During the course of "helping" the embassy worker, he suggested that perhaps it was a problem with the phone line: "Which phone number are you dialing in from?"

You would also want to ask if there were any alternate numbers to try.

Unlike typical reverse engineering, this particular case involved no physical entry of the computer site. Normally, access is needed to set up a hardware or software problem of some sort, and to set up advertising for your unique brand of assistance. How to gain access is touched on elsewhere in this book.

Solving The Sabotage

When they call you, after going through the login procedure and finding the error still there, you must tell the user what he or she can do to correct the problem. This can be done by giving explicit instructions such as: "Type 'rename WP.A to WP.EXE'..." But if it is a knowledgeable user who calls you, he or she will notice something fishy going on.

So how to get around this obstacle? You have to give instructions which will soothe the wary user. If the sabotage is software-related, put a software solution on disk. For example, "Go into the word processor directory and type 'SETUP' and press Return. Now try running the program again." In this case, SETUP was a file that *you* put on the disk, which contained the renaming instruction, and also a command to delete itself at the end of its run.

Hardware problems may be difficult to fix or explain over the phone, but then, most RSE won't involve hardware anyway; if you had enough on-site time to physically mess up their computer, you should have had enough time to glean the information that you are trying to get.

RSE Advertising Methods

Here are five general advertising techniques that can be used to get *them* to call *you*:

- *Switch notes.* If you see a slip of paper taped to or nearby the computer, with the phone number of the computing department, get rid of it and slip a note with your own phone number in its place (or some number at which you can wait for a call from them). Elite hackers will simply dial into their local telco computers and change the number of a local pay phone to the listed computer help desk number. Also look for business cards and Rolodex numbers to either hide or switch.

- *Post a public message.* On a bulletin board (thumbtack style, not electronic!) put up a huge, brightly colored, professional-looking sign that says something along these lines:

Technical Helpline

— — — — — — — —

COMPUTER PROBLEMS?
CALL US FREE AT
OUR NEW NUMBER:
(123) ABC-WXYZ

— — — — — — — —

Technical Helpline

Be sure to put the name of the company you're hacking, and their address and logo somewhere on the poster to make it look like it's endorsed by the company. Put these signs up all over, or drop them as flyers on people's desks, especially in view of the computers you sabotaged.

* *Social engineering.* Call up the day before — or even a few hours before — the sabotage and tell the person who answers about the computing department's new phone number helpline (your number). Ask whoever answers to put it in the Rolodex, or to keep it otherwise close by and handy for whenever anyone needs it. Ask if he or she is the only one who uses that terminal; if the answer is "no," tell the person to make sure others know about the new number too.

* *Directory tailoring.* Get a company's internal phone directory and add your number to the list, either by crossing out the existing technical support line and writing in your own, or by inserting a visible printed addendum to the book.

* *On-line advertising.* When doing the initial sabotage, see if you can post a note on the bulletin board (electronic this time!) concerning your computer helpline. Alternately, have part of the sabotage program give out the phone number. For example, rename WP.EXE, then create a simulated word processor which crashes to the operating system after the first few keystrokes, leaving behind garbled characters and colors, and this message:

```
<Beep!>
XERROR 3 - - - Consult fdox 90v3.2a or
call Jim at technical support @ (123)
ABC-WXYZ
```

In your advertisements, make sure the user realizes it is an *outside* line they are calling (so they know to dial 9 or 2 or whatever to exit the company PBX). That is, do that unless you have managed to appropriate an inside office or phone (by sneaking into an office while someone's away on vacation, for example).

Trouble For Nothing?

Okay, granted the initial setup and planning and sabotage is an exciting, amusing kind of thing to do. But is it worth the effort? Why not just stick with the easier social engineering and not worry about the remote possibility that the guy on the other end will be wise to you?

Well, first of all, that's foolish. Especially considering that many of the people and places you will want to hack most will be very security-aware. You *must*, in many circumstances, assume that they know what you're up to when you're bullshitting them. And if they know what you're doing, you shouldn't be doing it.

Another factor, one related to both this and a remark I made earlier: when you reverse engineer a situation, you create a friend on the inside. Once you start hacking big-time you'll never know if somebody's on your tail unless you have an inside connection. If you've proven yourself to some user by solving their computing problem, you can then call back a short time after breaking in and ask questions like, "Hi, remember me? I helped you with that problem... I was wondering if you heard about anyone else having that problem, or any other *weird stuff* going on with the system?" If they've heard about attempted break-ins or system failures, you will be the first to know. You might want to tell them to call you if they ever hear about "hackers" or whatever. This way if you are discovered and, let's say a memo is distributed telling everyone to change their passwords because a hacker is on the loose, your contact will innocently call and let you know about it.

The continuing loyalty and assistance you will receive from the inside is well worth the beginning trouble you may have in setting up the sabotage.

Part Two
During Hack

Chapter Seven:
Public Access Computers
And Terminals

Introduction To The Three Kinds

Have you been to a mall lately? I mean one of those huge, sprawling malls that not only have clothing stores, electronics shops and food courts, but miniature golf courses, arcades, banks, post offices, and anything else you can or can not think of?

Instead of the large "You are here — >" maps they used to have, you now often find computers set up with touch-sensitive screens that help you find your way around the mall and inform you about mall happenings.

Personally, I've never hacked a mall computer — but the potential is there — and the motivation to do so is there as well. Hackers hack because they are in love with the idea that any accessible computer has a secret side that can be broken into. The computers at the mall have a secret side — the general public is not supposed to be able to change around the names of the stores on the computerized map of the building — but there is a way of doing just that. Similarly, when you go to Ellis Island and look up your ancestors in the computers, there is obviously some rear end to the system that you are not being allowed to see. All public com-

puters have a secret side. A hacker is a person who wants to get at it.

This chapter addresses two aspects of publicly accessible computers:

- How to get into the behind-the-scenes parts, and
- using public computers to collect information you're not supposed to know about the people who use them.

The computers and dumb terminals that are publicly available are a great boon to anyone interested in hacking. Even if a general-access computer doesn't have a modem hanging off the back, or does not allow out-dialing, hackers can benefit by using the computer to gather information about legitimate users of on-line databases, school networks and other computing systems.

Computers are publicly available in lots of places — lobbies of office buildings, malls, museums, airport club lounges, public fax machines, public and private schools, and in stores. However, the place they are most often seen is at libraries; consequently, the following discussion is based mostly on the computers found there.

Computers for the use of the general public are available now at most public and academic libraries. They fall into three groups:
- CD-ROM databases and information computers,
- public access terminals, and
- general purpose microcomputers.

Let's look at each one of these in turn, and see how these can help the hacker help himself.

CD-ROM Databases And Information Computers

CD-ROM databases, like InfoTrac and News-Net, are computerized listings of periodical articles, updated monthly. Other databases are available with slants toward business news, census data and the like. Some libraries have CD-ROM encyclopedias, and many government depository libraries will have databases listing government publications available.

In a similar vein, I've seen libraries with computers (usually Macintoshes) set up with user-friendly programs designed to teach patrons how to use the library and to dispense other helpful advice. All of these computers are useful to the hacker only for the information they carry, due to the fact that they are set up on independent machines, without modems, and without access to telephone lines. They usually serve the single purpose of dispensing information on their specific topic.

Finally — this is rare and a bit odd — but occasionally you will see a computer being used as a "register". As people walk into the computer room, office, or wherever, they sign into the computer with a name and ID number, and perhaps answer a few questions about themselves. The purpose of this sort of computer setup is to keep a timed and dated record of who uses the public facilities. Of course, unless a light pen or graphics tablet is used, signatures can not be collected and so their use for security purposes is lost.

Unlike databases and tutorials, there is a bit more you can do hacker-wise with a guest record computer, though not much more. One application might be to use the computer to see who else has been using the facilities. This information could be helpful if the facility in question is a computer room. You might be able to find exploitable patterns in computer usage by certain individuals, or an overall tendency for less people to be in the room at certain times, both of which are helpful to know, as we will see.

If the guest register program itself doesn't let you see who was there before you, try exiting out to the operating system and checking for relevant data files. This will be discussed in the upcoming section on general-purpose micros.

Access to CD-ROM databases and information computers is not usually of much use to the hacker. There are exceptions of course, and it's well worth investigating any computer of this kind that you find.

Public Access Terminals (PATs)

These are usually dumb terminals (although sometimes you see IBM compatibles) set up in libraries as electronic card catalogs. They have names like IRIS and GEAC. These systems allow library patrons to search for materials (books, magazines, videos) by various search restrictions; to see the current status of materials (On the shelf? Charged out? Overdue? Missing?); place holds on items; get library news, and other library-related functions. Often dial-in lines are available, especially at university libraries.

The challenge to the hacker is this: He knows there is a secret side to every library computer. How can he get into it?

Every library computer system is divided into two parts. There is the publicly-accessible catalog, and the private stuff. The private stuff (the secret side) includes procedures to discharge materials, get confidential patron information, add or alter fines, block library cards, etc. These private functions, used by library staff, must rely on the same database of information as is found on the PATs. (If the librarian checks out a book to somebody, the fact that the book is not present in the library must be shown on the public terminals.) Therefore, the functions that are available to the public are a subset of the entire library program. That is, the program the public uses to make inquiries on books is part of a larger program which includes higher managerial functions.

The two program parts are obviously separated, otherwise anyone could walk into the library and erase all the fines off their library card, or put $100 worth of lost items on an enemy's card. So, how is the public side separated from the private side? Take a guess.

Yup, a password.

Actually, it's usually a combination of two things: first, a hidden menu command, and then the password to authorize usage. Go to the main or earliest menu on the library system and try various commands like BYE, END, EXIT, X, XXX, SYS, SYSTEM, LATER, and OFF. Usually this kind of system will accept either three-character commands or single-character commands, but of course things vary widely as you go from one system to another, so vary your tactics accordingly. If something like BYE works, and you are exited from the public portion of the system, you will probably be asked to supply a password. Well, you know how to get passwords! On the other hand, it may not ask for a password at all...

Several library systems use bar code identification to determine who gets to go backstage. If your library card has a bar code on it, then it is possible — but not certain — that achieving system operator status relies not on uncovering a password, but finding out some sequence of little black stripes. I have a story about this.

The Bar Code Hack

A certain academic library, close to my house, has dumb terminals and IBM compatible micros set up throughout the building for the public to use. The IBMs also have light pens attached. On those computers, patrons can access and change information about themselves, using the bar codes on their library cards for security.

One fine day I decided I wanted to hack the system. I knew from random trying that BYE from the Main Menu brought me to a screen that asked for my bar code number. Naturally, I was not allowed staff access, so scanning my library card did nothing. I needed a staff card — preferably one with high access levels, like the library card of the library director, or some supervisor or someone like that.

I was not about to become a pickpocket to get a card. There was a better, more flexible, more hacker-like way of solving the problem. I would use computer technology to defeat the computer.

When you look at a bar code, you will generally see little numerals printed below the stripes. This is the number that the bar code is encoding. On a library card (or the bar code put on library books), the number is about sixteen digits long. There is an initial grouping which identifies the bar code as belonging to that particular library, followed by some zeros, and then a concluding seven or eight digits. This kind of numerical arrangement applies to your checkbook account number, and many other numbers used to identify you.

Now, the only part of the number that really matters is the last group of eight digits, following the zeros, since the library identification portion doesn't change from one person to the next. This meant that if I wanted to try a brute force entry of every bar code number until I found one with high access levels, I wouldn't have to try trillions and trillions of numbers — only a hundred million or so.

Naturally I wouldn't be able to type in those bar code numbers from the keyboard (and who would want to, anyway?). You see, the computers do not allow people to walk over and type in bar code numbers. If they did, then anyone who knew anyone else's code number could easily access the private records of anyone else. That meant, even if I found out the bar code *number* of the library director, I still wouldn't be allowed into the backstage areas of the library program. I would still need the director's *library card*.

A way you might be able to get around this is to scan your bar code, and look at what happens. Did the computer put a carriage return at the end of the number? If not, see if you can back up and alter digits.

If a carriage return *was* added, try scanning your bar code again, this time sending a break or pause signal as soon as you do. You might be able to make the computer *think* it's receiving the entire bar code, although you will be able to change and add numbers to suit your needs. If you pushed control-S to pause the bar code — and it worked — try pressing control-C and see if this stops it from reading in more digits from the scanner.

The bar code will be read in and placed on the screen rather quickly, so it may be difficult to stop it halfway through. If there's a printer attached to the computer, try sending output to it. This might slow down the bar code enough to let you break it at the right time. Also, if it is a computer you're working on (not just a terminal) there might be a "Turbo" button that you can press to take it out of turbo mode. If there is no button (but you know it's in turbo mode because there is a "Turbo" light lit up), there will be some way of disabling turbo mode through either the software (break into the DOS shell and see if there's a SPEED command or something similar), or through the keyboard (often something like Ctrl-Alt-Minus sign will take it out of Turbo).

Another difficult thing to do is to try giving the scanner only a partial or erroneous code. Occasionally bar code readers can be duped into thinking a bar code of a kind it's not supposed to be able to read is the correct type. Then it may read that code and stop halfway through, to wait for the rest of the input.

Lastly, if there is a way of accessing terminal parameter menus, by all means do so: often there is some sort of switch which toggles automatic sending of input, or the key code used to send input. By disabling the automatic send, you can manually input the bar-coded information.

All of these above suggestions imply that you have managed to get ahold of the bar code number of someone important in the library hierarchy — someone whose ID number you can use to access the rear end of the system. If you *do* happen to know the number, then you can try to print up a bar code for it, either by using bar code generating software, or by carefully examining bar codes until you have determined what thickness and pattern of lines are used to represent the different digits.

But I didn't have anyone's number. The purpose of my hack was to *find* one. So I had to find a way of using the light pen to scan in a hundred million bar codes that I didn't have, until one was discovered that could access the library program's secret side.

I could've used a bar code program to print out all of those different combinations of digits but that would have been a huge waste of time and effort.

The light pen (also known as a "wand," "bar code reader," or "scanner") works like this. Light is emitted from an LED inside the pen, focused through a sapphire sphere (which acts as a lens) onto the bar code. The light is then reflected off the

page, and now focused through the sphere onto a photo-sensor, which converts the reflected light into bursts of voltage. The electrical output of the photo-sensor is amplified, thus generating a signal proportional to the series of black and white lines of the bar code label.

The pen is attached to the computer either via some external box, or an internal card. This box/card decodes the on-off firing pattern of the voltage into usable ASCII characters. At the time of decoding, voltage corresponding to white lines is approximately 0.11 volts, and 0 volts for the black lines. My plan was to send voltages into the scanner, making it think it was reading a bar code, when really all it was doing was being victimized by a clever hacker's brute force attack.

If you are programming a computer or signal generator to create fake codes for you, some fidgeting around might be necessary before you arrive at the correct numbers for that particular system. Also, the time it takes to generate a complete code will have to be adjusted accordingly: usually scanners will accept bar codes at up to 45 inches per second. Perhaps you can manage to locate appropriate technical manuals or some source code listings, or call up the company and ask to speak to a technician about what ideal values are for voltages and timing.

If it is a computer you are working with, rather than a dumb terminal, it is possible the bar code decoding program is memory resident. You might be able to circumvent that program, or trick it into reading input from a disk file you supply. A good idea would be to copy the contents of the fixed drive, then at home see if there's a way of making the scanner decoder think the keyboard is the correct RS232 serial interface to look at for input data.

Finally, remember that there will be a check digit at one end of the bar code, or both ends, although it will almost never be printed on the label itself. If the check digit is printed on the bar code label, study some sample bar codes and try to work out the method used to generate the check digit. You don't need to look at only bar codes on library cards — which you would probably have difficulty finding enough of — you can examine bar codes on books and come up with the same result.

For example, the check digit formula used by the Universal Product Code found on supermarket food packages is the following: 210 minus three times the sum of the alternating digits (starting with the separated digit to the left of the bar code), minus the sum of the remaining digits. The check digit is the last digit in your answer.

Figure 6

The UPC check digit system. The initial digit may appear in either of the spots marked with a 0. The subsequent digits are placed under the bar code, with the check digit appearing in either of the two places marked with a check mark.

The UPC check digit formula is:
210 - 3 (a + c + e + g + i + k) - (b + d + f + h + j)

For this sample bar code, the formula is:
210 - 3 (0 + 2 + 4 + 6 + 8 + 0) - (1 + 3 + 5 + 7 + 9) = 125

The last digit of the answer is 5.
Thus 5 is the check digit.

Back to the target of my attack, that academic library near my home. The light pen at one of the computers was attached with a telephone-style modular clip. It could easily be removed. I bought a receiving jack of appropriate size and used a cable to connect it to the modem port of one of my smaller portable computers. Then I modified an auto-dialer program to spit out bar code numbers in the range I needed. I was all set.

A few days later it was Saturday, and it was a gorgeous day. I had expected to pull off this stunt on a Sunday because I'd seen the results of a user survey which indicated that less people came into that particular library on Sunday than any other day of the week — the last thing I needed was a bunch of onlookers. But it was such a beautiful day I figured everyone would be at the beach. I was right; practically no one was there.

I detached the light pen from the library's computer and connected the plug into my portable's jack. I typed BYE, which brought me to a prompt which asked for my bar code before it would allow me to go backstage. Then I started the program running. It worked fine — the program was sending bar code numbers through the modem port and into the light pen cable. The library's computer had no way of knowing that the data it was receiving was not coming from an actual bar code.

I closed the cover of my little portable, and hid the whole thing under a newspaper. Then I sat there and read a magazine while it went through the numbers.

After a while I did find a bar code number associated with a privileged account, and I was able to use it to change the status of my own library card to a virtual superuser.

That was great in and of itself, but having superuser status allowed me to go one step further. Since I now had access to patron records, I could find out the addresses, phone numbers, student IDs, social security numbers and birth dates of everyone with a card at that library. This meant I had background information on virtually every student at the school, and every professor and staff member. I could also find out what books were checked out to people, and therefore the subjects and hobbies that interested them. Using all this information it was a simple task getting into many network accounts I should not have been able to get into otherwise.

Hidden Commands

Whenever you're hacking any public terminal of this type you have to remember that it's common to have different levels of security for potential users of the system. With each level, the various commands may or may not appear listed in the menu — although you may still be able to activate them via an inadequacy in the program. If a menu is given with options ranging from one to four — try five! And six... and zero too. Always try Z, Q, X, and other "weird" letters — anything else that has a possibility of working. It may not be enough to try these unlisted commands just once; sometimes you can have the program display an error message once or twice, and then suddenly crash out of the system or enter private territory. I grant you, usually you *won't* find that programs have been so badly coded as to allow misuse, but you'd be surprised at the number of bugs that do go unnoticed by the authors and testers. This is especially true of early program editions.

Also, remember this: There are many functions you may not think would be on a library computer (or whatever computer it is you're working on).

There may be mnemonics used which, on your own, you would never think of trying. So you must therefore try everything you can. What I mean is, let's say a library's PATs allow you to enter these three-letter commands to do different things: INQ (to make an inquiry on a book), NEW (to get new user information), and PAT (patron information, to find out about yourself). Naturally the system doesn't only support those three commands. There are dozens of other commands that you simply don't know about.

Try things like CON, ILL, CHG, DIS and other three-letter combinations (or whatever number of characters is appropriate). On some systems, all commands are three characters except for one called NEW USER or RECALL or something. If that's the case, then you know the computer will support commands of more than three characters. Consequently, you should try longer commands as well. The commands I've chosen above are abbreviations for CONversion, InterLibrary Loan, CHarGe and DIScharge, respectively. Before I told you what ILL stood for, you may have been wondering how the word "ILLness" or "I Love Lucy" could have anything to do with a library. But ILL happens to be a very commonly used abbreviation.

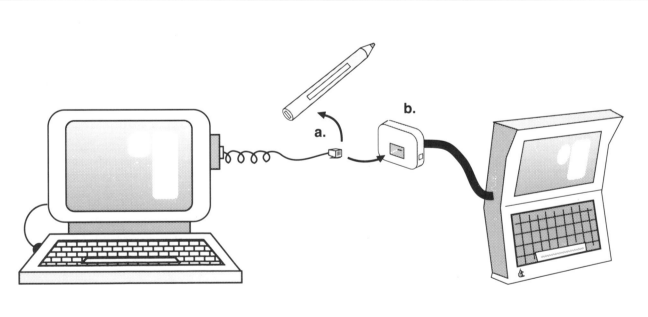

Figure 7

To fool the PAT into believing you are feeding it bar codes, first (a) remove the light pen from the computer.
Then (b) plug the jack into a receiver that is connected to your laptop via the communication port.
You can then output bar codes through the comm port, straight into the PAT.

If you're trying to break into a system you know nothing about, it's more than likely they'll use codes and abbreviations that are related to their field. Consequently, ongoing research is a must.

One United Kingdom system uses things like LCO and LIN for Library Check Out and Library INquiry. Also, due to certain overseas privacy laws, staff members are not supposed to access patron accounts to see personal information like addresses and phone numbers, and what books are checked out to patrons. This poses an obvious problem to the librarians who MUST know how to contact people who refuse to return borrowed items (and for countless others reasons, must know what items people have borrowed), so the people who wrote this library program installed a command that is invisible to EVERYBODY — even library employees. Pressing "X" at the book inquiry screen will access a patron inquiry mode. This is something that the library staff obviously knows about and uses, but is not supposed to have even heard of.

Anyway, the point is this: dumb terminals often include exits to controlling programs. You can access these secret parts by either issuing an exit command (a "trap door") and entering a password, or by entering a hidden menu item or command statement. Access may also be unintentional and due to an error, as with a program that lets you in even though you are not situated at a valid terminal, or have not entered the password.

It is also advisable to turn off the terminal, wait ten seconds, then turn it on again to see what happens. Some terminals respond to various combinations of Ctrl, Shift, and Alt. (Sometimes Alt is labeled "Compose Character" because if you keep it pressed down while typing out a number 0-255 on the numeric keypad on the right side of the keyboard, the corresponding ASCII character will be produced.)

Also look at the function keys, and combinations of Shift, Ctrl, etc., with the function keys. Try various other control codes like Escape, Ctrl-C, Ctrl-X, Ctrl-Q, Ctrl-G, Ctrl-Break, etc. You can never tell what's going to do something, or if anything unusual will happen at all. But sometimes you can get pleasantly surprised.

College PATs

There is also another kind of publicly accessible terminal, one easily found in the computer rooms of any college. These are different from the information-dispensing ones found in libraries in that these are meant to be used solely by authorized users — people with accounts and passwords on the system.

You should try the different function and control keys on these terminals, too. This isn't likely to get you anywhere, but often you can use various control codes to access parameter menus or change screen colors.

Press ? or type HELP and see what commands are available to you. Most colleges run an information system, possibly connected with the library system, which gives you information on such things as student activities, phone numbers, office hours, campus news, and might also allow you to connect with other college information systems around the country, or possibly federal or state systems. It should be a trivial matter to find out if a public information system is present on the system you're using, and if so, how to access it. If you don't know, call up the computing department and ask. (Remember to ask for the dial-in phone numbers, too!)

Generally you will be able to use telnet or other networking protocols to connect with computers all over the campus, country, and possibly, the world. However to do so will more than likely require you to login as a registered user first. This section deals with some techniques hackers have used to uncover passwords and IDs through the use of public access terminals at colleges.

Here's story #1.

Doing It The E-Z Way

Barry, a computer enthusiast from Las Vegas, Nevada, used a quite easy way of finding out info without any programming skills or special equipment.

At the university Barry attended, there was a computer lab that had Macintoshs set up in the center of the room and terminals around the perimeter. He had his own account on the system, but he wanted to do some serious hacking. He knew if he tried anything logged in under his own name he might end up in trouble. All he needed was some measly low-level account from which he could hack without risk.

The public terminals at his school worked like this. Available commands or menus were displayed on the screen with an underline _____ of appropriate size placed at the bottom, where the user would input his choice. You could move around on the screen with arrow keys and type elsewhere, but when you pressed Send, only the characters written in the space where the underline had been would be acknowledged.

Barry went to the main menu of the information system. He used the arrow keys and space bar to erase all the text on the screen, then proceeded to reproduce the login screen that was used to access the mainframe. At the bottom, he put the appropriate prompt...

ENTER NAME/PASS IN FORM
nnnnnnnn,pppppppp_____

...and positioned the cursor at the beginning of the underline. He switched the Caps Lock key on, and he shut off all the other terminals. Then Barry took a seat at a Mac near his prepared terminal, and waited.

Everyone seemed to want to use a Mac that day. He had to wait more than an hour until a person finally came in to use a terminal. As Barry had hoped, that person walked straight for the one that was already powered-up. From Barry's position at the Mac he could easily see what the person typed in.

As you can imagine, when someone uses the actual login screen, the computer covers up passwords with asterisks. The woman who was using the terminal did not seem to realize that anything unusual was going on as she typed her vital data.

When she pressed Send after her password, she got the usual beep of disapproval (because she had pressed Send without entering anything in the space that was supposed to be used for commands, which Barry had erased). The computer redrew the information system main menu, and the woman, surprised, logged in again and went about her business.

Another computer user, who had sat down beside her shortly after she entered the room commented, "They've been acting weird all day." Barry was elated; on his first try, with almost no effort on his part, he had a name and password and could do all the hacking he wanted to without having it being traced back to him. *Plus*, the bit of strangeness he had caused was being blamed on unrelated system malfunctions.

There are many variations of this tactic that should also be considered, depending on the nature of the command system, the terminals used, layout of the room, etc. You will want to adjust your strategy accordingly.

Some terminals allow you to change screen color. I've worked a ploy similar to Barry's on one such terminal. First I erased the screen and typed up a fabrication of the login screen. But it wasn't an exact reproduction — I put my underline one line below where it normally would be.

I then moved the cursor over to the place on the screen where commands were supposed to be entered (above my fake underline). I used a color-change function key to make the characters I entered next appear in the same color as the background. I typed "log-on." It was black letters on a black background, so only I and the computer knew it was there.

Then I repositioned the cursor at the beginning of the underline, used the function key to change the text color back to bright white, and took a seat on a nearby armchair.

I didn't have to wait long. About twenty minutes later a group of people came in, and one sat down at my terminal. Unfortunately, he saw the screen, thought someone else was using the terminal, and he got up to leave. I told him, "No, no one's using that one." So he reset the terminal and proceeded to log onto a totally different system!

A couple hours later I got luckier. I set up the terminal again and took my position on the chair, pretending to study a numerical analysis book. After a long while a guy sat down, typed in his name/password combination and pressed Enter. All this I was easily able to see.

But the computer couldn't see what he was typing because he hadn't entered it in the special input space. The computer only recognized my hidden (black-on-black) "logon". The computer then connected to the ungradx machine, and asked for the user's identity. The user, thinking he had made a typing mistake, entered them again. I was already out of there, as I had the information I needed.

This will only work with systems that allow you to enter all login codes on a single line, or on machines with certain appropriate capabilities and setups.

Another way is to use a text editor to simulate the login screen. If you don't have an account on the system, and therefore do not have access to the e-mail text editor, there is probably a "Send Comments to Sysop" section in the public information system that you are able to access. You would probably want to use a public editor anyway, to avoid having this evil-doing being traced back to your ID.

One way of using a text editor to simulate the login screen is to write up a document such as this:

>login

Enter Name:
Enter Password:

Above this you may want to have the tail end of a commonly seen menu, list of commands, or a body of text one normally sees when turning on the terminal.

You position the document so the last line visible on the screen is "Enter Name:". You put the cursor right after the colon, and turn off the Insert key, if there is one.

A person sitting down at the terminal will think someone else before him typed in the "login" command. He will type in his name and press Enter. Pressing Enter scrolls the document up a line, making it look as though the computer is asking him to enter a password, which he then does to your utter bliss, because you are sitting there watching this unfold.

There are some problems with this method (and all these E-Z methods, actually). What if the first person to sit down doesn't want to log onto his account? Or what if he makes a typing mistake which goes unnoticed until after he presses Enter? In both cases your little deviltry may be found out. There's always the possibility that some guardian of the computer room will switch off any terminals he sees left on needlessly, and then all your work

might be lost. Additionally, if you're doing this on a university terminal that has access to lots of different computers, there might not be a reasonable way to set up the screen.

There are plenty of things that can go wrong with this ruse, but for the small investment of time to set it up, then who-knows-how-long of waiting, it's worth it.

If you try this, remember these tips: Do what you can to make reading the screen from a distance easier. Switch on the Caps Lock key if it helps. Brighten up the screen if you're able. Tilt the monitor a bit to reduce glare from your viewing angle. And if possible, select large fonts. Before you choose your waiting spot, make sure that when a person sits down in the chair, his or her body won't be blocking your view. While you're waiting, keep yourself busy to avert suspicion, but don't get so involved that you miss your quarry.

Shoulder Surfing

The above two methods are slightly involved examples of what's called "shoulder surfing." Shoulder surfing is when a hacker looms over the shoulder of a legitimate user as that user logs onto a computer system. While the user types, the hacker watches the keyboard to pick up the password as it is entered. Remember, most login routines will not display the password on the screen, so you must look at the *keyboard* to get any useful information.

Pure shoulder surfing can only be done under certain circumstances, such as if you are legitimately helping the user with a problem and you have to stand there for the user to show you what's wrong. Most of the time you will not be able to just stand behind a person without drawing suspicion to yourself; you will have to rely on more crafty inventions.

A strategically placed mirror, in the upper corner between wall and ceiling, can do the trick. It must be small enough to stay put with duct tape, but big enough to be read from a distance.

Binoculars are frequently used by calling-card number thieves to illegally obtain people's code numbers, thus enabling the thieves to make free long distance phone calls. You can do the same to read passwords off keyboards. It might be necessary to tilt the keyboard to a specific orientation to better enable you to see what is typed. If the keyboards have kickstands to prop them up, make sure you use them before you take your stalking position.

You might have to do your watching outside, through a window. Before you do, make sure you won't be visible to those inside. Even at night you will be easily seen through the glass if the building has outside lights. Do some detective work before hacking; go into the computer room and see how visible someone outside the room would be. Perhaps you can partially close the blinds or drapes, to further shield yourself from view.

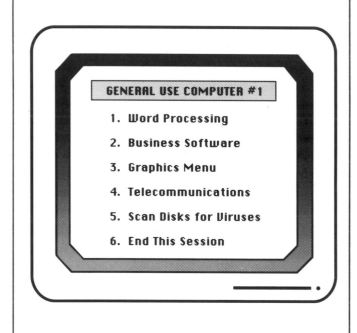

Figure 8

An example of a menu on a public computer. Tricks can be used to break free from the menu, then either alter the menu or the application programs to collect private user data.

Finally, think about this. Perhaps you don't need any of this advice at all. Over the past two weeks, every day that I've visited a certain school's computer rooms, there was at least one instance where I would switch on a terminal and find it stuck inside somebody's account. Apparently the account owners didn't know that shutting off the

terminal does not log them out of their account. Occasionally I would find more than one terminal left in a logged-in state. It was a hacker's paradise!

Doing It BASICally

If you have an account — or if you go into the computer lab and find someone else's account logged in and abandoned — you can write a simple BASIC program to *simulate* the login procedures, then leave it running. Here is a very simple example:

```
10    PRINT "Welcome to Y University Com-
      puter Network!"
20    PRINT
30    INPUT "Name? "; N$
40    INPUT "Pass? "; P$
50    REM Now store these two variables in a
      file
60    REM and logoff from the account, giving
      an error
70    REM message. Or, use the inputted data
      to have
80    REM the program login to the system.
90    REM Finally, delete this program.
```

Remember to program in necessary time delays, if it usually takes a few seconds for commands to register. Also remember to have the program print asterisks (or periods, or dashes, or whatever's appropriate) on the screen instead of the user's password.

Sometimes commands are available to users before logging on, like allowing them to see who else is currently logged on. You may or may not be able to program phony responses to a user's queries. The program doesn't have to be extremely elaborate, however, as most users will probably just sit down and login right away. You might want to sit around in the computer room awhile and look to see what commands get used the most, so you will be able to program simulations of them.

After the user is done typing his name and password, the program should store the information, and exit out of your account. If you wrote the program in another person's account (like the ones I mentioned finding logged in already) then the program will have to transmit the data to you somehow[1]. After all, once you log out of that account, you won't be able to get back in again. On the other hand, the operating system might allow you to save the file in your own directory if given the right access codes, or if you can make your own account temporarily less secure, allowing others to write to your directory.

Hacker security is very important — you never know what superuser is spying on your activities. Therefore, it would be wise to encode volatile information like other people's passwords before they get stored in a file in your personal directory. I use a simple code, such as storing 13 + ASCII code of each character, with every other number stored being random. So for the name/password combination SMITHERS/RANGERS my program would store 96 90 86 97 85 82 95 96 / 95 78 91 84 82 95 96, with random numbers between each of these numbers.

An expansion of these ideas is found in an upcoming chapter.

Hardware Methods

One thing I've done is to take an old, unused terminal I found hiding in a basement storage facility, and wire it up to a portable computer. At about four in the morning I smuggled the thing into the computer lab, and replaced a terminal that was already there with my own, connecting the cable to the portable.

I hid the portable under the table. It was a wooden table with an overhang. I used an electric stapler to make an old pair of cut-off jeans into a pouch that hung down from the underside of the table, and I enclosed the portable within it. I had the portable programmed to save on disk the first ten characters that appeared after "Username:" and "Password:". Basically, the portable acted as a monitoring device, working between the terminal and the mainframe. It worked well.

The only thing that didn't work out was when I replaced the computer room's original terminal a week later. The guy thought I was trying to steal it.

There have been hackers who've taken old terminals, opened up the plastic casings, and hidden little computers inside the terminals! There was not enough room in the terminals I was using to do that, but in certain situations that would be a preferable thing to do. Make sure the computer you put in and any wiring associated with it stays separated from the internal goings-on of the dumb terminal. When hackers hide portables in this way, they are generally putting their computer inside an otherwise hollow, bulky base of the terminal.

General Purpose Microcomputers

Now we come to the third type of Public Access Computer from that list I gave several pages back: the General Purpose Micro. I'm going to be talking here about IBMs and MS-DOS machines, although nowadays we're seeing more and more Macs out in the open for public use. Of course, all techniques I discuss can be translated to any computing environment.

Let's say you call up your local library and make an appointment to use a computer there, for word processing or business or whatever. Ordinarily these are non-network machines, although if there's more than one they may be connected to the same printer, or to some other peripheral. At colleges, the word processing software may be on a non-writable disk — on some sort of mainframe or minicomputer. There are also businesses set up now where people can go to rent time on a computer to type up their résumés or reports, and have them printed out on a good quality printer. Set-ups such these can be exploited to the hacker's benefit.

Breaking Free

The first thing you'll notice is there's some kind of menu system on these micros. The people who run the joint don't need some snot-nose kid coming along and formatting their hard drives or leaving behind obscene messages, so certain protective devices are used to guard against such activities. It is generally a trivial matter to get out of the menu program, even though its very existence — at least partially — is to keep you from doing just that.

If the computer is turned on already and at the main menu, look on the screen for any indications of commands that shouldn't be there, such as "Alt-X to Quit." Try it — does it work? You might

---

[1] Methods to covertly transmit data are discussed in the chapter "What To Do When Inside."

exit the menu, only to get a message like this: "Error! Press any key to return to Menu." What happened is this: when the computer was first turned on in the morning, the menu system was called up by the AUTOEXEC.BAT file. By typing Alt-X, you have been returned to the AUTOEXEC.BAT shell, and are experiencing the next line of that BAT file. Simply Ctrl-C your way out of there.

Even if it doesn't say on the screen how to leave the menu, you will want to try various function keys, the Ctrl-Break key, the Escape key, and different combinations of Alt and Ctrl with C, X, and Q.

Often menu systems will have you enter a password before allowing you to exit to the operating system. If this is the case with the one you're hacking, by all means try various passwords — starting with blank lines, the name of the building or company, and other obvious work-related and business-like words.

Computer systems are at their weakest when they're moving from one program to another, so try choosing a menu item and using Ctrl-C as soon as it's selected. Actually, for best results you should repeatedly tap Ctrl-C and the Ctrl-Break key simultaneously.

If none of this works, turn the computer off, then turn it on again and see if you can Ctrl-C or Ctrl-Break your way out of the AUTOEXEC.BAT startup procedures. Alternately, you should have your own program disk ready to boot. If both of these tactics fail, use the menu system to run the various programs listed and see if any of them have an escape to the operating system.

For WordPerfect, you can shell out with Ctrl-F1. Wordstar allows shelling or single commands to be entered with Ctrl-K, F.

Freedom Means Free Roaming

Once you are able to exit the menu system you will be able to explore the computer.

If there are lots of computer-wise people around, or people looking over your shoulder, or people in charge running all over the place, then you'll want to get back to authorized sections of the computer ASAP so you're not discovered in the private parts and thrown out of the building.

My recommendation is to copy everything relevant to your cause onto floppies, then take them home to examine them at your leisure. This is akin to the burglar who steals the entire unopenable safe so he can work on it in his basement with noisy power tools and blow torches.

Copy the AUTOEXEC.BAT file and the menu system first of all, and any directories you find containing files with BAT, DOC or TXT extensions; miscellaneous disk utilities (especially public domain-type programs); security, maintenance, or updating programs; anything having to do with telecommunications; memory resident programs; other explanatory text files.

Especially if the computer's on a LAN, there may be a D: drive, F: or H: or an L: drive, or some higher-lettered drive that you wouldn't ordinarily even think of looking for.

Check for hidden files and directories. Copy them, too, if you find any. Also see if any files have been deleted, and try to recover them if they appear applicable to your needs.

Depending on the situation — the computer, the place of business, other relevant factors — you may or may not find anything on the computer. Often it's worth hacking a public computer like this just for the thrill of getting by security measures. However, the computers are often so poorly protected that even this thrill is a minor one.

Many times I've found public domain and shareware utilities that I'd never seen before, so it's worth doing this just to see if you can pick up anything new along these lines. You may even pick up some valuable programming hints or ideas — some of the batch and script files you'll find can be impressively complex.

Another thing that's common is to find in-house programs on the system — things like employee schedulers, databases, or other programs that are not available for public use, and are reserved for use by the managers of the business or library.

If the computer has telecommunications or networking abilities, there may be handy phone numbers or sign-in protocols you will be able to use.

If you have encountered prompts for passwords in your exploration of the computer, try to find out where the master list of passwords is stored on the disk. One time I broke out of a public menu program in a special library, and after looking around awhile, found a carefully hidden file called PASSWDS. I typed it to the screen and was surprised to find a list of about six user names, along with passwords, addresses and other personal information for each name. Naturally I was overjoyed, but to this day I haven't figured out why they were there. I tried those names on all the systems in the area without success. I tried fingering the people ("finger" is a UNIX command that allows you to look up information about system users) on the major computers, to no avail. The people listed in the file seemed to not exist anywhere I looked for them! Perhaps someone was just using the file as a test or demo, or on some private computer system... but then why was the file hidden away so well?

Sometimes you will discover red-herring clues of this kind, trails that seem to lead nowhere. It's all part of the nature of being what you are. Hacking is frequently a matter of intense research, with the goal being to establish a hypothesis, a question that needs answering. Once you have decided on a question ("Will this password list work on the Raamses 3?" "Does the President of Moroll Corporation have a secretary with system access?"), then you can do higher level research and try to answer it.

PACK

When you go out on a public hacking expedition, you'll want to be prepared by taking along your PACK: Public-Accessible Computer (hacking) Kit. This kit should include:

- Plenty of blank, formatted disks, in both 3½" and 5¼" sizes, so you can quickly copy the menu's security programs. Make sure these disks are the proper density for the drives you will be using.
- Auxiliary programs, such as superzappers and other utilities. You will also want to bring any special programs you have written (such as menu simulations, as discussed in the next section). Public domain programs are available to shut off the internal speaker. This can be useful if you're hacking a computer that lets out a loud and suspicious beep every time a wrong password is entered.

- Other tools: A Swiss Army knife is good, or at least bring a little screwdriver. Very often, especially on CD-ROM workstations, you will find locks or covers placed over the disk drives to limit access. A large, unbent paper clip is handy for hacking Macs. If you have to leave in a hurry, you can slip the end of the paper clip into the hole next to the disk drive, and your disk will pop out. That's often the fastest way to eject a disk.

Menu Simulation And Other Sneakiness

For protection and simplification purposes, just about all general-purpose public computers will boot up to a menu program. There are three fruitful programming ideas the hacker can employ with these:

- altering the menu,
- altering the menu *program*, or
- creating your own simulation of the menuing system.

Menu programs will have a menu-editing option. This allows the people who maintain the computers to create menu categories such as "Business Programs," "Word Processing," and the like, and to add and edit the programs available for public use. The way to work menus to your advantage is to use the editing feature to add or change an option that will appear to be taking the user into an area where a password is required. However, what the menu will really do is take that user to a program that *you* wrote, that simulates an environment the user is familiar with. The user innocently enters his user ID and password (which your program stores), then an error message is given and the user is returned to the menu. Later, you can go to where the computer hid the passwords and IDs, and retrieve them for your personal use.

The first question is, how does one edit the menu?

The menu-editing feature may be part of a secondary program, such as INSTALL.EXE or SETUP.EXE. You may also be able to do editing directly from the menu program itself, by pushing a function key or control code.

Problems start arising because you were not meant to be able to change the menu setup on publicly available computers. The menu-editing feature may have been eliminated once the menu was set up, or a password might be required to do anything.

Maybe you can re-install the program, recreating the present menu from scratch, while putting in your own additions (to be discussed soon, hold your horses!). Alternately, you might be able to use a text editor or superzap program to change the file where menu information is stored. If you start getting error messages when you try to change the file, the ATTRIB command might have been used to "lock" the file. Just type "attrib filename -r" to unlock it (on MS-DOS systems).

The way these menu programs work is, the person doing the editing must supply a short phrase that will be displayed on the screen. He then must choose a file to be executed when that phrase is selected, possibly providing a drive path, and other information.

Suppose you want to infiltrate a university computer system. Your initial target is a public computer with word processing, spreadsheet and telecommunications abilities. When someone sits down and selects "Telecommunications" from the menu, he or she is either connected to a host server, or asked which computer he or she would like to connect to. Then the connection is made.

That's what it's going to *look* like is happening. What *actually* happened was that when the user pressed "T" for "Telecommunications," the menu ran a program that *you* snuck onto the system, instead of actually connecting to the network.

The program you put on should look like it's doing whatever normally happens when someone selects "Telecommunications." For example, it might prompt for which computer the user wants to connect with, and then pretend to connect to that computer. Your program then presents the name and password prompts, and saves those lovely words to disk!

Next, you can have the program give an error message and return the user to the main menu, but that looks suspicious and will cause the people in charge to take a closer look at their computer setup.

You'll be better off having your little simulation program being called from a batch file. When it's through executing, have the next step in the batch make a real connection to the system. It might be possible to have the batch file feed in the name and

password the user entered, thus eliminating any trace of weirdness. Otherwise, have it print the standard "password not valid" message, and then connect to the network.

In other situations, the "Telecommunications" option will bring the user to a commercial terminal package such as ProComm Plus or SmartCom. Again, it is easy to make your own fake version of one of these programs. But there is a catch. When the user enters your fake terminal program, he will select a phone number from the list, and attempt to dial it. He will be awfully suspicious and confused if the speaker is on and yet no dialing sounds come out of it! (Remember, you somehow have to make the program appear to dial out, so you can then simulate the network that is called. Then the user will enter his password thinking he has actually accessed the network.)

The most reasonable way to solve this dilemma is to have the program give an exotic error message like:

Operating Error 2130 : Line Noise Interference. Shut off your speaker and try again.

Of course, this message should closely conform to the other error messages that the terminal program actually puts out.

Once the user shuts off the speaker, the program can then pretend to dial out, and give the standard login screen for that network. The name and password is taken and quietly stored to disk, and then an error message is given and the user is logged off.

You may want to have the computer just put a lot of garbage and random characters on the screen after the name and password are entered. Make it look realistic — like the kind of line noise that we've all gotten at one time or another — but make it excessive. The user will be forced to log off almost immediately. If he doesn't, or if he tries doing anything, just have the computer display the standard "Logged off. Good-bye!" message. It may be possible at that point to have the computer load the real terminal program, so it will look like nothing very unusual has occurred.

It is unusual to find commercial terminal packages on public computers, mostly because that would lead to people coming in and placing calls to halfway around the world. But offices and businesses might have them, so consider these ideas when you think about hacking on-site.

Let's go back to the menu program.

The menu program might not be a commercially available one. It might have been designed in-house, or in an interpreted language such as BASIC, or for some other reason the source might be readily adjustable. The program might be just a batch file.

If any of these are the case, you will be able to effortlessly change the menu program itself, either by building subroutines that store names and passwords, or by adding a telecommunications option if one is lacking.

The final variation on the menu ploy is to compose a simulation of the menu. That is, if you are not able to change the already-existing menu, you will have to write a program that *looks* like the established menu, but with your own embellishments on it.

It can take a while to replicate the menu program. If the menu uses pop-up windows you will have to write routines for screen dissolves, or program-in windows that explode open and implode to a close. You will have to carefully take note of screen colors and special characters displayed, how the actual program handles invalid data, and other peculiarities of the menu.

While the programming may be difficult, you are better off using your own menu because that will make it easier to hide the captured passwords and other goodies that are the goals of this project in the first place.

Hiding Your Goody Basket

All of the above menu methods, as well as many of the techniques explained earlier regarding simulating network login sequences and capturing keystrokes, result in a file being saved to disk. There are two things you have to worry about: That your file will be discovered, and that your file will be read. Let's look at how we can prevent both of these from occurring.

The thing is, since most of this takes place on public computers, anyone at all may locate your precious files. This includes the people who run the computer labs, those who fix the computers, other

hackers, and the oh-so-curious general public. It also includes the computer itself.

Most public computers you encounter will have a self-cleaning routine installed. Weekly, monthly, or perhaps every night, the computers will have all their old data files erased, to keep room on the drives for new material.

Most public word processing computers have notes attached that beg people to bring their own disks on which to save their work, but there usually is a special USERS directory, or some other area where anyone can save files.

The cleaning program is used to clear away old files from this directory. The program will often scan the rest of the drive, clearing away files that users have stored in other directories. Often on public computers you will see dozens of empty directories scattered about; usually these directories have human names to them. These are private directories that people made for themselves in the hopes that other users wouldn't read or delete their files — never realizing that their files would be deleted by the computer. Often the cleaning program is too dumb to recognize that the directory, too, should be deleted.

Before you put your altered menu program or whatever onto a public computer, you must do some experimenting to see what kind of cleaning system it has, if any. There's no sense in spending hours on a project only to have it erased soon after it's implemented.

If a cleaning program does exist on the computer, you should have it copied over, along with everything else, from your initial investigation of the computer. Take a look at the program; there will be plenty of ways to defeat it. The cleaner probably has a data file that holds information on which directories it should examine, what should be done with the outdated files it detects, what calendar date constitutes "oldness," and other pertinent variables. You may be able to use this file to your advantage by adjusting it so that your own special directory or program will be ignored by the cleaner.

If the computer activates the cleaning program automatically, your explorations might lead you to find the trigger that sets it off and causes it to delete certain files and not others. For example, the cleaning program could be connected with a logoff function, so that before the computers are shut

down for the night, the drives are scanned and unwanted files are removed. The cleaner could also be
activated as part of a start-up routine, or a regu-
larly-performed maintenance check. In any case, a
careful exploration of the files on the system will
reveal the pattern they follow. Once you find the
program that sets the cleaner off, you will be able to
make alterations to your own file so that it is ignored, rather than deleted.

Often the cleaning program is an all-or-nothing
monster that wipes out everything in its path as it
crosses the hard drive. However, there are consid-
erate versions that only delete old files. You can get
around these gentler kinds by writing a simple
program. Here is an example of an MS-DOS batch
file that changes the date of your hidden goody
basket in the example (a text file called "filename")
to one far in the future. Append this batch file to
the end of the AUTOEXEC.BAT, or to the point in
the system's maintenance routines directly before
the cleaner is activated. Your file will never be
erased.

```
@echo off
ctty nul
date < command1 > temp
edlin temp < command2
date 12-31-1999
edlin filename < command3
edlin command1 < command3
edlin command2 < command3
edlin command3 < command3
date < temp
del *.bak
del temp.*
ctty con
```

For this to work, you need to make up three
auxiliary files. Here we are calling them
"command1," "command2," and "command3," but
you would want to name them something more innocuous. "Command1" contains a single carriage
return (Control-M). "Command3" is a file containing only the letter e. "Command2" is a bit longer:

```
2d
1rCurrent date is
1rSun
1rMon
1rTue
```

```
1rWed
1rThu
1rFri
1rSat
e
```

The batch file works by using the "date" command to change the date to December 31, 1999.
EDLIN is invoked to save the password file
(containing the goods), and the three auxiliary files,
under this new date to protect them. Finally, the
date is returned to normal. Note that MS-DOS can
be set up to display the date under various formats.
You might have to alter the batch file and
"Command2" if your target computer is set up in an
irregular way. Also, realize that "temp" is a common filename. You would do best to use something
exotic in your own program.

AUTOEXEC.BAT files get changed often, and a
batch file like this sample is bound to be noticed by
the maintenance staff. To keep your coding discreet
you may want to keep this and similar batches in a
separate file far away on the hard drive from the
AUTOEXEC. BAT. At the point in the AUTOEXEC
where your Trojan batch would have been
executed, you can use the DOS "call" command
("call BATCH.BAT" will execute your Trojan and,
once it's done, return to the AUTOEXEC batch file).
Your batch file can be suitably camouflaged as
described below, and there is now only one
imposter line in the AUTOEXEC batch for a
maintenance worker to notice.

Also remember that under certain operating
systems, such as MS-DOS, the "ATTRIB" command
can be used to make filenames invisible in the
directory listing ("attrib FILENAME +h" turns on
the hide factor). ATTRIBing a filename is not really
secure, as there are many ways someone can either
accidentally or purposely find out about invisible
files on a hard drive. But eliminating the name
from the directory certainly does much to halt the
casual discovery of your Trojan files.

Things To Watch Out For

I'm going to list a few things to be careful of
when you implement a program of this kind. My
remarks will be directed toward this program in
particular, but they are far-ranging enough to be

applicable to just about any program like this that you hide on a system.

First, make sure EDLIN is there, as well as DEBUG, TREE and other external DOS commands. They may not be available on the computer you are using, and you can end up with a mess on your hands, and discovery of your intentions. When you attempt to copy these files you may find that the DOS directory has been write protected. In that case you may have to put the necessary commands in an alternative directory. This might expose them to the ravages of the clean-up program. If the cleaner *does* delete these external commands you will have to figure out some solution to get them onto the disk and protect them from the cleaner. This batch only works on text files — EDLIN will mess up binary files.

Second, you will have to make sure beforehand that the DOS directory is in the PATH. What that means is, for a particular file to be executable, it must either be located in the current directory, or in a directory that has been predefined (usually by AUTOEXEC.BAT) as a place for the operating system to look for files to execute. This is no problem of course — just add a PATH or CD statement before the first EDLIN — but it is something you could easily overlook, especially if you had to add the special commands yourself to an unusual or unfamiliar directory.

Also notice before installing any programs: will there be enough space on the disk? Enough memory? Does the program try to create the *temp* file in a locked directory? (If so, open *temp* in a USERS directory, or some other writable one.) Does a file named "temp" already exist? How about "Command1," "Command2" and "Command3"? There are alternate ways to use this program. Instead of having the date-changer execute before the clean-up program, it could be run every time the password file gets updated. Though it takes a few seconds to run and that time might be enough to noticeably slow down the user's application program. Recall that this program is meant to be used in conjunction with some sort of Trojan horse you've installed; the horse itself will slow down the computer somewhat already, the combination of the two programs might be too much to go unnoticed.

The clean-up program might use some other criteria which helps it decide which files to save and which to throw away. You will have to use similar programming techniques to thwart its advances accordingly.

If there is no special clean-up program, the hard drive will be cleaned by an actual human being. That human being might not be clever enough to look outside the designated USERS directory for files, but you have to act as if that person is as clever as you. Anyhow, you never know who else is using a public computer, so you will have to take measures to hide your precious password files from view. Here are a few suggestions:

Change the hidden-file attribute so that it is not listed in the directory.

Place it in an obscure directory or in an *unreachable* one. Try this experiment. Put the following commands into a batch file:

```
:Start
mkdir dir
cd dir
goto Start
```

and then execute it from the root directory. After sixteen nestled directories named "dir" are created you will get an error message. Press Control-C and look at what has been created. You will find that within the innermost directory it is impossible to make any more directories — there's a limit to what the computer has been programmed to handle. However, you can use a disk management utility or your own system calls to prune and graft many more directories inside the deepest one. Those grafted directories will be impossible to see or access from the DOS shell. If the clean-up program uses the DOS command TREE to scan all the directories, it will crash or freeze once it gets to those illegally nestled directories you put there. You don't want that to happen: that would lead to discovery of your secret files hidden within that directory. Accordingly, this trick requires that you have the programming prowess to write prune-and-graft programs on your own. Your Trojan horse would have to be able to move the data file from its protected position, then back again afterward.

One thing you are certainly DOS-sophisticated enough to handle is to camouflage the files you want to protect within their directories. DON'T use filenames like SECRET.PSW or HACKER.HA! Use a bit of creativity when naming them. Go into one of the applications directories and see if there are any patterns to file namings. If you see for example, that a spreadsheet has files named AFGRAB1.OVL, AFGRAB2.OVL, AFGRAB3.OVL, then name your files AFGRAB4.OVL, AFGRAB5.OVL, etc. Do you think anyone will bother to look at them then? You might want to split up the files, putting each in a separate directory; don't forget to specify the proper drive paths in the batch file that uses these files.

Trojan horses on public access computers can be an excellent way to slowly-but-surely collect passwords for your enjoyment. However, all will be for naught if, when you come back the next day to see what you've reaped, all of your files are gone. Protect yourself, and your handiwork.

Keep in mind as you read about these special programming tricks, that I'm not implying you should actually sit out in the open and edit menus or sift through files looking for passwords. *Never* do that! You must always first make a preliminary examination of the computer as I described earlier. You will have already copied over the important and unusual files — in this initial exploration of the computer — and you should have the entire menu program at your disposal. At home and at your leisure, you can write the programs necessary for this kind of hacker attack. Then, once you've finished the programming and editing required, you can go back for a second session at the public computer, this time secretly installing your mutated versions of their programs onto the system. This reduces the amount of time you will have to spend in a public place doing questionable things to somebody else's computer. It also reduces the chance of error in the things you do.

You must be especially careful with computers that are meant to be used only for short periods of time. Guest registers, as described earlier, are used for the few moments it takes for a person to enter his or her name and identification number. You will look extremely suspicious fiddling around there for forty minutes, taking notes and inserting disks.

It is not the other users you have to be wary of: they couldn't care less about you, and if anything, will probably mistake you for someone who works in the building. Depending on where you are, you might not even have to worry about being caught by the office or lab managers, computer aides, or whatever the official designation is for the people in charge. If it's a college computer lab being monitored by one or two students, they might be curious, but won't pry as long as you don't stay longer than you're supposed to at the computers. It is almost never a good idea to come right out and admit you are snooping around for the express purpose of gathering data to be used in hacking. A comment such as, "Oh, I just wanted to see how they did this batch file," or some other appropriate explanation, is a good enough excuse for most such people.

Some computers are public; many more are private. That is the topic of the next chapter.

Chapter Eight:
On-Site Hacking:
The Trespasser-Hacker

In the previous section we discussed methods of exploring publicly available computers, but there is another side to on-site hacking. It is one that you might think would be best left to spies and thieves, but one that you can actually participate in yourself. I'm referring to the on-site hacking of, not public computers, but private ones. Basically, I'm referring to trespassing.

It is risky and possibly dangerous to walk into a company headquarters and simply start using the computers you find there. But it's also thrilling! It is an electrifying experience to first maneuver one's way into a restricted place and then, while there, to explore both the building itself and its computer system.

Sometimes, on-site hacking is a necessity. In many situations, computers will not be connected to outside phone lines. More secure setups might use some facet of the hardware to validate authenticity. You might have to use a particular kind of terminal or modem, or install a certain security chip to access the system. In these cases you would *have* to hack on premises. Furthermore, reverse so-

cial engineering often requires admission to the computing site. Hacking is about computers; there are lots of reasons why a hacker will need to be able to touch and see those computers in person.

You might think it would be virtually impossible to do this, but more often than not it can be an easy thing to do. For example, security expert Robert Farr, in his book *The Electronic Criminals*, explains how he penetrated the "heavily guarded company headquarters... [of] ...a well-known office machine company" to win a bet. Farr also tells an anecdote of his entry into a vault at the Bank of England: "There I was standing inside a vault containing millions of dollars with a bewildered look on my face, wondering what to do next."

Farr did it with prethought, planning, and sometimes blundering. You can do it too. In some ways it is easier to enter large organizations like this than the local insurance office or small business. Wherever you go, you will often have cameras, guards and possibly biometric devices (see below) to deal with. All of these can make it tough for a hacker to get close enough to even touch a computer on site, let alone infiltrate it.

Closed-Circuit Television

My home computer broke a little after 5:00 p.m. one night. I called up the store where I bought it, trying to reach the service and repair department. Nobody answered the phone. Finally I spoke with someone in the computer department who assured me that people would be in the store until 9:00 p.m. to deal with my broken computer. So I drove over there, lugged my computer downstairs to the repair department and — guess what? The place was empty.

The door was open and unlocked, the lights were on, thousands of dollars worth of broken appliances were lying around, and there were two of the store's terminals up and running. All I had to do was step behind the counter and I'd be able to see what made them tick. But surely *someone* was there? I yelled for assistance. I rang the bell. I walked behind the counter and into the back areas of the shop. The place was absolutely devoid of life. And there were those two terminals there....

The only thing that stopped me from fooling around with them were the hidden security cameras I spotted. Now, as it turns out, I did some checking around the store until I managed to find a room that appeared to house the viewing monitors associated with the store's security cameras. Naturally no one was paying any attention to them, so I went back downstairs, closed the door behind me, and had my way with those terminals. Even though the monitors were not being watched, it was good that I had seen those hidden security cameras. You, too, should be wary of such things when you attempt to hack on private property.

The correct terminology for security cameras is Closed-Circuit Television, or CCTV. Both black & white and color transmissions can be sent over privately owned cables from distances of a few feet to hundreds of miles. Usually black & white is used, as it is less expensive and color is generally an unneeded feature. No licensing is required for most private CCTV installations, so given the relative cheapness of the technology, such security measures can be found in many settings.

The cameras employed may be either openly visible or hidden (as my department store cameras were). Another approach is to place an empty camera frame in an obvious location, while hiding an actual camera in an unusual spot. A trespasser will then cringe from the dummy camera, straight into view of the well-placed real camera. Dummy cameras may also be used to give a false sense of high-security, when in reality only a few, or maybe no security precautions are in place. If you see some cameras visibly panning back and forth, but one or two remaining stationary, it is likely those motionless ones are either broken or fake.

Many cameras, especially ones used out-of-doors, will be contained in some sort of housing. This housing may be a conventional metal box, or one more suited for covert surveillance. For example, cameras are often placed in housings made to resemble a light fixture, smoke detector, loudspeaker, or utility box. Cameras may also be placed behind grillwork, pipes, or a one-way mirror, or hung from the ceiling inside a translucent plastic dome.

If you are trespassing you must be aware that hidden cameras exist, but you shouldn't necessarily try to seek them out. After all, you don't want to give a camera a full-frontal shot of your face and body. You're better off, when walking where you oughtn't, to walk tall and proud, but don't stare at the corners or ceilings of rooms. If a shape protrudes from a wall or ceiling, pay it no mind — it won't do you any good to stare.

Note that many surveillance systems are not all that great. Images picked up may be fuzzy, dark, full of shadows, and generally hard to see. Others, however, give perfect views of a point or an area within the camera's range. Concealing a camera may hinder its usefulness. Placing a concealing grillwork in front of a camera will result in a loss of detail in the images the camera picks up. Hidden cameras are more likely to be stationary and focused on a single point, such as an entrance or exit, or a particular point in a hallway.

You often see cameras outside buildings, near rooftops or over doorways. These will be protected from the elements with suitable housings, sunshields, fans, wipers, and/or defoggers. Outdoor cameras are often contained in a white or aluminum housing with vents on the sides. If they are outside, they will have night viewing capabilities, and so you may be detected even before you enter the building. I remember walking across the lawn of a Johnson & Johnson building one rainy night, and as I got closer to the building, I looked up to see two guards with their faces pressed against the glass, staring at me.

If you absolutely must trespass a building or its property to get to its computers, try to go at night during a thunderstorm. Visibility will be poor, you can use your umbrella as a face-shield, and if you get chased away they will be reluctant to chase you very far.

Biometric Systems

Controls based on personal characteristics are the ultimate in computer access control — when they work properly. Known as *biometric systems*, these devices limit access to a computer or the computer room by verifying physical attributes of a person. A biometric system may look at any one of these individual traits to verify user identity: fingerprints, voiceprint, handwritten signature, palm print, hand geometry, or retinal patterns.

Biometric systems are costly to implement, but they are not always as accurate as television would have one believe. For example, a legitimate user's voiceprint may be rejected because of a change in voice pattern or voice speed due to illness or stress, or because of interference from outside noises. One system I tested would occasionally offer responses to the noise my finger made as it scratched the microphone!

Similarly, finger and palm print technology can be thrown for a loop due to cuts and scratches on the hand, dirt on the hands, bandages and blisters, or scrapes in the glass tray on which a user places his finger or palm for scanning. Signature and handwriting analysis systems sometimes fail to pick up nuances in pressure, style and velocity; people do not always write their names the same way every day. I imagine this would be especially true for someone rushing into the computer room to print out a report three hours past deadline. Hand injuries could also make a person's signature look different.

Hand geometry devices — those which measure the length and translucency of fingers — don't seem to have much going against them, although again a Band Aid or scraped machine tray could easily cause the rejection of an otherwise legitimate

system user. Finally there are retinal pattern recognition systems, which look at the pattern composed by blood vessels in the eyes. These too have been shown to be reliable in their acceptance/rejection rates when user complicity is high.

I point out the flaws in these systems so you will get a feeling for what it must be like to work in a building where you're required to get your eyeballs scanned every time you want to walk through a door. Or imagine being in a place where you have to speak foolishly aloud to switch on the computer. The first few times it may be seen as a novelty, but soon these gadgets become another ho-hum part of office life. Add to that the time delays these devices cause, the frustration when they don't work properly, the feeling of subservience that comes from having to remove gloves and glasses, speak distinctly into a microphone, present a clean hand, or hold one's face immobile, and you will find a bunch of people who — even under the strictest of security conditions — are sick of the whole damn thing!

Unless there is some incentive for workers to use these biometric devices — for example if their time cards will be punched depending on the time they register in, or if their actions are being monitored by guards — unless there is a motivation to follow the rules, you know very well that everyone is going to try their hardest to break them. People *like* showing how friendly they are. People like to show that they are not a part of the stupid bureaucracy that runs the place — they *like* holding doors open for others, even for strangers. They don't mind allowing others to use their own clearance to gain access to a room. Nobody wants to look like she is so caught up in protocol that she has ceased being a human being! And after a while, people don't like that their humanness has been reduced to a digitized picture of their thumbs, or the snaky red rivers in their eyes.

So, you will sometimes find these costly machines turned off and unplugged. You'll find garbage cans placed in the doorways to prevent them from shutting anyone out. You will find helpful, smiling personnel who will open doors for you and hold doors open behind them to let you through — even when they've never seen you before in their lives.

Look what has happened here, and what *does* happen: the most effective way of ensuring user legitimacy is overthrown by the users themselves. Well, that's good for you, the hacker. Don't abuse the access that has been offered you by being malicious in your explorations of the facilities you find laid out before you.

Always A Way

Think about the enormous amount of power government possesses over us. Think of the billions of dollars it can spend to pry into our lives, to photograph us, record our movements and our daily activities. Think of all the *expertise* available to such a powerful entity. Anything that government — or big business, or anyone in power for that matter — wants to know about, wants to happen, or wants to change, *will* become known to it, *will* happen, or *will* be changed.

When we start to think about all the covert actions going on around us, and all the myriad ways in which we don't even know we are being manipulated or spied upon, we begin to think of government agencies as unbreakable, unstoppable... un*hackable*. And even if we think we have a chance at hacking it, we know we will end up in prison.

But all of that is simply untrue!

Government agencies are limited in what they can do and in what they know. You only have to look as far back as Operation Sun Devil a few years ago, when Steve Jackson got his games taken away because they were thought to be a menace to society. Sure, the Secret Service and the FBI may be powerful, but maybe they are *feeble-minded* too.

We read about all these scary spy gadgets that have been developed that can read our lives like a README.DOC. We hear about the "impenetrable" government computer systems that have been set up, and we are scared away because they sound so hermetically protected. For example, we know that any transmission of an interesting nature has a 100% chance of being intercepted. Therefore, all those spy guys in Washington have set up ultra-secure network links in an effort to protect their valuable secrets. Their most safeguarded lines are fiber-optic cables buried deep below the surface of the earth and sealed in gas-filled pipes. These are strictly isolated systems — no connections to outside phones or computers, so no hackers can gain access by dialing in. Even if a hacker were to discover where the (unmarked) underground lines are, and even if that hacker were to manage to dig down undetected, and cut open the pipe to tap the cable, the drop in gas pressure instantly sounds an alarm.

This is heavy protection, and sounds like it would be impossible to hack, especially when you realize that even if there were some way to get at those lines, you still need various levels of permissions, passwords and access codes to reach the highest and most secret classifications of data.

But think again. Never forget that behind every complicated system, is nothing more than some human beings. And what are human beings if not fallible? In the case of this seemingly impenetrable system, we can imagine the humans who sit night after peaceful night, watching their TV monitors, waiting for the alarm to sound that signals a breach. They're probably asleep more often than awake, especially if the temperature and humidity is high in their work area. If ever the alarm did sound, they probably would ignore it, or wouldn't know what to do. Or they would take a quick look out the window and go back to sleep.

Even if the guards *did* go out and check the wires to make sure everything was okay, do you think they would continue checking them after five or six false alarms? "The boy who cried wolf" trick always works, especially on a dark and stormy night. *No* guard is going to go out sloshing through the mud and rain to investigate an intruder he knows won't be there. There is *always* a way. Don't be fooled by first appearances.

And here are some more ways you can beat the security:

Acting For The On-Site Hack

On-site hacking requires some acting ability — the ability to act like you have a valid reason for being where you shouldn't be and undertaking questionable activities while there. There's nothing difficult about this — just pretend you own the place. Strut down the center of hallways holding your head high. Smile and say hello to the people you pass. I learned this trick in school, where we needed hall passes while classes were in session if we wanted to leave the classroom. All throughout junior and senior high, I never got stopped once by a teacher or hall monitor for not being in class, simply because I acted as if I was on some official mission for the principal. (It helped that I was a "good kid.")

So do your best to keep your cool. Have a reasonable story prepared in case you are stopped and questioned, and try to tell it without fumbling for words. Here's a hint to help you do that.

After rehearsing a story in your head for the umpteenth time and finally repeating it aloud to a security guard, the *quickness* with which words come to your mouth may seem to you to be too well-prepared, too fake to your ears, and you start throwing in "uhhmm"s and "uhhhhh"s to slow yourself down. *Don't do that* — it sounds really bad and it takes away from your credibility and sincerity. Talk at a normal pace. Say your prepared script without worrying if it sounds fake. And throw in some company insider lingo or gibberish to give yourself an extra believability edge.

Piggybacking

There are two kinds of piggybacking. Electronic piggybacking is dialing up a computer and finding yourself connected to the account of the last person who logged off. Physical piggybacking is using another person's access to gain entry to a computer or computer room.

One way of getting in at hospitals, offices and other buildings which require the insertion of a magnetic card to gain access is to stand around and wait for someone with access to open the door for you. Many offices stay open late at night and on weekends, for people who need to come in to clean or work overtime. I especially like going into big office buildings on Sundays. Just wait around outside until you see a car pull up, then time yourself so you will be behind the employee as he or she heads toward the door. Let the person unlock the door and hold it open for you. If you can get in, the whole building is yours for the asking. There may not even be a maintenance crew around to get in your way.

The thing is, though, you have to plan ahead to be successful at this and not arouse suspicion. If you're going to try piggybacking your way into an office building, dress like an office worker. Perhaps carry a briefcase or a lunch bag.

I know these things are possible because I have done them. I spent last week at the regional headquarters of a large bank, doing temporary work for them. From the moment I drove into the parking garage I was inundated with all sorts of warnings about security measures. First there were the signs hanging up in the parking garage about how my car would be towed if I parked there without a hangtag. A guard was sitting in a little booth near the entrance of the place. I went over and explained to him that I was a temp worker and I didn't have a hangtag. He told me not to worry about it, that they don't really tow cars unless there is some problem with them, like if they are double parked.

Then I went into the building, up to the seventeenth floor, and came out of the elevator facing a locked door that required a magnetic card to get in. A sign informed me that I was supposed to buzz the receptionist and have her open the door for me, but there was no receptionist sitting at the desk. I waited a few moments until an office worker approached the door from the other side, held it open for me, then went on his way.

The entire week I got in and out of the office without a security card, and in fact later on I even found a concealed door that allowed entrance to the same offices, without a key or card of any kind.

So you see, piggybacking — the use of another's legitimate access to gain entry into a building or computer — is an on-site hacker's best friend!

Other Successful Tricks & Antics

There have been hackers (and thieves and spies) who dress as one of the maintenance crew to get into a place and get closer to the computers there. Grab yourself a ladder and a can of paint, and see if there's any work you can pretend to be doing. This sort of impersonation works best in large companies where no one will question you, because everyone assumes you're there because someone else wants you there. As long as you act like you belong, you will be accepted.

One hacker/spy completely re-wallpapered the employee lounge while learning codes, names, and procedures over a five day period. You may not have the stamina or the patience to invest in a scheme such as this, but similar actions can be worked effectively on a smaller scale. Besides, you may find that you're suited to being a delivery boy or sandwich girl for a few days.

You can gain access to dozens of offices by signing up at a few temporary agencies. Then, even if the jobs you are assigned don't take you near a computer you will be able to later use your temping as justification for a return visit to the site. That is, you wouldn't necessarily come out and tell people you're there on another temporary assignment — you would let them *think* it, meanwhile roaming freely around the building.

Cubicles are great — I love cubicles! Because once you're in one of those gigantic gray ice-tray rooms, you have the entire area to explore: no locked doors and lots of corners to hide behind. If you ever trespass into an office of cubicles, you can roam from one cube to the next, finding passwords taped to ink blotters and stuck to walls. You can find pictures of kids, people's names, hobbies, etc., from which to guess more passwords. You can easily eavesdrop and find out inside dope on people, as well as shoulder surf with ease. Yes, to a hacker, those yucky gray cubicles can be wonderful!

Sometimes you will be trying helplessly to hack an on-site computer, but for whatever reason the data you type refuses to be entered. Note that on some terminals (or computers), non-standard data entry keys are used. Thus, instead of pressing Return or Enter following a command, you type F1, or Home, or Insert. I know, it's crazy, but I've seen it.

On-site hacking doesn't only have to imply the hacking of computers behind closed doors. In airports one can often find unattended terminals. Step behind the counter and you can hack until you're chased away.

Before concluding this section on the hacking of private and on-site computers, I want to touch on an area that is connected to the subject by a tenuous thread.

Electronic Passive Computing

I don't like to use the term, but active computer hacking can be thought of as a "sport," or a game that is to be won by the hacker. That's the way many hackers view this activity of hacking — as an intellectual exercise in which the hacker tries to out-think either the computer, the user, the Goliath corporation, or the computer designer.

Passive computing, or "lounging," is like watching a sporting event on television, rather than going out to the field and playing the game yourself. Passive computing is the act of eavesdropping — monitoring computer usage and surreptitiously collecting the information that is transferred.

In seventh grade I was amazed, the first day of my intro to computers class, when the teacher told us that each of our Apple computers were connected to his. Thus, by a flick of a switch he could send any of our screens to his computer monitor, to make sure we did the work we were assigned and didn't goof off. He was screening our screens! Some paranoid bosses do just that to their employees today, to make sure they do the work they're assigned.

Actually, it's no great technological feat to connect two or more monitors to the same computer and switch between them. If you have access to the computer your target will be using, you can attach an RF adapter to the back and secretly run the cable to another monitor or television set. Then sit back and watch as what occurs on your target's screen unfurls on yours. You won't get to see your target's password, since it will be covered by asterisks, dots or spaces as it is typed — but you can get other information this way. This is a good technique if your target has a lot of encrypted files for which you don't have the key. Monitoring your target like this will let you read whatever he reads; and if he decrypts his files, you get to read them, too.

It may not be possible to sit down close to the target at your own monitor and watch. You may have to attach a broadcaster to the RF connector, and listen from outside the building with a receiver, which in turn is connected to a viewing screen.

If you hook up a VCR to your monitor, you'll get a hard copy of your target's activities. It may even be possible to directly connect the VCR to the computer your target will be using. If you do so, it is best to have a remote way of turning the VCR on and off, so you don't record while the computer is idle. If the target has a regular schedule you can simply program the VCR to tape at a certain time.

There's no law saying all screen output has to go to a screen — if for some reason you can't use any of the above techniques. An alternative is to have information sent to a printer buffer. Make sure that either the printer is fast or the buffer is large. Otherwise the target's computer will slow down tremendously and he won't know why. Also, of course, the printer has to be located far away from the target, preferably in another room or another building entirely.

As an example of one limited way in which this can be accomplished, consider the "print from keyboard" option found on many word processors. "Print from keyboard" causes that several thousand dollar machine to act like any old junky typewriter, printing characters directly as they are typed on the keyboard.

While your target slips away from his word processor for a coffee break, you can slip over and activate the "print from keyboard" feature. From then on, anything further he types within the program will be sent to the printer. As I said, this is of limited use, but it shows one more way that even impromptu situations can be exploited by the computer-knowledgeable investigator.

By printing "Shift-PrintScreen" on any DOS computer, the "print from keyboard" mode will be activated. However, if the printer is not ready, the system may hang up.

As an example of passive computing which is really very *active*, in that hacking is required, it might be reasonable to log on to a network and use programming to direct the target's output to your own terminal. If you have the target's password, the host computer would have to be tricked into allowing the same user to be logged on twice simultaneously. Additional programming might be required if the computer refuses to send the target's output to your screen, or if the target is getting your output.

If you have a password other than the target's, some programming could send the target's screen to yours, or yours to the target's (if you want to get into simulation). On UNIX systems, you would be thinking in terms of altering already existing programs such as TALK or WRITE to get the job done. These two programs induce a link between two separate accounts. Any time two accounts are joined, there is a potential for misuse of that linkage. But these programs are written with security in mind; the hacker's job is to rewrite the programs, eliminating the security measures.

Another option is to make use of monitoring software which is commercially available — or write some yourself, to satisfy your own personal needs. Managers of offices routinely spy on their secretaries, data entry clerks and other computer operators through the use of software which stores key presses. Other monitoring software keeps track of which programs are being used and how, often time-stamping such information as well. Doing this form of research does not, as you might at first think, necessitate going back to your target's computer to see what keystrokes have been recorded. I hot-wired one such keystroke-capturing program to print a weekly report to a hidden directory. When secretly installing the program (visiting the site, posing as a confused user who had a virus-attacked disk that needed repairs), I also altered the computer's startup file which executes upon login. I altered it to look for that hidden report on certain days and e-mail it to me through an unknowing third party. Now I get weekly reports on this one poor system manager's every last keystroke!

I didn't think of it at the time, but it would've been a good idea to add a few lines to the startup batch to look for the existence of a piece of mail from me containing a few key words which would signal the program to remove all incriminating files and program lines from the computer.

You might ask, "Why would you need such a thing — don't you have the guy's password and everything from reading those weekly lists of his keystrokes? You can delete the evidence yourself." Good question, and actually I do have his password, but it took a long time to get it.

You see, the keystroke-capturer can only go into effect once the user has logged in and the startup file is executed — by then there is no need to enter one's password. (You can tell that even though I put a lot of thought into this hack, there were a lot of things which I didn't ever consider before the actual results starting coming in. Hacking often involves making assumptions and then seeing how one's assumptions were wrong.) It took awhile, but eventually I did get the password, when the system manager invoked a second sub-shell within his logon.

Tapping the phone line or intercepting microwave transmissions are always open options, or bugging the phone if the modem is coupled to it.

Then you get the added bonus of hearing the target's voice-phone conversations as well. Printer, modem, monitor, and other computer cables can also be tapped to good effect. One nice method is to tap the modem line, making a recording of any modem calls that take place. You go home, call the number that the tapped computer called, and play back the recording for the remote computer to hear. Remember, the high-pitched squeals and cries in the recording you made will include that lawful user's access codes. Your goal will be to synchronize the playing of the recording with the remote computer's prompting. If you can get it right, you get yourself in.

You know, once someone gets their computer all plugged in and set up, it is only on very rare occasions that they ever look at the backside or underneath it again, especially since they probably have a messy tangle of cords running out the back, an office cleaning staff to keep it dusted, and the back of the computer pushed against a wall. That RF adapter or extra wire coming out will surely go unnoticed for a long while.

Radiation Comprehension

If you like to watch television while you use your computer, you may have noticed something funny happening when the channel is turned to certain stations. With the computer on, channel two on my television is complete static, while channels 3 and 4 get decreasingly snowy. This happens when electromagnetic fields radiating from my computer and cables are picked up by the television antenna. If I'm watching channel 2, I can even make out a very fuzzy representation of what I see on the computer screen.

There is a simple reason for this happening. The various components of a computer — amplifiers, cables, the coupling between cables, the power supply to power line coupling, switching transistors, the ground loop, internal wires, and even printed circuit boards — all act as antennae to conduct electromagnetic radiation. The components, cables and whatnot will not only pick up the radiation, but transmit it as well, sometimes re-emitting it at some distance from the source equipment.

Nearby electrical wiring and metal pipes can further act as antennae.

Computers operate at radio frequencies and so they are also radio transmitters. That's why the Federal Communications Commission must approve all computers (and many other electronic appliances) before they can be sold in the United States. The FCC wants to make sure those radio emissions aren't strong enough to interfere with other licensed radio receivers (such as television sets). In fact, there have been cases of unregistered computer monitors whose screens have been picked up on the next-door-neighbor's television set. This sort of thing is more likely to occur when the neighbor has a black and white television and the computer has a composite monitor, because a black and white set can more easily adapt the synchronization signals that it picks up from a composite monitor (especially if the TV has an antenna amplifier attached).

When my television receives computer frequencies, it is doing so accidentally. Imagine the consequences of someone setting out to *purposely* receive radiated information. Indeed, such a thing is possible, and has been going on for quite some time. For years the Department of Defense has stashed away its most hush-hush computers and communications devices in copper-lined rooms to prevent radiation leakage. They have also produced guidelines for a security standard called TEMPEST[1], which defines how military computers are to be constructed so that the radiation leaking from them is minimal.

Special military computers might be well protected, but your run-of-the-mill PC or terminal is not. The FCC ensures that equipment won't interfere with other equipment; it makes no promises that equipment is safe from prying eyes. In fact, those eyes don't even have to be at the scene of the crime. There is an electronic marvel called the Van Eck device which picks up your favorite leaked radiation and projects it onto a television screen. Hook up a VCR to the television and you've got a living document of everything that goes on in your target's computer account.

---

[1] Transient Electromagnetic Pulse Emanation Standard.

Van Eck And Britton

In 1985 a group of Swedish engineers, led by one William "Wim" Van Eck, presented a paper called "Electromagnetic Radiation from Video Display Units: An Eavesdropping Risk?" at the Securicom Conference in Cannes. The paper, which was published in *Computers and Security 4*, described how one could easily and inexpensively convert a normal television set into a non-trespassing, passive device to intercept and reconstruct the information from any digital device, most notably computers. Scientist Don Britton had already gone public with a virtually identical device in 1979, but it was the Van Eck paper that got people to sit up and take notice.

We were talking before about how you could set up a radio receiver to pick up the mess of signals coming from cables, wiring and circuit boards. This is possible, yes, but you would end up with an unintelligible mishmash of signals. It would be difficult to separate and decode the various signals — though not entirely impossible. Doing so would enable you to determine what a distant computer was "thinking" as those electrical pulses shot through its system.

"Pulses" is the key term here. We all know the story about how computers are digital beasts, processing streams of ones and zeroes to create the fabulous tapestries of color and sound that we get to appreciate every time we boot up a copy of the latest Sierra game.

In reality, there aren't actually tiny 1s and 0s coursing through the wiring. What's going on is a high or low electrical current passing through. We think of these high and low currents as being 1s and 0s because it is convenient for us to imagine them this way. *Any* electrical device is going to have radiation emissions. But only a digital device, like a computer, will have pulses of high and low. Keep all this in mind while we take a little side trip.

Computer screens operate on the pointillist school of display painting: what you see as continuous shapes and lines on the screen is actually composed of thousands or millions of tiny dots, called picture elements, or pixels for short. Each dot is a little speck of some substance that glows (fluoresces) when energized, and the inside of the screen is covered with the stuff.

Video control circuitry located either within the monitor or plugged into the computer, controls the position of an electron gun, which repeatedly scans the screen top-to-bottom, firing an electron where appropriate to energize a bit of the fluorescent substance. Light up the appropriate pixels and keep them lit, and you end up with glowing dots that can combine to form the lines, characters, symbols and graphics that make up our daily experience with visual computer output.

You may ask yourself, "Well, once a pixel is lit up, how do you darken it to clear that portion of the screen?" The answer is simple. Hitting the phosphorescent matter with an electron only produces a very brief burst of glow before extinguishing. That's why the electron gun must systematically scan the entire screen sixty times a second to constantly refresh the image appearing on it. If we wish to cancel a pixel or series of pixels, we simply discontinue firing an electron at that section of the screen.

Every time the beam fires we get a high voltage pulse of electromagnetic emission. Britton's and Van Eck's idea was to simply use a television receiver to listen for those bursts of high voltage as a monitor emits them, and have the television respond by firing a pixel in the corresponding place on its own screen — thus ending up with a display screen that exactly matches, pixel by pixel, that of the target computer. A good thing for a spy to have, huh?

The problem is that while a television can *receive* those bursts of high voltages, they don't know what to do with them. There's nothing inherent to a high pulse that signals where on the receiving television that pixel should go[2]. The Van Eck or Britton devices bestow this function upon any lowly TV receptor, by producing an artificial synchronization signal. Two adjustable oscillators are used to create the vertical (picture) and horizontal (line) synchronization. For technical reasons, proper reception requires a constant re-tuning of the oscillators. This could theoretically be done by hand, but this *is* the computer age: the signals are

---

2 Actually, such signals are readily available from the mishmash, because the originating monitor's synchronization components also generate signals as they function. However, the pulses are too weak to pick up from a distance.

mathematically combined and fed into a logic circuit which performs the job automatically.

The difference between Britton's and Van Eck's designs are that Britton based his system on United States NTSC technology, while Van Eck's model is based on European PAL receptors, using European voltages, and includes a built-in digital frequency meter. If you have the techknowledge you can build one of these for $10 to $15. Models are also commercially available through spy shops.

Besides the oscillators and the logic processing sync restorer board, you will want to hook up a directional antenna to help focus in on exactly what you're after. Someone using one of these devices should be able to fine-tune their receiver to the point where multiple CRTs within the same room may be distinguished. This is due to differences in the components making up the monitors. Pieces that come off of different assembly lines or from different countries will have varying radiation-emitting characteristics. Your suitably engineered Van Eck or Britton device can discriminate between the several traits presented. Just pick one line of signals which you wish your machine to follow, and off you go.

Ups And Downs

This method of on-site computer cracking is safer than most because it involves no trespassing at all to get at your target computer. Van Eck has reported that he was able to use his invention to view the contents of computer screens from distances over a kilometer away. His working group housed the device in a van which they parked on the street, usually right in front of a target's home, without incident.

These devices give us hackers the opportunity to do what we always say we want to do — innocently look around in computer systems without hurting, without changing, without destroying. But Van Eck and Britton machines also deprive us of freedom of direction, of choice. We can only use it to see what the user himself sees; there is no chance for us to *hack*, only to spy. Very rarely do passwords appear on a computer screen, so we most likely won't even be allowed the opportunity to use a bit of learned knowledge to coax what other exciting information we can from the system unless the user chooses to allow us entry into those secret realms.

Seeing the contents of a forbidden computer screen from a kilometer away is marvelous in and of itself when one is discussing, as we were, pulling flutters of distant radiation from the ether. But traditional hacking methods — through the telephone — allow us to delve into the forbidden from much further away than a kilometer. In the following section we will start looking at how a hacker can roam through all the confidential computer systems of his neighborhood, his country, and, if he chooses, the world.

Chapter Nine:
Hacking At Home:
Dialing Up Computers
With Your Modem

Now we get to the stuff of which dreams are made. You flick the switch on your computer and a few moments later it's purring away. You press a few keys, type in a phone number and after some beeps you hear the wonderful shriek of connection. The handshaking is fine, but you're looking for a lot more than a handshake.

You press Enter a few times. "What's your name?" it asks. You respond — not with your own name of course — with someone else's. Then you let your fingers whisper that sweet secret word through the keyboard and the screen lights up with a luscious display.

Menus! Options! Choices to be made! Files to read and to learn from, software to run, games to play. You let the directories sift past you, letting yourself be mesmerized by their framework. So much to do, and then you see connections to other sites, and more sites, and more secret files to read! You smile as you realize something: every hack, no matter its size, leads to new hacks, new computers, new horizons of exploration and gain.

Reality

When I say "Hacking at Home" I don't really mean it. Most computer hackers nowadays won't hack from their houses for fear of Caller ID, line tracers, tricks, traps and federal agents. When I say "Hacking at Home," what I'm really referring to is the phenomenon of dial-in lines. Ways in which, if you are so inclined, without even leaving your house, you can connect yourself with the world.

Who To Connect To

Who can you expect to connect to, calling from home? Lots of places. There are other home computers, mainframes, minicomputers, companies, government offices, clubs — you will be able to call any organization or individual who owns a computer, and has need to communicate via computer with other entities.

You might also find yourself calling on-line databases and pay-for-play services.

Paying For The Pleasure

A hacker named Rebel was recently telling me how enthralled he was with CompuServe, except for one aspect — the stiff price one pays for using the service. For this reason, CompuServe is often known as Compu$erve, with an oversized dollar sign replacing the S. CompuServe is not the only vendor charging the public a fortune to pay back their huge advertising budget. There are literally hundreds of on-line services to which one may subscribe, or hack one's way in if that's more your style.

Databases are available to look up any sort of data: census data, news, stock market information, results of government research, science and technology reports, books, personal information, history, and popular culture. There have been times late at night when I needed one crucial piece of information for something I was writing, or just to satisfy my curiosity. Anybody can access one of these databases and find what he or she needs any time of the day or night. Of course, we must be prepared to pay through the nose. There is usually a charge to subscribe to the service, then there may be any number of the following charges:

- A display charge for each piece of data presented on the screen, or a search charge for each query made to the database.
- Minute-by-minute charges as long as you stay connected to their computers.
- High-speed surcharge for using a faster modem (thus gaining the ability to grab more info per minute).
- Long distance phone charges if the service doesn't have an access number in your local-dialing area.

Many hackers refuse to pay the inflated bills these services can run up, though they also refuse to give up the service, particularly when so many special and useful features can be gained by dialing in. On-line gaming, electronic mail, multiple-user chatting, bulletin boards[1] and a plethora of other goodies make the services attractive to the hacker. The many ways to get past paying for them are also

very attractive. You will find many ideas throughout this book.

You'll be interested to hear about one trick a pair of high-school-age New Jersey crackers used to get some service for free. One brand of personal computer was being sold in a special package that included several pieces of software, along with a trial membership to one of the on-line services. They hacked the system of one of the stores that sold the computers and obtained a list of customers who had bought it. Many of those customers were individual people or families, but a good number of the computers had been bought by stores and businesses. They went to these businesses and snuck around in their back rooms and offices. Sure enough, pushed aside on bookshelves, unopened and untouched, lay the envelope that included the "Getting Started With StarBase On-line" manual and trial access codes that had been included with the computer. They helped themselves.

Packet Switched Networks

There are corporations and government agencies all across the country that have computers you will want to get your hands into. But you're not going to want to get your hands into your wallet to pay for all those long distance calls. The solution? Public Data Networks (PDNs).

A PDN is a network of hundreds of computers scattered nationwide. You call up one local to you, then type the address of the computer system you want to connect with. The "address" is usually something like a phone number. When you enter a valid address, the login display for the desired system will appear. You are then able to interact with the system as if you were directly connected to it, when in reality everything you type is being broken down into chunks of text (packets), possibly compressed and encoded, then shipped across the country, from one computer to the next, until it reaches its destination.

There may be hundreds of other sessions going on simultaneously from points throughout the network, as thousands of users interact with the many computers on the net. Sending messages this way is known as *packet switching*. The intermediate computers that do all the work are called PADs, or Packet Assembler/Disassemblers, because they

---

[1] Many of the fee-based services which offer bulletin boards even have a message base or two devoted to hacking.

take incoming packets of data, strip away the encoded insulation which tells that PAD where the packet is headed, then reassemble the data with new directional information, sending it further along the route.

Hackers take great glee in connecting with a PDN. Once there, a hacker can try out various addresses at random. In a matter of minutes, he will find himself with a wide variety of login prompts to crack, all made through a local phone call.

The most well-known PDNs are Telenet and Tymnet, and there are also international packet networks, and networks in other countries as well. Generally you can call any one of these services to get a list of PADs in your area you can dial in to.

Other Networks

The only other network that counts is the Internet.

Internet is an international network of networks. There are academic networks, government networks, businesses and organizations throughout the world, all connected together (by PDNs) to exchange ideas, software, technologies, gossip and guacamole recipes.

Before Internet there was ARPANET, a military network which has since been replaced by MILNET (a well-guarded network of United States military sites) and other smaller networks used by the US military. Altogether, these make up DDN, the Defense Data Network. DDN is now just one of many networks participating in the Internet.

Others include the National Science Foundation NETwork (NSFNET), which includes supercomputer centers and other research sites funded by the NSF. CSNET is a network established to encourage cooperation between sites doing development work in computer science. JANET is the United Kingdom network, one of many national networks around the world that is bridged with the Internet. Internet is truly a global community.

Some of the pay-for-play services offer access to the Internet. Many university computer accounts are connected to it. Basically, having an "in" with the Internet allows one to travel around the world and back without leaving your armchair.

We were talking before about packet switched network addresses. An Internet address is a series of code words punctuated with periods, and refers to one particular computer in the millions that make up the Internet. A typical Internet address might be "danielk@cs.zowie4.uboulder.edu." We can deduce that at the University of Boulder there is a computer in the computer science department called zowie4, and on that computer there is a person whose first name is Daniel, and last name begins with K. The "edu" is a standard thing stuck at the end of educational computer addresses. Other identifying components used are:

COM for commercial sites,
MIL for military sites,
GOV referring to governmental organizations,
ORG for non-profit organizations, and
NET meaning Internet administrator sites.

An Internet address may also end in a two-character country abbreviation. Some examples of these are:

AU AUstralia
IL IsraeL
US United States
JP JaPan
UK United Kingdom
DE Germany (tricky! DE is for DEutschland).

Finding Dial-Up Numbers

To "direct connect" with computers, you will need their phone numbers. Very often you can call up a company and ask the switchboard operator for the computer department and/or computer lines. If that doesn't work, try calling individual offices at the firm and ask if they know how to access the company computer from their home computers. If they don't know the phone numbers, perhaps they have a terminal program on their office computer which has the phone number stored for use.

Phone books are a big help. First there are the internal kind: companies and other organizations will have a directory of people who work there, with their extension numbers. Internal directories might also be of the kind that list numbers for the different departments; some go so far as to list home phone numbers and addresses of the people who work there. Names can be used to pretend familiarity with the people you speak to when you call. But you won't even have to call and ask for dial-up lines if those numbers are listed in the directory.

A second useful source is phone company data grade line directories....

When a person speaks on the telephone, it doesn't matter if every once in a while the voice on the other end gets a bit fuzzy, or if the tone gets momentarily higher or lower. When you're transferring data between computers, however, audio noise can be a problem. So the telephone company has special lines which offices can install (for a price) to ease the flow of data between telecommunications devices such as modems. If you can get a data grade line telephone book, you will have found a huge and wonderful collection of computer phone numbers (and fax numbers too). Many hackers get theirs by scavenging.

The third way phone books can be helpful is by looking in the public white pages and yellow pages that every phone owner gets for free. Large companies will own big blocks of telephone numbers, with each office or extension being one digit different from the preceding one. To call the different departments at Company J, you would dial 390-WXYZ. The 390 stays the same for every department, but the last four digits change for each phone line. So turn on your computer and type up a text file listing every occurrence of those last four digits you see listed for that company in the phone book. Then sort the list and try calling everything in that exchange that is *not* on your list.

It can be helpful to use a criss-cross directory for this task. Criss-cross directories are sorted by *number*, not name, so if you know that Company J's numbers fall into the 390- range, using such a directory you will have an even bigger list of numbers to avoid. This makes the job of calling every potential number much quicker and easier.

Software is available to repeatedly dial up a series of phone numbers, reporting on whether a modem is connected. These programs, often available on hacker and cracker BBSs, are known by many names: "WarGames Dialers," "autodialers," or "demon dialers." If you can't find such a program, write one for yourself; it's simple to do and will cost you only a few hours of time.

Once you have your autodialer, be very careful how you use it. The phone company security patrol knows what you're doing when you make that many calls that quickly, and with such precision. I've often thought it would be a good idea to combine one of those computerized telemarketer machines with an autodialer. That way everything looks legit: if a person picks up, they get a short recorded message: if a modem picks up, they get a callback later.

Dial-Up Security Measures

Some security directors get themselves into a bind. They recognize the important value of having direct dial-up lines for easy access, but they also understand that anytime a person is able to call a computer directly, a security breach is not only possible — it's unstoppable.

To overcome this, security-minded folk will not allow direct dial-up access to the real computers. They will only allow access to an intermediary device or computer which firewalls important data from potential hackers.

For example, one may dial-up a computer whose purpose is only to check authorization codes. When access is confirmed, the caller is transferred to a line connected to the actual computer. There, the caller may have to identify his or her private account by username and password. As long as the password to the initial computer is kept secure and changed frequently, the important data on the actual computer is free from harm.

In states where Caller-ID service is legal (and even in those states where it is not, or isn't available) it is possible to set up a modem to only handshake with a user who is calling from an authorized phone number. The system administrator keeps a list of the home phone numbers and office numbers of legitimate users, and if the computer sees that the incoming call is not from one of those, there is an immediate disconnect. The call would also be disconnected if the caller had enabled Call-Blocking, which disallows the Caller-ID from reading one's phone number.

Where Caller-ID is unavailable or unknown, a ring-back feature may be put to use. Once a caller inputs correct identifying information, the host computer disconnects and calls back a stored telephone number which goes with the identity that has been entered. This is the normal way ring-back works, but in some instances (such as the RBBS-PC electronic bulletin board system) the ring-back option means that a caller lets the phone ring X times, then hangs up and calls back again. This time the BBS will answer the phone. If the caller had originally let the phone ring more than X times, the computer would have ignored the call completely, thus providing a layer of security. So if you have a number you know belongs to a computer, but there is no answer, try letting it ring a different number of times, then call back immediately.

A host computer may also not connect a caller until a certain code is played on a Touch Tone phone. Since the code would ordinarily be played by the terminal program of the calling computer, this code may be very long and complicated, thus difficult to crack by chance or force.

As you can see, all of these dial-up security measures make life difficult for the hacker. One may social engineer the knowledge out of a legitimate user of the system, but often the hacker won't even know that such extreme security measures are in effect to begin with.

You may be randomly dialing through a range of phone numbers because you have reason to suspect that a computer line exists within that range. If one of the numbers is never answered no matter how often you call, you can surmise a ring-back or similar device is connected to the other end. If you call one number and hear a computer at the other end but aren't connected, suspect that the computer is looking at your phone number and seeing if it's valid.[2] (Either that, or what you're really trying to connect to is a fax machine.) Caller-ID type systems, and those which call back a phone number, will be especially common on computer systems whose users are situated within a close regional area. The remote system may also be trying to detect special tones encoded in the modulation. Though it is a dial-in line, special equipment may be needed to connect with it.

Sometimes the system managers get so tricky as to disguise the fact that they have a dial-up computer available at all. When a user calls up to use the computer, a special device answers the phone.

Instead of hearing the characteristic modem noises, a user might get a recorded voice, static, or nothing at all until a specific password is sent from the calling modem to the remote system. You can see how this would easily foil any WarGames dialer.

All in all, devices which inhibit access to the actual computer are nothing more than one more layer of security to get by. Luckily, the majority of computers do not employ such tactics, and are easier to crack than a hard boiled egg.

Scrutinize The Login Environment

The login environment is the area of the remote computer which you are allowed to access before identifying yourself as a valid user of the system.

The login environment of most computers is limited to a username and password prompt. Some environments are more expansive, giving a general command prompt, at which you can type any number of instructions. Those instructions won't necessarily be carried out (you probably have to log in first) but they can be helpful.

There are a number of common commands that one can type at a board command prompt, and a list of these is given in Appendix C. Try typing "help" or "?" first, and see if that does anything. A command like "users," "show users," or "who" will be helpful, in that you can see the names of people who are on the system and try to guess their passwords. The advantage of having certain other commands may not be as apparent, nor will there necessarily be any advantage at all to the hacker.

One good thing about general command prompts is that often one is reverted back to them after failing a login. Thus if three incorrect username/passwords are entered, instead of disconnecting you, the computer will bring you back to the command prompt for another go-round.

When you find yourself at a general command prompt with no help available, try doing different things, paying attention to the error messages you receive. Try entering commands in all upper or all lower case, then mixed cases. Look at the maximum and minimum lengths of commands. See which characters are recognized. All of this is helpful in that it narrows down the number of unknowns. It helps you more easily figure out what you should be doing to get things moving. If every time you

---

[2] A knowledgeable hacker could temporarily change his phone number to one that the computer recognizes, by hacking the telephone system mainframes. However, it is still necessary to know that phone number.

type "HELP" you get a "Line too long" error, then you know the system is probably looking for three-letter commands. That is useful information.

If you type "CONNECT," and the system responds, "The verb CONNE is not available" it implies that only the first five characters of input are examined. If, on the other hand, your entire entry is examined, advanced help may be available. For example, if by typing "HELP" you get a list of commands, typing "HELP COMMANDNAME" may give you help with that one particular command. Such help systems are common.

Let's look at the actual entering of username and password. Some terminals tell you you're wrong when you enter a bad name, others wait until you've given both name and password to inform you. The first way is preferable, as it is less secure and requires substantially fewer guesses to crack than the latter. The IBM VM/370 was insecure in this regard; it immediately informed you that the username was no good with a "userid not in cp directory" error message. One system that I know of (Dynix) follows the same format. First it helpfully prompts for your "Nine digit ID code" (hint, hint, what could that be? A social security number perhaps?) and when the correct one is entered, it will say, "Good morning Samantha. Now type your password." This particular computer allows you to easily break into one of several command languages and reprogram the menu interface. It also comes equipped with dial-in ports. Dynix is a joy to hack.

If you get a computer of the second type (one which asks you for name and password before saying if your login is accepted), then time how long it takes to display the password prompt on the screen. This can help you decide if a username you're entering is valid or not. Let's say you try the name "Jim," and it takes two seconds for the computer to respond with the password prompt. Every time you type "Jim," it takes that long. Now try the username "Zzzzzzz." This is obviously a made-up name that the computer won't be able to find in its files. If it consistently takes longer for the password prompt to appear after typing the name "Zzzzzzz," you know that "Jim" is a valid username, and you should continue guessing passwords for him. That is, on systems where sequential search is in effect, it takes longer for the computer to search for a nonexistent entry in its data files than an existent entry.

In any case, source codes are often available, especially for UNIX files, and so you can look them up to see how the inner workings of the login prompts function.

If you have no idea what kind of username and/or password is required on a particular system, do the same kind of checking you would do at a general command prompt, checking for which characters and lengths are recognized.

A completely different way you might like to research the login prompt is by control codes. Pressing certain keys, or combinations of keys, delivers codes to a remote computer which may force it to act in ways that it was not meant to behave. For example, you can send an ASCII code to command the remote computer to stop reading a password file. Sometimes it is then possible to quickly retype the password you entered, and make the computer believe it has found your input as part of the password file, thus letting you into the system. Sometimes pressing Control-Z (the end-of-file command) at the right time will bring strange results too.

Look up all abbreviations, weird letters and other things that appear on the screen. Any decent library will have an encyclopedia of acronyms. (Any *indecent* library will have *this* book.) Very often you will call up a packet switching network, find a valid address, then get something like "Welcome to VHMSD! Password?" on the screen. So, you do your research and find out that VHMSD stands for Viking Horn Manufacturers of South Dakota, and the whole task of hacking the place becomes infinitely simpler. Remember, when you are hacking a computer, you are really hacking the people that run the computer. Thus, if you can find out who is running the show, you have a multitude of resources at your disposal, including all the research tools mentioned earlier. Otherwise you're just taking random stabs at a computer identified only by some strange abbreviation.

Chapter Ten:
Electronic Bulletin Board Systems

The Electronic Bulletin Board System (EBBS, but usually referred to simply as a BBS) is how most people get introduced to computer telecommunications. A BBS is a computer program that anyone can set up on his or her computer. The program watches the computer's modem, waiting for the telephone to ring. When it does, the BBS program answers the phone. If it is another modem calling, the two computers are connected. The person who is calling is then able to use the computer on the other end of the line as if he or she was sitting directly at that computer's keyboard. The BBS program allows the caller to choose various options from menus, letting the caller write messages to be displayed to other callers, read messages, send files back and forth, or play games on the remote computer. In essence, the caller actually controls the computer through the phone lines. However it is only the BBS program that he or she is allowed to control. The BBS program separates the caller from the computer itself. At least, it tries to.

BBSs are generally run by computer hobbyists on their home computers, and are used as a way to share information in the spirit of the original hackers. Usually there is no charge to call these up and look around, but that is at the discretion of the per-son running the BBS — the system operator (sysop). Schools, libraries, stores, user groups, churches, and organizations often run BBSs to spread the word about activities and to keep members in touch with one another. Sometimes companies will set up electronic BBSs as a way for customers to mail order products from them, to see new product information, or to report problems with products or services.

The US Congress has even set up a bulletin board system. Run on RBBS software, the BBS was created in late 1991 by Congressman Bob Wise and his House Government Operations subcommittee on government information, justice and agriculture as a way for government employees to anonymously inform inspectors about wrong-doing at the workplace.

Other BBSs are private ones, the phone numbers to which are not made widely available. For example, the FBI runs the National Crime Information Center (NCIC) which makes use of a BBS to keep track of wanted persons, missing persons, and people with criminal records. Franchise businesses such as fast food places often use BBSs to upload inventory or financial data to their company headquarters on a daily basis. And of course, there are otherwise "public" BBSs which maintain silence because the people who use them do so for illegal purposes.

Access to most BBSs is controlled by a name/password combination. When you call up a BBS you are asked to enter your name, or NEW if you have not called before. If you are a new user, you will be asked if you wish to register for the system and, if so, you will be asked some questions, welcomed to the system, perhaps given a short tour, and shown the rules of the house ("Please keep messages clean... No discussion of illegal activities such as computer hacking, fone phreaking, stolen credit card numbers, etc...").

After that, you might be given guest access to the BBS until the sysop can validate your request for admission, or you might be logged off and asked to call back the next day. This isn't always the case, of course, but sysops like to make sure you are who you say you are — if you registered with a phony phone number, they want to know about it. They want to make sure the people they will be allowing to use their computer can be trusted.

Electronic bulletin boards are important to the computer enthusiast and to the hacker for many reasons. They enable us to communicate (possibly anonymously or semi-anonymously) with other computer users. We can learn from those who have more experience than us, and we can use BBSs to help newcomers to the world of computing.

And of course, there are the immoral and illegal ways of using BBSs, ways to exploit them and the people on them for your benefit, ways to make contact with the underground and deviant computer users of the world, including hackers.

Finding BBS Numbers

Once you find one BBS number, you will automatically have literally thousands to choose from. The sysops of BBSs are not competitive. They don't care if you use their system exclusively, or if you call up every BBS in existence. Thus, you will almost always find a BBS list on any BBS you call. The list may be nationwide or local, and will detail BBS names, phone numbers, perhaps the sysop's name and special features of the systems. BBSs also usually have a BBS message center, or a place where other sysops can advertise their BBSs.

So once you call up that first BBS, you will have the phone numbers for many more. The trouble, for beginners, is finding that first number.

To start with, if you know anyone who has a computer and a modem, ask them if they have any BBS numbers.

Many computer users groups, libraries, religious organizations and schools have BBSs. The companies that manufacture modems and other telecommunications equipment, as well as the software companies, often have BBSs. If one isn't advertised in the packaging, call them on the telephone to ask if they have one. Hayes, for instance, has a nation-wide 1-800 BBS you can call to get product information and lists of BBSs from all over the country. The number is 1-800-US-HAYES.

Computer magazines often list BBS numbers. There are many books on telecommunications, some of which have listings of BBSs across the country in an appendix. There are also several computer phone books that give listings. Additionally, you might find BBSs advertised on community bulletin boards or in neighborhood computer stores.

Finding Hacker Boards

The most adept hacker BBSs will not advertise themselves, but don't worry: Once you establish yourself as a knowledgeable hacker, you will learn of their existence and they will welcome you with open arms.

There are plenty of hackers and wannabe-hackers who will openly advertise their BBSs as catering to the kind of thing you are looking for. Perhaps they have worthwhile information. Probably you'll log onto these boards and find nothing more than some no-brain kids cursing at each other. You can ask on overtly hacker/criminal boards if the members know of any other hacker boards (or look in the BBS listings there), but you probably shouldn't stick around on overtly criminal boards, as they are more likely to be busted. Since they generally don't contain anything but publicly-available or useless information, don't feel you're missing out on much by shunning these places.

Occasionally you will find an electronic conversation with some intellectual value to it. Embrace it, add to it, and pretty soon you'll find yourself accepted into its underground. If you find such a BBS, one whose members proclaim themselves to be hackers, and yet the conversation is smart and conservative, you can bet that there are secret subboards lurking behind trap doors, where all the *real* hacking news gets discussed. Prove yourself as a worthy member of the above-ground community, and after awhile the sysops and assistant sysops will vote you into their elite society. To be accepted as a hacker you must be willing to exchange information. You must *have* good information to share and to give.

If you log on to a respectable BBS which you suspect contains a secret hacker subsection, accidentally try a different unlisted command each time you log on. (Don't do more than one per login, to avoid generating suspicion.) If you find a command that works, and you're asked for a password, then you'll know you're on the right track. Talk to the sysop or other group members about your feelings on hacking, and ask them what they think about it. Modestly tell of your hacking achievements. You will already have impressed them by *finding* the secret section, but you don't want to agitate them by hacking it out.[1] And you certainly don't want to post a public message stating that you found their trap door; you can bet there are plenty of others without that secret access who are also roaming about. Talk to the sysop and assistant sysops *privately* about your find, via e-mail or online chats.

---

[1] One of the criticisms that law enforcement officers make about hackers is that they say we live by a double standard: That we think it is no crime to violate other people's privacy, but we can't stand the thought of being probed ourselves. Well, I don't find a need to defend myself. If a hacker can get through the safeguards I've set up, that's fine, because I know that hacker will not damage me by it.

As far as hacking a hacker BBS is concerned, since the users of that BBS do not know you, they don't know that your intentions are honorable. Thus, to invade them is to get their guard up. In your talking to the sysop you might want to mention that you refrained from hacking the hole that you found, in order to reassure them that you are a fellow hacker and not a cop.

Making Connections

Many of the BBSs you encounter will be strictly legit operations. There will be no talk of hacking, no trading of break-in secrets, and certainly no sensitive information of any kind being distributed to newcomers. You will have to start by jumping into already established, possibly ho-hum conversations.

Be polite, try to be helpful. Add thoughtful comments to the discussion. Having an experienced hacker as a friend will do more to boost your skill in that area than anything else — except perhaps some persistence, research and luck.

Soon you will have a few favorite systems that you'll call on a regular basis, but you should also be constantly branching out, trying all the new systems you find, your goal being to eventually find an access into the "computer underground."

There is no single, organized underground per se, but there *are* groups of hackers and others interested in technology scattered here and there. They will keep their conversations of illegal activity secret, so it will be difficult to find them. The message boards they use to communicate will often remain hidden to the uninitiated, and the BBSs on which the most interesting tales are traded will not have their phone numbers publicized at all. Your best bet is to keep searching. If you start to get the feeling that someone on one of the bulletin boards may be inclined to deviant computing, you may want to send him or her a private message (tactfully) asking if he or she is interested in that sort of thing and if so, would that person want to trade information? But remember: any message you send on a BBS can be read by the sysop, co-sysops, and possibly other system managers lower down the hierarchy, so be discreet if the people who run the show are anti-hacker.

A lot of people own computers with modems, and you will run into a lot of different kinds of people on electronic bulletin boards. If you look in the right places you are sure to find computer hackers. What may be more difficult is getting them to accept you as one of their own. Hackers like to show off, but they don't usually like to explain how they do their tricks. You will have to demonstrate to them that you are a thoughtful, resourceful, logical person who can hack just as good as they can — and one who has information to share.

As you wander through the bulletin board forest, keep track of where you've been. Keep a list of the different BBSs, making note of the software used to run each BBS, and what features are available on each one. Particular features to keep track of are file transfer capability, extent of BBS list, user lists, and doors.

BBS Features

BBSs are more than just bulletin boards — that is, they are more than just a place to write and read messages.

BBSs with file transfer sections will allow you to upload (send) computer programs and files to the BBS, and download (receive) files from the BBS computer. Many of the more serious BBSs have renounced file transfers as a waste of good time and disk space, but this feature is still common, especially with sysops who cater to software pirates (or bootleggers) who deal in software that has had its copy protection removed.

There are various kinds of user lists and logs on BBSs. These range from user responses to a poll or questionnaire, to a little introductory message from the user, to brief one or two word descriptions of the user's affiliations and interests. Often usage logs are available; these will let you see who logged onto the BBS before you arrived there. These usage logs may go back to the beginning of the day, or farther.

"Doors" are used to go outside of the BBS program. When you walk through a door (by selecting a command from a menu) you enter a completely different program. Usually doors are used to play games on-line, but any kind of program can be accessed through doors. It all depends on the BBS software being used, and the whims of the sysop.

Other BBS features include:

- Graffiti walls. These allow users to put up a short note, advertisement, or a joke.
- E-mail (electronic mail). Lets users send private messages to other users of the system.
- Chat (also called "page operator"). Allows you to have an on-line conversation with the sysop, if the sysop is at home.

- Text file libraries. These contain anecdotes, jokes, "Welcome to the BBS," handy information, technical files and other sorts of things that people might like to read.

Once you get started BBSing, you'll get a handle on the kinds of things you tend to find on BBSs... and the ways you can exploit them to your mischievous hacker advantage!

BBS Exploitation

It used to be, long ago, that if you wanted to break into a computer system, it was easy to exploit bugs in the system software, or default passwords, to work your way in. Nowadays, things are a bit tougher. Those bugs and default passwords have, for the most part, been done away with.

Oh, they're still there if you know what you're doing — but unfortunately, for the most part you'll be stuck if you rely on those methods. What you have to do is exploit the *new* line of system bugs.

Unless you have some phobia, you are not afraid of being struck by lightning every time you leave your house. That's just not the kind of thing that makes sense to worry about, so you probably don't worry about it at all. But what if someday you *were* struck by lightning? That would change your perspective on things, wouldn't it?

My point is this: the weakest link in any security system is the people involved in making sure everything stays secure. Joe Blow, the average computer user, doesn't care about security matters — why should he? He has no reason to even think about security. He's never had files erased by a virus, never had his credit card numbers stolen, or his DIALOG account breached. Joe Blow is the weak link.

How is Joe Blow — the weak link — to be exploited? Joe is a typical computer user — and a typical human being. He's a bit into computers, but not a fanatic like maybe you are. He's human, so he has trouble remembering fifty different passwords. So he uses the same password for every computer system and BBS with which he has an account. Joe uses easily guessed passwords, or maybe none at all. He's not a computer whiz, so he doesn't always understand what's going on when people start talking computer language to him — this makes him vulnerable to being exploited.

And guess who's going to be exploiting Joe Blow?

Yes, you.

Getting To Know You

What I'm about to say here will sound like heresy to some, downright evil to others, and superficially it will appear to break the very fundamentals of the hacker's code of ethics. Well, in some ways it does, but there are a lot of things I say in this book that are like that. It's true: life often breaks it's own rules. Sometimes you have to break your own rules to have some fun. So anyway, here's my warning: Watch out! Taboo subject ahead!

If you've followed my earlier advice, you have this huge list of BBS numbers, and you've been calling them all to get more numbers. Why did I say to do this? Because the people you will meet on these systems are people who are into BBSing. A lot of them have accounts on other local systems or databases, or at their jobs, or schools.

If you call up Fred's BBS, and you go to the "Computers" Discussion area, and Joe Blow is there talking about CompuServe, you have just found out a very significant clue! All you have to do now is find out what password Joe uses on Fred's BBS. More than likely it's the same one he uses for CompuServe and every other computer account he owns (not to mention, this password is probably the key he uses to encrypt files). This is easier said than done, of course.

This is what you should do. Many BBSs have a listing of which users have signed on to that BBS, where they live, what their interests are and what they do for a living. These lists are like gold to a dedicated hacker. Use your program's data capture facility to record the most useful lists you find, then edit them down and print out the essentials.

Let's say you're looking through your captured user list from Fred's BBS, and you see Joe Blow's entry. Under interests, Joe put down "bowling, SCUBA diving, Star Trek & lacrosse." Now you have some clues. It's more than likely that Joe Blow's password is a word taken from one of these areas of interest.

When you look through these user profiles, you are learning more about these people, you are getting to know them. It is vastly easier to figure out

the password of someone you know than the password of a complete stranger.

If you've been having conversations with these people on the bulletin boards, you've found that some are computer experts and some are not. Obviously, it's better to try to focus on someone who is not an expert BBSer — although some expert users are so smug they become complacent and lazy, and so perhaps become better targets. Use your judgment. A newcomer will be more likely to choose a bad password. Newcomers (or people disinterested in computers) will tend to choose certain obvious passwords over and over again.

To sum up: If you find out what things a user (especially a new user) is interested in, it's "easy" to guess his or her password. If you know that person uses a computer at work or school, it's likely the same or a similar password is used for both systems.

I'm not trying to suggest that guessing a password is simple. It's not — you have to have patience, and a lot of time on your hands. But there are faster, smarter — and consequently, more technical — ways of getting into Joe Blow's BBS account than a brute force attack. Let's look at these.

Bypassing BBS Security

Even though BBSs employ security features, there are at least eight factors which serve to make them vulnerable to any resourceful hacker. These security loopholes are:

1. Hacker is familiar with the remote hardware.
2. BBS run on home computer.
3. Hacker is familiar with the BBS software.
4. Hacker is familiar with the people involved.
5. Diversity of people involved.
6. File transfer section.
7. Hacker knows when sysop is and is not watching.
8. Hacker knows usage patterns.

Each of these vulnerabilities offers numerous opportunities for a hacker to break into the BBS of his or her choice. Taken as a whole, it should be pretty much impossible for a hacker to NOT be successful at a BBS breach.

Unlike other hacking situations — such as when dialing up a large government computer for the first time — you will be familiar with practically every aspect of the BBS you select to hack. BBSs often have a menu option that gives you the rundown on what equipment is being used to operate the system. The brand of software will also be known to you, and from regular conversations with the sysops and users, a personal familiarity will develop. Knowing all these facts gives you a great advantage in the writing and uploading of Trojan horse programs, in the seeking out of bugs to profit by and, yes, in the guessing of passwords.

BBSs will generally tell you upon login whether or not the sysop is available to chat. Naturally there is no guarantee that the sysop is not present when the notice says he's not present, but the "Sysop is IN" sign can at least warn you of when you should definitely be most cautious.

Even if the sysop appears to be unavailable, the BBS software itself might be watching you like a hawk, printing out your every move, or every attempt at crashing the software. For example, RBBS-PC bulletin board software allows the sysop to keep a continuous printout on each caller's name, files exchanged, and error messages that occur. As we will see later in this chapter, this can be troublesome depending on the type of attack you wage against the BBS.

Running A BBS

The least difficult way to collect passwords is to have people *give* them to you. If you start up your own BBS, that is exactly what will happen.

But being a sysop takes a lot of work, and it also involves the use of your computer, modem, telephone line(s) and possibly even your printer. That leaves little equipment to hack with!

The original three motivations for hacking local BBSs were for: 1) the excitement and curiosity-satiating value of it, 2) the opportunity for low-risk practice and, 3) to obtain passwords which might also be used by the same users on other computer systems. When you set up your own BBS, the first two of these reasons are suddenly gone. Only the third — password collection — remains, and there are more efficient ways of collecting passwords than this. However....

There are some advantages for the hacker who runs a BBS, whether or not the hacker is willing to abuse the trust users place in the sysop. For example, the hacker can set up a BBS specifically as a place for other hackers to pose questions and exchange information. If you decide to do this, you will want to make sure you are *overly* wary in your advertising and in your group's initiation procedures, to ensure that you're not accepting law enforcement officials or hostile hackers onto your board. So as not to get too off the topic, I will come back to the security subject later, at the end of this chapter.

Running a BBS — or at the very least, setting one up on your system, even if you don't go public with it — will teach you more about how BBSs operate than anything else. It's always beneficial to a hacker, and soothing to the true hacker's mindset, to be fully conscious of how a computer system works. Also, you can try setting up a limited BBS and practice breaking into it from a friend's house, or challenge others to do so (you're best off making this challenge only to close friends). This will show you what can and cannot be done on the particular BBS software you're running, and might teach you something about hacking as well. Then you can go out and infiltrate other systems which run the same software. And you can alert other sysops to the security risks inherent in their systems. I've never run a BBS by myself — I've never wanted to devote a computer and phone line, nor my time, toward the maintaining of a bulletin board system. But I have been an assistant sysop with full operating abilities on several BBSs, and in so doing I've seen a lot of tricks that people have tried in an effort to break into those systems.

Midnight Masquerade

One night, at around 1:30 a.m., the Treacherous Den BBS received a visit from a hacker. The hacker tried logging in a few times using my handle, The Knightmare. The sysop of the system, my friend DR dendryte, was sitting there watching the hacker go at it unsuccessfully until finally he pressed the function key which brought the two of them to chat mode. The following is a transcript of the ensuing conversation, copied exactly as it appeared in the sysop's printout, but with unnecessary carriage returns removed. [My own comments are in brackets, like this.]

SysOp wants to Chat!
— —- — —- — — —-
This is DR dendryte, Who RU?

this is Knightmair i Forgot my password. Log me on.

[At this point, DR dendryte knew for certain he was dealing with an impostor. He knew that I never called that late at night, and that I would never forget my password, considering that it was the same password I'd been using for several years. DR dendryte, however, decided to play along.]

How Did you forget your password??!

!
I dont know it just slipped my mind. i guess!

I can't just give out passwords like that

you don't have to........you can just log me in.

If you're really The Knightmare then tell me, what is your REAL NAME?

[A pause, and then:]

don't you trust your own best friend & co-sysop?

come on.....
.
i cant beleive you!!!!!

You are definitely NOT The Knightmare...

[Here DR dendryte was referring to the hacker's bad spelling and grammar; DR dendryte knew that I am meticulous in my on-line chat writing.]

he never makes stupid spelling mistakes like that, or uses bad grammar or

[Here, both are trying to type at once. DR dendryte lets the cracker speak:]

That does igt! I don't want to be your friend anymore! Just delete me off the BBS.

If you are really who you say you are, let's go voice!

[That is, DR dendryte is asking the hacker to turn off his modem and pick up the telephone — go voice.]

i Don't believv you don't trust me

GO VOICE

Theres no phone in the room..

Sure there is! On the bookshelf next to you!

It broke

HA!! You should have said, "WHAT bookshelf?" There IS no bookshelf in the room! HA HA HA HA HA A

+++

[Click.]

The next day, when DR dendryte told me this story I said, "You should have told him, 'I AM The Knightmare!' That would've really embarrassed him!"

Impersonations of this kind *might* work, but only if you are already intimately familiar with the person you are attempting to impersonate. In this instance, the hacker chose to login as me, correctly assuming that I would not be at the sysop's home at midnight. Perhaps the hacker also supposed that DR dendryte would be asleep.

It seems to me that a ruse like this is more likely to work on a large corporate computer, where nobody knows each other and workers may not have the great love for their computer system that sysops have for theirs.

Hackmail

The Treacherous Den BBS was a particularly sweet target for hackers to try and infiltrate. It was a large system, with many users (many of whom were sysops of other BBSs), and it had dozens of games and digitized pornographic pictures that could be downloaded.

The system was run off a pirated copy of a popular BBS software package, but DR dendryte had altered it so that it appeared to have been officially registered in his name. Once a long-time user of the system asked DR dendryte an innocuous but technical question about the BBS, over the phone. DR dendryte told him to hold on a minute, he would look up the answer in the manual.

"Oh, you *bought* it?" the user asked, apparently referring to the BBS software.

"Yeah," DR dendryte replied, referring to the instruction manual, which he had found at a used book store for a quarter.

DR dendryte answered the user's question, chatted awhile longer and then hung up. He didn't think any more of the conversation until the following month, when a cardboard envelope arrived in the mail. It was a disk envelope, with a computer-printed return address label affixed that gave the address of the company that produced the BBS software. DR dendryte opened the envelope. Inside was a letter addressed to DR dendryte's real name, and signed by the author of the BBS software, the man who also owned and had started the company. The letter read:

Dear Mr. L___ H___:

K___ Software has adopted a new software upgrade policy. All customers who have purchased non-entertainment packages from before July 1986 are entitled to a yearly free upgrade.

This new version of your software is fully compatible with all previous ones. To upgrade, simply insert the enclosed diskette and type START.

Thank you for purchasing fine quality K___ Software. We hope to have you again as our customer in the future.

Very Truly Yours

(Signature)

P___ I. B___

Not only did DR dendryte know immediately that this was a total crock, but he knew who had had the gall to send it to him. At once he reduced login access for that user he had spoken with on the phone, down to one-time visitor status. Then he wrote a nasty note and e-mailed it to him. That particular user was the only person, aside from myself, who knew about the manual. But of course, I already knew that DR dendryte had not *bought* the software, but had obtained the manual through alternate means. The user had assumed incorrectly that because DR dendryte had the book, he must have bought the BBS.

Upon examination of the disk that had been mailed to him, we found that the disk contained eight files:

There was a text file which explained all the "wonderful and exciting features you will enjoy having on your new version of L___ BBS Software." There was an instruction file called START, which read the contents of that text file. START would then "update" the old version of the software with its "new" version.

There were four files on the disk that exactly matched ones found in the actual BBS software (apparently these were there to misdirect our attention), and a fifth program that matched *closely* but not exactly! (It is possible to compare two files by using the "comp" command under MS-DOS, or by using a relevant feature of a Norton or Norton-type program.) Finally, there was a blank file called T on the disk, which served no purpose at all.

It took us hours to figure out what the user had programmed his "new" version to do. As it turned out there were two things different. A copy of the user information file was programmed to be e-mailed to a user the first time he logged on; a trap door had also been inserted that would give temporary operating system access to anyone who typed control-E, control-X, control-I, control-T, control-! at the username prompt.

You won't be able to pull a stunt like this unless you can gain access to the source code for the software, as he must have been able to do (unless you want to recreate from scratch an entire bulletin board system).

Once again, another of those pesky hacker attacks was thwarted!

Crashing BBSs

On another BBS that I was a part of, the sysop would come home from school every day to find his system had crashed. It had simply frozen up and would have to be rebooted. Eventually he found out from someone that there was a bug in that version of that particular BBS. A "\x" typed at the password prompt caused everything to halt. Key portions of the BBS software were written in easily changeable, interpreted BASIC. To remedy the problem I simply added a line after the prompt that would disconnect anyone who tried typing in the dreaded "\x."

It worked.

I've always wondered about that "\x." Why would such a harmful thing be there? I can't imagine the programmer putting it in purposely, unless perhaps it was a means to bother unlawful users of his software. Maybe it was some trap door that had gone awry. Maybe if I had studied the program more I would have figured out its meaning.

Maybe — this is a credible possibility — that bug had been placed there by the person who had given the copy of the software to the sysop, or by the pirate who had first bootlegged it, or by anyone at all along the line. Pirated software travels so rapidly across the country and around the world that literally thousands upon thousands of persons might have had the chance to add the "\x" thing and distribute the buggy code. Hey — are you starting to get an idea there? I know I am!

You could either write your own BBS program or alter a currently existing one, with some secret features such as an exit to DOS, or whatever trap doors tickle your fancy. You could put in a line which checks to see if a very obscure and unlikely control code is entered at the login prompt, and if so, highest system access is gained.

A twist to this tactic is to write or change a terminal program, which you give to the user. When it receives an internal code while connected to your BBS, you gain access to the calling computer. For example, a user would be running your special terminal program while calling your BBS. The BBS would send a code to the caller's modem, which would allow you to wander around the caller's hard drive. To cover up the fact that you're roaming around in there, entry would have to take place during a long file transfer or, if it is a slow modem, during those time lags between modem action. The terminal program could continue pretending to receive data while you surfed the remote user's drives.

PRODIGY, a graphic-oriented interactive, online service, was accused of engaging in a variation on this theme in the summer of 1991. Users were finding personal data buried inside the software that is used to dial up PRODIGY. After complaints and outrage, PRODIGY's senior vice president mailed out a utility to those concerned, which would erase non-essential data from the service's terminal software. In an accompanying letter he sincerely asserted:

> As we have stated publicly and written online, *the PRODIGY software does not read, collect or transmit to PRODIGY Services Company any information or data that is not directly connected to your use of the service.* We want to assure you that we will continue to work to safeguard the privacy of all of our members.

Maybe theirs doesn't do those things — *but yours can!*

Years ago, one group of enterprising hackers distributed their own homebrewed, broken terminal program for the Macintosh line. The program gave users the convenient option of allowing them to store passwords and other login procedures on disk so that one would never have to worry about forgetting them. The information was stored in encrypted form on a hidden part of the disk. The program was developed to "go bad" after several phone numbers and passwords were stored, the hope being that users would send back the disks, and the hackers would end up with a bunch of precious login information.

This should be taken as more theory than actual practice: PRODIGY can get away with requiring users to boot from their software because of the unique graphics and mouse interface provided. Unless you work something like that into your term program, who's going to want to bother installing and learning your software when they are already familiar with one or several commercial packages? In fact, this is what happened to that group of hackers. Initially there was great interest in their terminal program (which they gave away free), but no one wanted to go through the trouble of using it. The problem was, the hackers gave the program out to *experienced* users who had already developed an intimacy with one or more commercial programs. No one needed the hacker's terminal package, and so what seemed to be a great idea netted the hackers nought.

As for the first idea — changing a BBS to include trap doors — now that *is* a viable possibility. There will always be plenty of people looking to set up their own bulletin board system, or who are looking for ways of acquiring new software. Distribution is less of a problem than the programming, especially considering that you will not only have to interject code for the trap door but, for best results, determine a way to hide that code from interested eyes.

Trojan Horses

It is usually easy for a hacker to infiltrate a BBS with some version of a Trojan horse program. The hacker writes a program which performs some interesting function, such as playing a game or putting pretty pictures on the screen. Hidden in that program are instructions to read BBS password files, or carry out some other covert operation. The hacker then uploads the program to a BBS and — here's the important part — *hopes the sysop runs the program.*

You will want to procure a copy of the BBS program before writing a Trojan horse, so that you know exactly what those secret instructions should be doing. Otherwise, how will you know what files to look in or where to go on the disk for information?

What kinds of things can you program a Trojan horse to do? Here are some suggestions:

Have it secretly reprogram the BBS itself to include a trap door. If the BBS program is written in an interpreted language, you can have the Trojan horse add some lines which would give you sysop access upon entering some code word. This actually has been done on a popular Commodore 64 bulletin board system that was written in BASIC.

You can program the Trojan horse to look into the password file and send data contained in it back to you somehow. Many BBSs have a text file section. You can have your program encrypt the passwords as it routs them out, then append them to the end of one of the text files. Then you simply log on, view the files, obtain the encrypted passwords and decode them. People reading the text files on-line will interpret the seeming random characters as line noise or harmless file corruption.

Another way to get password information back to yourself is to use the BBS's e-mail function. To avoid suspicion (because sysops love to read the e-mail users send to each other) you should, again, encode the information and imbed it within an otherwise boring piece of e-mail.

A Trojan horse may contain a rough version of some key portion of the BBS program itself. The Trojan then extracts that piece of itself, copying over the legitimate version already on disk.

Covering Up
Trojan Horse Activity

There are two things you have to worry about when you upload a program containing a Trojan horse to a system:
• That your Trojan horse will be discovered while it is running.
• That it will be discovered either before or after it has run.

I will talk about each of these problems in turn.

While It Is Running

The rational hacker has an easier time of this than does the malicious system crasher. You see, if Junior Joe writes a program to covertly format hard drives, something has to be happening on-screen to divert the user's attention while the hard disk drive light flashes on and on and on.... It takes quite a while to format a hard drive. Junior Joe has to cleverly devise some *non-interactive* time-killer that will hold interest for the length of the format or file deletions. The time-killer could be a pornographic display (perhaps accompanied by digitized sound effects: "Ohhh! Ooooh baby! Yummm-mee...!") or a digitized musical score, or perhaps the program could send graphics to the printer. Meanwhile, you will be using rapid-action Trojan horses (sprinters) which do their thing in short, quick bursts.

Never have your program access the hard drive (or any unauthorized peripheral) for what the sysop will think is no reason. When the Trojan horse is actually going about its business, there should be a note on the screen to misinform the sysop as to what the program is doing. For example, if the Trojan horse is hidden in a game, you could have it display the message, "Saving your new high score...", while the program changes around user access files (or whatever your horse is trained to do). Don't forget, the program actually should be saving the user's high score as well, and the entire drive access time should be very short. As soon as the Trojan horse is finished operating, the program should erase the note from the screen; this will ensure the drive access time goes unsuspected. If possible, have the note be erased midway through the Trojan horse's activities, to deliver the illusion of very quick drive access.

Another way to access the drive unnoticed is to have the program say something like this when it is started up:

AutoCheck Virus Detection Program v1.3
(c)copyright 1992 Paul Bradley Ascs.

Scanning file FILENAME.1 for viruses......
Scanning file FILENAME.2 for viruses....

Meanwhile, the Trojan horse will be scanning the computer's hard disk for passwords!

For FILENAME.1, FILENAME.2, etc. in the above, substitute names of the program and data files that were uploaded with the application. A nice extra touch is to not have the ellipses (.....) written to the screen immediately. Instead, have the periods appear one at a time between disk accesses, to make it appear that the program is really scanning through the different files.

Trojan horse activities can also be covered up under befitting circumstances by such messages as:

Opening data file

Reading data

Saving selections before quitting

Loading text

Messages should always follow naturally from whatever's taking place on the visible program.

Trojan horses that perform BBS functions (such as changing passwords) should do so via direct disk access if possible, and not by utilizing the BBS program. That lets you bypass any security logs and printouts that are made of suspicious activity.

Before & After

Sysops, system administrators, and even regular users are now wise to the hazards of bulletin board file transfers. They understand at the very least the threat of viruses, and so are more likely nowadays than ever to examine a program carefully before using it.

This means they will use a virus scanner to check your uploads for viruses. This is almost a given, but it is nothing to be feared since the available virus detection programs will not locate your Trojan horse in an otherwise valid file. What you do have to be careful of, is that the sysop or system manager will manually examine your uploads for filthy words or erratic programming.

As before, malicious crashers and system vandals have a bigger job ahead of them than you. *They* have text they have to hide within their programs. For instance, who hasn't heard of a virus or logic bomb that screams "GOTCHA!!" as it overwrites the File Allocation Table? Programs are available that specifically *look* for this sort of thing in files. Even if the sysop doesn't have one of those programs, if he or she is cautious enough, that crasher's "GOTCHA!!" will certainly be discovered before the program is ever run.

Your Trojan horses won't have as much to hide. All the text in your programs will be text that gets written sensibly to the screen anyway, text that is either part of the application program, or text that looks like it comes from the program, but is actually used to blanket your Trojan horse. Also, your program won't have any "format c:" commands sticking out like sore thumbs. Thus, your job is easier than the crasher's, though it's far from being a snap.

There may be commands in your program to read or write, or to rename private BBS files. These commands, and more importantly, the filenames, must not be discovered by the sysop. It is not good enough to use a simple one-letter-higher cipher to encode commands and filenames; for there are programs which can scan a file and display readable text it contains. If you just push everything up one letter higher (i.e., "PASS" becomes "QBTT"), those programs will still locate this encoded text — and the sysop might be smart enough to discover what it means. You're better off encoding text using numbers, symbols or foreign alphabets.

A program you upload may be an uncompiled source listing or a batch file. In this case, you will have to do some fancy fingerwork to keep your Trojan horses hidden. NEVER simply upload a batch file in its raw form. Imagine if you were the sysop who got this from a user:

```
cd BBS\USERS
open USERINFO.TXT
read USERINFO.TXT: User #44
set systemlevel 3 == systemlevel 99
close
exit
```

This isn't real code. It's meant to illustrate the kind of brazen attempt at upgrading access that would catch a sysop's attention.

One way to eliminate this problem is to have the main application program *create* batch files and other programs it needs. The batch commands start out as encoded gibberish in the application program. A subroutine is called, which opens a text file, decodes the commands, fills the file with them, then goes about its business. The creation and use of the file should probably be done on separate occasions, to keep illegal drive access time low.

Also for easily-readable sources, the Trojan horse part should not be standing right in front or at the end of the listing. Put it deep within the program. Add comments that will tend to mislead the careless reader. Remember, if your cover program is particularly clever, the sysop may want to analyze it, to see how you achieved such a wonderful thing! This means your cover program could be under some heavy scrutiny; and your Trojan horse could be discovered by accident.

Consider having your program delete the Trojan horse after it has been executed. That is, have

the last few steps the Trojan horse takes be to erase itself from the program.

Alternatively, have the *sysop* delete the application program (and thus the Trojan horse). This can be tricky: how can you get the sysop to delete all those files you uploaded, without letting on that something shady is going on below the surface? Ways this can come to pass are by having the application program be something that you know the sysop already owns, or something similar yet inferior to the sysop's version.

Or you could just write the sysop some e-mail, saying that you found a potentially dangerous bug in the program, "so if you would delete it I will send you a corrected version." This can only be done when the application you sent is a compiled program, elsewise the sysop would be able to correct the problem himself — wouldn't he!

A particularly paranoid sysop might transfer any uploaded files to a different computer before he tries them out. Or the directories could be set up different than expected, or the BBS might be set up to upload files to a floppy instead of the hard drive. Take these things into consideration when you program, and have your Trojan horse only work when the computer is set up as it is supposed to be. That is, it will only run when it has access to the password files, or whatever else is necessary for the Trojan horse to function. It's also necessary to do this because, if the application that hides your Trojan horse is good enough, the sysop will make it available for other users to download.

A Few Tips For The Do-It-Yourselfer

We talked earlier about hacker BBSs. What if you make a dedicated effort at finding a suitable BBS on which you can learn and share, but none turns up in your search? You may want to start a BBS of your own to suit your needs. Get ahold of the proper software, gather your most trustworthy friends together, and put together your own bulletin board system!

Running your own system means that you won't get much use out of your home computer and the telephone line to which it is connected. This would be no problem if all you did on your computer was hack, since your hacking can be taken on the road through the use of laptops, publicly available computers and the like. But you most likely use your computer for other sports: game playing, word processing, programming, and legal modem usage. Consider this before you get all excited about setting up a BBS.

One way to get around this problem — and to simultaneously overcome many of the problems that arise when one sets up a BBS — is to use your hacking skills to break into a mainframe far away from your house, and use *it* for the site of your electronic bulletin board.

Whatever home you give to your system, you should install it with a false front to make it look legit, and a back side that encompasses the private area for accepted hackers only. Invite the hackers whom you know to be wise and trustworthy into the inner sanctum, while leaving the rest of the board open for unknowns to explore.

I have seen some fantastic BBSs go up, only to fail miserably. And I've seen so-so BBSs that quickly establish themselves as the "in" place to be. As a hacker BBS, you won't experience this to such a great extent since you aren't going to advertise as much as a generalized BBS would — after all, you're trying to keep out all the riff-raff. But you will still want new users to come and enjoy themselves, and if they turn out to be the kind of folks you'd like to invite behind the scenes to your secret hacker sub-section, all will benefit by it.

The strategy for getting users to come in and stay awhile is to set up your BBS, turn it on, then *leave it on*. Many first-time sysops, excited with the prospect of running their own system, continually take their BBS off-line to make improvements. Don't do that! If someone calls and finds no computer is there to pick up, they aren't going to call back a second time.

Advertise your BBS on other BBSs whose members you would like to have on yours.

Have members of your BBS run scouting missions to the above-ground hacker BBSs. You will find out what, if any, useful information is exchanging hands over there, and you may be lucky enough to discover a hacker who is worthy of becoming a member of your club.

Before you allow an unknown hacker into the secluded realm of your hacker sub-boards, you should make doubly and triply sure that he or she

is not a cop. Real hacker BBSs verify their members by having them go through an initiation procedure which includes recommendations from respected hackers, full disclosure by the hacker of personal information so that it can be checked, and an autobiography detailing what he or she has done, and what he or she can contribute to the group. Don't be fooled! Verify that this self-proclaimed hacker is not an FBI agent by checking out credit ratings, telephone company data, and positions on other computer systems. You will have to use every inch of your hacking skills to ensure that the personal information that you are given matches a real human being. This isn't paranoia — it is common sense. Many, *many* hackers have been fooled by impostors pretending to be hackers. The safest thing is to not accept new members into your BBS; but that may not be the smartest thing because it eliminates a possible world full of information that will never expose itself to you.

Exploring electronic bulletin boards can be a pleasant pastime. It can sharpen your skills and teach you much about a lot of things. There is such a startlingly large number of BBSs around that a hacker could find himself spending all hours of the day and night connected to them, never to enjoy the thrill of the hack itself. Considering the dangers of hacking, that might not be such a bad fate.

In an upcoming section we will explore more ways you the hacker can protect yourself from the law. But for now let's get back to hacking — some of the best and most useful techniques are yet to come!

Chapter Eleven:
Borderline Hacking

I want to talk about some non-hackerish ways of dealing with hacking problems. There are times when some need forces a hack to be accomplished under time constraints. When that is so, the usual time consuming methods may fail us, and so one must resort to desperate measures. For the most part this is a topic related to doing hacking as a job, which I feel is important to bring up because lately being a hacker-for-hire has become an issue in the hacking world.

Hacking For Ca$h

There are hackers who have "made good," becoming security consultants for corporations and governments. These turncoats have received criticism from two directions. From the hackers: "How dare you do this to us!" (Rebuttal: "Obviously you are not a real hacker. A True Hacker would delight in trying to outwit another hacker's attempts to beef up security.") From the law-abiding citizens: "We couldn't trust him before, why should we trust him now?" and "Just because you know how to break into systems doesn't mean you know how to prevent them from being broken into." These are all valid points.

If you wish to enter this line of business, you are not alone. Companies have paid as much as $20,000 — possibly more — to have a hacker attempt to gain access to their computers. "Tiger teams" is the term for groups of hackers or sometimes lone hackers who are hired by an organization to put their security to the test. If you decide to pursue such a path, you will want to project an air of professionalism and sincerity. You have to prove to them you are a competent hacker, but you can't let them know that there is a rebellious spirit in your heart.

Remember that computers are vulnerable not only to crackers. There are also viruses, improper computing environments, loose-lipped employees and other hazards that can make even a tightly sealed ship sink. Preparing the owners for any catastrophe will earn you extra respect and recommendations for other jobs.

To touch on the second criticism of the "law-abiders," it is important to offer solutions to any security loopholes you uncover in your investigation. You are a hacker, so you know how hackers think.

You know their minds and their methods, and so, yes, you have the expertise to recommend action that will prevent invasion of their system. Explain to your employer why it is important that each of your suggestions be followed. Tell them what you did to get in, the weaknesses you saw, and the potential trouble spots for the future.

Other suitable clients are private individuals who are concerned with the information being stored on them in databases. Hackers have been hired to alter phone numbers, find unlisted numbers and addresses, remove fines, look up license plate data and change school grades, among other jobs. Hacking a business's computers under contract for that business is a perfectly legal occupation, but when you start helping people access and perhaps change their data files, you have stepped into the unlawful zone. Therefore, you should be very careful about who you deal with and how much you let those people find out about yourself.

Hacking is a hobby. Once you start getting paid for it you run into a problem: What happens if you can't complete a job?

True, nothing should be too tough for the Super Hacker like you, but occasionally you might have a deadline or unexpected difficulties and the system that looked so fragile when you began now looms as a large and impenetrable monster that is beyond your capabilities. That's where foul play comes in. Hopefully you won't have to resort to anything less than hacker's methods. On the other hand, if you have reached a point where you must choose between balking the job or finishing it in an untraditional way, you might decide to do the latter to keep your good reputation intact.

Besides, there's no sense in restricting yourself to hacker techniques when the bulk of penetrators are going to use these uncouth methods anyway. If a company is paying you to stop intruders, you'll want to make certain that there really is no way that these blunt methods, commonly used by non-hackers to gain access, will be viable. Therefore, you might have to try them out on the system you are being paid to protect.

Filthy Tricks

These tricks are filthy because they are the kinds of things a rank amateur would do. These "techniques" are strictly for non-hackers. I'd go so far as to say these are the kinds of things a non-computer-user would do! When I say "computer user," I mean someone who uses a computer because they want to, as opposed to someone who does so from necessity.

Often these tricks are used as a precursor to some sort of theft, or espionage — topics which lay on the fringe of true hacking only because they involve computers. A true hacker must know these tricks exist, but would use them only as a last resort — and then only with severe motivation to break in.

Bribery

You might not want to bribe the system administrator, but there will probably be some underlings who also have "God access," who may be willing to lend same to you, for a price. I would suggest you use bribes to pay for access to the system, rather than bribing the person to carry out computer work for you. After all, you want him to remain uninvolved in your affairs; if you're spying by computer, the last thing you need is a company insider knowing that you're doing so.

Have the bribe pay for either access to that person's account, or to a newly created superuser account. If the latter, only log on when the bribee is not on duty, so that he or she won't get curious and look to see what you're up to.

Offering money in exchange for a specific service to be performed (like offering $500 to change a grade from an F to an A) is even tackier, and more dangerous, than just paying for system access. For instance, in 1973 a computer operator employed by the Illinois Driver Registration Bureau was given a $10,000 bribe to steal a tape reel which contained personal information about drivers registered in that state. Considering that Departments of Motor Vehicles are some of the easiest and safest of computer systems to hack into using social engineering, it was both foolhardy and expensive to pay that much. My source of information on this case does not mention whether or not the people who offered the bribe were apprehended, but just the fact that we know about the bribe implies they were not successful. (Or at the very least, that future attempts would be less likely to succeed.) This is why you should hack if you can hack, and use other methods ("filthy tricks") only as a last resort — and then only to get into the computer, not as payment for the information you seek.

Besides, with system access you can try-before-you-buy, and you will be sure to get your money's worth, especially since once you have logged on, you can create your own superuser account that the person you bribed doesn't know about.

Booze And Broads

Yes! It sounds like science fiction but it's true!

There have been reported cases of crackers gaining access to computers by supplying alcohol, drugs and even prostitutes to the security personnel at a company. An article by Douglas Waller in the May 4, 1992, issue of *Newsweek* reported that a Japanese competitor to a "Midwestern heavy manufacturer" had outbid them one too many times. Upon investigating, it was found "that the Japanese firm had recruited one of the manufacturer's midlevel managers with a drug habit to pass along confidential bidding information." This sort of dealing sounds risky to me, because who knows what someone's liable to do once you've gotten them drunk or high? But that's why I'm saying these are the "techniques" used by the computer illiterate.

Bad Feelings

This isn't exactly a dirty trick, but it feels like one. If you can manage to find yourself a worker who feels maligned by the company, possibly one who is about to leave, especially one with programming ability — then you've got it made. Play up his or her bad feelings toward the company. Remind them how the company screwed them, didn't recognize their good work, and continuously passed them over. Without being specific, say you want to help them get revenge on the company. Of course, a hacker does no such thing, but if you can incite the disgruntled employee into action, he will get the blame for your own hackerish misconduct. (I know, I'm cruel sometimes.)

In any case, employees who are moving on to greener pastures, or those who are disgusted with their bosses, are a great source of inside information, including company lingo, phone directories, procedures and policies and, of course, passwords.

If your goal is to penetrate a system run under top notch security, getting a friend on the inside may be your only hope. But an ex-employee doesn't have to leave angry to be of use. Anytime you hear of an employee either quitting or being fired there is the opportunity to find out that blessed data. After all, computer accounts live on long after an employee has left a company. Once someone has left the company, what does he care whether you use his password or not?

Chapter Twelve:
What To Do When Inside

It seems straightforward enough. You're inside? Great! Take a look around! Of course that is what you'll do in most cases, after getting into a system and patting yourself on the back. But then what? To answer this we will have to begin with a re-thinking of our goals and morals.

Hacker Motivations Revisited

The true hacker is motivated by her or his desire to learn, to understand, to cleverly and harmlessly outwit.

Others who use hacker techniques might do so because they have a desire to learn about their competitor's secrets; to understand why they keep getting underbid every time; or to cleverly outwit the company or individual who they feel owes them something, and enact revenge upon them.

So let's see what we have here. There is the free-thinking, computer-enthusiast hacker, the economic espionage hacker, the politico-espionage hacker, the out for revenge cracker, and finally, the hacker for hire. Most often these assorted infiltrators will have breached security with a low-level account. This is because accounts with low security clearance are the most prevalent, and many hacker tricks focus on the naive user who is more prone to having a low-level account.

The hacker for hire and the hacker spies will have target computers, perhaps even specifically-targeted people in mind. They will want to go after either a particular username/password combination, or any access big enough to allow covert entry into their target's account.

Vandals and revenge hackers obviously would love to attain higher access than what they came in on, but unless they are sufficiently skilled, they will probably opt for the quick hit-and-run. That is, they will be content to break in under any password, do whatever damage is possible, send some nasty e-mail, and leave. Probably they will continue coming back over and over again until they are either arrested or shut out for good. If these "hackers" *do* have targets in mind (like the president of the company or whomever) they will most likely settle happily into whatever lower-level role they find themselves in. If they have any skills or computer know-how though, watch out.

The true hacker may or may not want to take the hack all the way to the top. He or she may feel it is not worth the effort for the amount of work that seems necessary to increase a low system access to a higher one. This isn't giving up, it's being practical. If the knowledge to be gained seems minimal or available elsewhere, there's no point in wasting time trying to get it. Or, the hacker may not feel secure enough in his knowledge of the computer, its users, or operating system to feel confident in his ability to achieve higher access. This is a valid feeling, and an intelligent one; if the hacker realizes he is somehow ignorant, then he can stop and do what is necessary to learn what he does not already know. If something like this comes up it's probably only a matter of research to put the hacker back on the track toward superuser status. As the hacker BrainMan put it:

I know the computer will be there for a long time to come. I like hacking, but I also like exploration. Sometimes I feel I'd rather wait for another day to do the exploration, the bookwork or social engineering, that will get me into an account, and I'd rather do some *real* exploration of a computer right now.

Besides increasing one's status in the system, a hacker has many options to choose from once inside. A hacker may:

- Read the documents that are available, and run the programs.
- Download files.
- Notify the system administrator of the presence of a security problem.
- Learn about the computing environment.
- See if other computers may be contacted from this one.
- Cover his ass.

Or a hacker might simply log off and never return.

If you have managed to work your way into some data that you feel might have market value, you might consider selling that data and thereby fund your next big computer purchase. I recommend *strongly* against doing so. Becoming a spy — for anyone — becomes a serious and dangerous business. It also helps to further degrade the image of the hacker in the public's eye, and will serve only to make matters worse for hackers in the long run — and you in the short run — if you are caught.

Although most courts and CEOs would disagree, I personally believe that there is no harm done in reading through whatever files are on a system, so long as no one is hurt in the process. At least, I don't think reading private files is a crime any worse than hacking one's way in, in the first place. You will have to construct your own set of ethics to guide you; I sincerely hope those ethical constraints are based firmly on the principles of the hacker ethic that both opens and closes this book.

Logging off and never returning is something the more fanatic and paranoid hackers tend to do. It is akin to B & E without the E, and I can not see how they can morally condone the "B" (breaking in) while shunning the "E" (entering). I suppose the hackers who disconnect without system interaction do it either because all that matters to them is getting in, or because they are intensely scared of discovery.

The other options I mentioned — increasing status, helping the sysops, and the learning — all require different degrees of familiarity with the computer system you have entered. Let us think about where you might find yourself, and what should you do when there.

To begin with, the account you have hacked yourself in with can be a single user account, a group account, root account, or "special account."

If it's a root account, congratulations! You now have the ability to do whatever you want. The root account is held by the system administrator (or one of several "sysadmins"). It may also be called by different names: avatar account, god account, sysadmin, superuser, demigod account, sysop account, or admin. Or you may never even know you've gotten into the root until you find you can do stuff only the Computer Gods high upon Mount Input/Output should be able to do.

A "group account" is one used by many people. It might be a departmental or store account, where everyone in a particular store or department can log in under the same name/pass combo. Depending on the situation, those who are of a certain rank or job may have their own shared account. For example, many companies like to set up limited accounts for secretaries, typing pool or temps. Other group accounts appear in places where terminals are available to a number of employees, but where employees have differing levels of security clearance. Thus, all may be able to search a database, but only those who log in with a certain password can enter new data, or can change the way the database is structured.

"Special accounts" include guest or demo accounts that allow one to take a sneak peek before subscribing to a service. They may be testing accounts put in by system programmers. Special accounts may also take one directly to a program, rather than logging you to an operating system prompt. Programs are set up this way for tutorial purposes, to dispense information, or so access to a particular application may be more freely available. If the account you've managed to hack is a special account, you might have to break out of it illegally and enter the operating system if you expect to increase your access level.

In any case, before any action can be taken you must understand what kind of access you have, what privileges you're entitled to, and how they can be exploited to your advantage. This may mean you'll need an intimate knowledge of the machine and its software. Before we can proceed there's one teeny weeny concept you must have full comprehension of. I've just mentioned it twice now — the operating system.

Operating Systems

Okay, clear your mind of any thoughts you've ever had about computers. We're going to start at the very beginning.

Let's say you had a computer that only did one thing. For instance, think of a coin operated arcade game. That's a computer which plays but a single game. With a one-game computer, as soon as you push the on switch, the game can start running. After all, there's nothing else to do with the machine except play that game.

Now let's add a second thing to our computer. Let's say, not only does the computer play a game, it also does word processing. So we now have a two-task computer.

What happens when we push the on switch? Does it go right to the game? It can't — what if we wanted to do word processing? You see, now we have to make a choice. When we turn on the computer, we now have to specify somehow whether

we want the game or word processing. How do we let the computer know where to go?

Well, we could have two separate switches, meaning any time I press the *left* switch, the game goes on and when I press the *right* switch, the word processor goes on. That may be a good solution for a little while, but what if I want to add a third thing to my computer? Or a fourth? Do I keep adding more switches?

What I do is, instead of adding hardware switches, I add a third program, a *software* switch. The third program is called the *operating system* (or OS), and when I push the computer's switch, the computer will automatically turn on the operating system program.

The operating system is a program that lets me choose between the game or the word processor. For example, when the operating system is started it may put a prompt on the screen such as, "Which program?" to which I would reply, "Game" or "Word Processor."

As you are well aware, this is basically what happens in real-world operating systems. In the early days of computing, when computers didn't do much more than run a few select programs, the controlling software was called "the monitor." As computers became more complex, there came the need to control multiple users, many peripherals, security, and an interlacing of program functionings. The monitor grew to become an all-encompassing program which did a lot more than just allowing the user to choose between a few programs. And so the term "operating system" is now used to describe this complicated piece of software.

Operating systems control the functioning of the entire computer; they control how resources will be allocated to the tasks at hand, how memory is used, which programs are to be run and in what order. It is the absolute master-control program; when you understand it, you have the understanding necessary to master the computer.

Some operating systems you are most likely to run into are "UNIX," "MS-DOS" or "PC-DOS" (on IBM compatibles), "PRIMOS," "RSTS" (on Digital Equipment Corporation's PDP-11 minicomputers), and "VMS."

It is important to understand operating systems because:

1. If you don't know the commands and syntax that control the computer, you won't be able to get the computer to do anything.
2. When you understand how an operating system works, you will be better able to look for bugs in it. Bugs invariably lead to security loopholes, which lead to a happier you.
3. You want to be familiar with the limitations of the operating system's security, so that you can exploit those limitations.
4. When you know how an operating system works, you will know what the computer's managers can do to trip you up, keep track of your whereabouts, and keep you from coming back.

All of this leads up to one big THEREFORE... Therefore, if you want to be a REAL HACKER, *you have to actually know something about computers.* If you want to control a computer, you have to know how to tame the software which controls that computer — you have to understand very fundamental things about its operating system.

Sure, a hacker may be able to get by using social methods and a tidbit of programming here and there, but there is no escaping the fact that real hacking requires real knowledge. And I'm talking about *self-taught* knowledge. You have to go out and learn this stuff on your own.

Does this sound intimidating? Then maybe you don't have what it takes to be a hacker.[1]

Realistically, there is no way to make a 100% guarantee that a particular computer system is safe from intruders. It is theoretically possible to break into *any* system. A *good* hacker should be able to break into *most* systems. An even better one will be able to get into *all* of them. And the absolute finest hacker will not only be able to enter every computer he encounters, but will be able to do something constructive once inside to make the trip worthwhile.

I mean, it's one thing to hack one's way into an on-line database. It's another thing entirely to figure out how to alter records in that database, and to do so without being caught.

If you want to have the ability to enter *any* system that you encounter and take action once inside,

then you must become knowledgeable about its OS. At the simplest level that means knowing the basic commands that any user of the system requires on a day-to-day basis to interact with files, to send and receive mail, and to perform any needed action on the machine.

A hacker needs to know the obscure commands as well, and should also be familiar with any files, software and directories commonly found on machines under that OS. He needs to know how the manuals are structured and the "jargon" of the OS. He needs to know who uses such an OS and how they use it. And he needs to know the meanings of error messages.

But we still haven't gotten to the hard part yet. You see, all of the above is just the tip of the iceberg. After all, all of this information is easily available from standard sources such as manuals and design specification guides. What a hacker needs to know about an OS is the secret stuff that doesn't come in the manuals, or if it is printed there it is so technical and obscure that it is information decipherable only by a select few. Those lists of "basic things a hacker should learn" describe what the OS is and what it does. But a hacker — to effectively enter and exploit *any* system he or she encounters — needs to know *how* the OS works, and *why* it works as it does.

Operating systems are so huge that they can never be adequately checked to ensure that every single bug has been worked out. They are sometimes altered to include features or functions that a particular computer manager finds desirable, but those alterations open up security holes. Sometimes multiple programmers working on different parts of the system don't communicate about vital aspects and so distant processes may explode if forced into contact. Additionally, the software that is used may have been designed for the plain-Jane version of the OS and so incompatibilities (and hence glitches) develop. Or two or more pieces of software being used together may open up sources of insecurity.

The casual user is oblivious to all of these possible security breaches. A hacker may be oblivious to them, but if the hacker has a fundamental understanding of the operating system which underlies all these sources of intrusion, then that hacker will, with a bit of thought, realize where the traps are and how they can be usefully manipulated.

---

[1] Hey, I'm talking Big Manuals here — thousands of pages long, and written in the ghastliest corporate/technical mumbo jumbo imaginable.

Needless to say, this book is not going to suddenly turn into an explanation of the technical aspects of every single operating system, and a true hacker wouldn't want it to be. So, go out there and find some operating system you can get acquainted with. Learn its basic commands, but then go a step beyond that and learn how those commands were programmed. Figure out ways you could simulate the command without typing it directly at the OS prompt. What happens to memory when the command is executed? Are there ways to change memory? These are the kinds of things that are important to a hacker who wants to accomplish big dreams.

Examples of such techno-oriented hacker methods abound throughout the rest of this chapter. The reason is simple and unavoidable: the best things in life are often not free. You have to work hard if you want to do great and exciting things after invading a system. Sure, you may find it convenient to learn certain things only as the need arises, such as a particular shell programming language, or the way an application works. But when you lack knowledge about underlying principles of the operating system, you are hacking blindly — you are just as oblivious to the exploitable faults and flaws of the system as any other user.

Let's get away from all this heady stuff for awhile and go back to the impetus for this discussion of operating systems: After you get in, what the hell comes next?

Looking Around

What should you expect to find, once you've made it onto a system or network? A whole lotta things!

There may be files to read, programs to run, or ways to move about from one computer to another, or one network to another.

Try looking for backup files and files that have been automatically saved on a timed basis. Some text editors leave behind files like this that are readable by anyone who happens to pass by. If the sysadmin has been editing the password file, or some other file containing sensitive data, you could be in luck. Electronic mail is often not automatically deleted, and it accumulates in (perhaps hidden) files on disks. Deleted files may not be deleted

right away, but become hidden or moved to a special directory.

See if you can find evidence of security logs. One of the most common errors for a user to make while logging in is to type the password at the username prompt. If you can find a readable security log it will often contain records of these login errors. For example, if George Washington tries logging into his UNIX account with his password, "cherrytree," but he types a little too fast, the following ensues:

```
WashingtonUs [Enter]
ername:cherrytree [Enter]
Password:
```

George realizes he has messed up. He has typed his name before the login prompt, and he has put his password (quite visibly) on the "Username:" line. He presses Enter a few times to clear everything, but the damage is already done. Somewhere in the administrative directories, there is a log file that reads:

```
Unsuccessful login of user cherrytree @ Tue,
Mar 24, 1992, 14:16:03
```

Now you just have to go through the various users on the system until you find the one who uses this password.

Security logs may also keep track of files sent and received, errors resulting from unauthorized commands, new accounts or new users being granted superuser status.

Speaking of security, the *first* thing you should do any time you log in to an account for the first time is try to get a sense of who this person is whose account you are borrowing (assuming you don't already know). When you log on you will most likely be greeted with a message telling you the last time that account had been active, and possibly which location or server the user had contacted it through.

If the message tells you that the legitimate user logged in recently then you may have a problem. Note the time of day the account was used and try to hack around it. Try logging in two times simultaneously on two separate computers and see what happens. Do you get an error message the second time? Is it possible to detect the presence of another person using the account with you concurrently? You want to know such things because you want to be able to deal with having the account holder coincidentally log on at the same time as you.

Let's look at this first scenario. You are logged into the account... the actual user tries logging in but gets a "User hjones already logged in on port 116" message. You have no way of knowing that this has occurred, but you can prepare for its eventuality by sending an e-mail message to the account, purportedly from the system manager, and leave it unread. So if the legitimate account holder were to log in she would find something like this waiting for her:

Message #01
From 1513 SuperUser
To ALLUSERS@calli.poo.mil

Some faulty wiring has led to problems with several of our port connection verifier circuits in the subchart group C of the local network system. If you receive a message upon login that you are already logged on, please hang up and try again in a few minutes.

We are sorry about this problem and we are doing what we can to correct it, but this will take time. It was a matter of choosing between a bit of inconvenience for a while, or shutting down the system entirely. I hope you will agree it is better to have some bugs in the system than no system at all.

We expect the problem to be cleared up before March 3rd. Thanks for your cooperation.

Often users will have personal history logs stored in their directory. There may be history reports detailing command activity, newsgroup readership, file transfers or files deleted. These can show you when and how the legitimate user is using the system, and also the level of competence of the user.

If your account has been used very infrequently, then you know that the actual account owner poses very little threat to you — although it also means the system manager is now a threat, since he will suddenly see tons of activity from an account that had never before been active.

On the other hand, if the account holder is in there night and day, you will have to be more wary of him than of the sysop — after all, any hacking you do from that account will get lost in the shuffle.

Commands To Look For And To Use

Most operating systems come with extensive online help. On UNIX, you can type "man commandname" to see the manual page for a command. Also helpful is "apropos" which will display a list of commands that are related to a given word. For example, "apropos password" lists all the commands, programs and variables that have something to do with passwords. You can then use "man commandname" to find out what each one means.

On TOPS machines you can type "help" or "help commandname" for on-line information.

Process commands tell you what is being done on the system and, generally, who is doing it. UNIX lets you type "ps -f" to see how other people are using the computer. Using such commands will give you a feel for what options are available to you. Also, it will show you which users have access on other computers, if they are logged into them from the one you are on. If you're extremely lucky you might even find an encryption key poised in the list of processes. If a person has typed something like "crypt key < filename" that entire command, including the key, will appear in the listing. Unfortunately, the crypt program acts to remove the key from the listing once it is activated, but there is a brief period when the key is public data, there for all to see. A "daemon" program could search for such occurrences (See glossary).

"Telnet" is a program that allows you to connect to other computers. Earlier it was mentioned that the account you've entered is most likely a low-access account. The reason a hacker bothers with regular user accounts in the first place is to give him or her a safe place to do *real* hacking. From that account you can do all the things you would never do from your legitimate account, like telnet to Pentagon computers and start a brute force attack. UNIX also has a "cu" (Call Up) command which allows the user to call up a specified phone number.

Calling one computer from another enables the hacker to avoid being traced. It also might be the most practical solution to the problem of connecting to a certain computer, since some computers can only be accessed through other networks.

File Transfer Protocol (FTP)

FTP is a program that allows users to copy files back and forth between two computers, usually two computers connected via the Internet. Strictly BITNET users will need to use e-mail instead of FTP to transfer files.

After typing "ftp" to start the program, one can input any computer address and try to connect with it. A username and password will be asked for. Many sites offer an anonymous FTP directory — users can log in with the username "anonymous" and have access to all the text files and programs that the site administrator has made available.

Often an anonymous FTP site is set up like a trading post. An incoming directory is set up with anonymous write and execute permission, but usually not read permission. Users can then upload files they want to share with others without those others knowing the files are available. The system operator can evaluate the files before making them publicly available.

One common security hole with anonymous FTP is that two auxiliary directories called "etc." and "bin" are often owned by the FTP account. If this is the case, and if they are not write protected, any user could upload their own malevolent versions of system programs and batches.

Fun 'N Games

You might see Xtrek or Empire, or any number of on-line, multiuser games available on the computers you crack, especially those at colleges. Because the games are multiuser, passwords are required to access them, and it should be noted that often the password-storing mechanism on the games is not as secure as it should be; the passwords are sometimes placed in a plaintext file. We know that people tend to use the same password wherever they go. Think about it.

The User Network

USENET is to local BBSs what the Taj Mahal is to anthills.

USENET is an Internet BBS that encompasses thousands of discussion groups and millions of postings. On USENET, you don't just have a "computers" bulletin board, you have boards talking about software, about hardware, viruses, hackers, individual operating systems and printers and spreadsheets and ethics and... you name it. Each topic area is called a newsgroup. There are groups engaging in talk about music, cars, sex, SCUBA diving, crime, parachuting, television, books, bestiality, flowers — it makes one dizzy to think about it all.

Some newsgroups are moderated. That is, some controlling organization edits the postings or picks and chooses which messages will be given display time. Most groups are an unmoderated free-for-all.

One accesses USENET by running a news program such as "readnews," "news," or "nn." You can read the posted messages, or write one of your own. Messages are sent out to all other participating sites worldwide, which means if you have a question about anything, USENET offers a huge international forum through which to find an answer.

Becoming A Superuser

Breaking into a system isn't worth anything if you find yourself in an empty home directory with such a low access level that nothing fun is allowable. When you hack into a low-level account belonging to a data entry clerk or some other restricted user, you will want to raise your access to the highest it can go. This is accomplished by doing research from the inside, spoofing, programming tricks, or social engineering.

As far as research is concerned, you will want to look around the system you've just penetrated and see what options are available to you. Read all files; run all programs. Most technical hacks involve bugs in established software. Generally this software is of a kind that interacts with other users' accounts in some way. Thus mailing and "chatting" programs are susceptible, as well as text editors. If you find a programming language of any kind you should be in Hacker's Heaven, as there are hundreds of variations on programming tricks you can use while inside to gain better access. Let's start with spoofing.

Spoofing

Spoofing usually refers to sending electronic mail in such a way that it looks like *someone else* was the one who sent it. Spoofing can also refer to any act whereby a hacker impersonates another user. Let's stick with the first, more common definition for a while, and look at some ways in which spoofed e-mail can benefit the low-level hacker who wants to make good for himself.

One prototypical scam is to spoof an e-mail letter from the system operator. Susie User, a highly powerful person on the system, is on-line, going about her usual business. She checks her mailbox and is surprised to find a letter has just been mailed to her from the system administrator. The letter talks about how, because of security breaches, they will now be issuing new passwords every six weeks. "Your new password is D4YUL," says S.U.'s e-mail. "You can change it yourself with the 'SET_PASS' command. Remember it! Don't reveal it to anybody! Computer security is an important issue that can not be taken lightly!"

A few moments later you notice that Susie has issued a SET_PASS command, and a few moments later you log on in her name, thus achieving her higher security privileges. It works every time! The trick is, you have to know how to spoof to do it.

Before you can spoof e-mail, you have to understand how such a thing is possible. Now, if you've ever used any sort of electronic mail program, whether on a mainframe or local BBS, you know that to send mail, the user enters basically three pieces of information: destination, subject and the body of the letter. Some mail programs allow further complexities, such as the inclusion of other text files or programs, return receipts, etc., but let's just concern ourselves with the most primitive of mailing programs, as those are the ones that get the most usage.

When you send electronic mail to another user, the computer automatically places a heading on top of the letter, which identifies it as having come from you. To spoof e-mail you will want to somehow change that heading, so it looks as though the letter was written by the person in charge of the system.

Usually one sends mail by running a mail program. The mail program includes a text editor and facilities to send mail to other users. But in many cases you don't have to use a special mailing program to send mail. There is usually a fundamental shell programming command that allows you to send text or a file, into a file on another user's directory. This is what the mailing program does: it sends the text of your message into a file called MAIL.TXT or something similar, and when Susie U. executes her mail program, it will display the contents of the file MAIL.TXT.

As you can imagine, it is a simple task to open a text file, type in a header that looks like a header from a superuser's letter, then add your own text to the bottom of the file. Next you use the "send file" command to put this file into another user's directory. Make sure the directory you put it in is one with higher access privileges than your own!

Sometimes the operating system itself foils this scheme. For example, one of the Internet protocols requires the two computers involved with the mail transfer to compose the letter headers. To spoof on the Internet, one would connect to a host through port 25, which is how e-mail is transferred to a site. Normally only two computers connect in this way; there may be security safeguards in place, but if there are not, you can pretend to be a computer sending the commands to generate an e-mail message. This includes "mail from" and "rcpt" which establish who the sender and recipient are. Use "help" to get yourself through this.

Earlier I mentioned that spoofing is also considered to be any form of on-line impersonation of another.

Many multi-user systems let users chat with each other by way of a command called TALK or WRITE, or something similar. When you issue a TALK command, a message appears on the recipient's screen, saying that you wish to talk. If the other user wants to talk with you, he or she issues the TALK command also. Then whatever you type appears on the other one's screen and vice versa. It may also be possible to filter the contents of a file onto another's screen by way of a TALK command. The hacking possibilities are endless!

One popular trick is to TALK a message like, "SYSTEM FAILURE. SHUT OFF YOUR TERMINAL WITHOUT DISCONNECTING TO PREVENT FURTHER DAMAGE. SYSADMIN," onto another person's screen. When they hang up, you piggyback a ride on their account.

As with e-mail spoofs, you can't actually use the TALK command to put text on another user's screen. You have to go into the source code of the TALK program, see how *it* writes to another screen, and use those commands. This bypasses the safety features inherent in the TALK command. (If you use the actual TALK command to send this sample error message, the other party will see that it's *you* sending the message, not the Sysadmin. You have to emulate the TALK header which announces the name of the user sending text. You also want to go down to the fundamental "send text" statements because you don't want the user to have the option of not talking with you.)

It's a recognized fact that spoofing accounts for a good majority of system security failings, mainly because they're so easy to do once you've gotten on-line and taken a look at the software source codes and manuals. Another trick relies on TALK-ing a message that an intelligent terminal will understand. When you use a TALK command you aren't putting words into the OS prompt's mouth — the OS is simply putting what you type onto the remote terminal's screen. One way to get around that depends on the remote hardware. Some intelligent terminals have a Send or Enter escape sequence that tells the terminal to send the current line to the system as if the user had typed it in from the keyboard. You can use TALK to send a message that contains a suitable escape sequence to do naughty things like e-mail confidential documents back to you and the like.

Not only e-mail and TALK, but other commands are also known to be rife with ways they can be misused to a hacker's benefit. Anytime you come across a command which allows interaction with another terminal, study it closely to see how it can be manipulated.

Look at programs, too, to see if they can be used to communicate out of your own directory. The GNU-EMACS text editor (used on UNIX computers) allows you to send the file you are working on to another person's directory. If you happened to name that file ".login"[2], then whenever that user

logged on, that ".login" batch would execute. And if part of that ".login" included mailing the user's secret stuff to your account, so much the better.

Cryptography And DES

Reverting to old tricks, brute force attacks can allow you to decrypt password files on your own time, on your own terms. Even with your meager account you should be able to copy an encrypted password file off a machine you've hacked and onto a safer one. At the very least, you should be able to view the contents of a password file, even though it is encrypted.

Then you compile a copy of the decryption software, altering it so it will read in a word from a specially-prepared dictionary file, use that as a key, and print the result. UNIX source code listings are available for every facet of the OS. Even if you *can't* get a decryptor of the type used by the computer to code the password (and other) files, you can still go to the manual, see which encryption algorithm is used, and write a program yourself that follows that algorithm. Brute forcing encryption keys on a password file is much faster than forcing one's way onto the system in the first place. Soon you should have found a key that unlocks the code, and soon you will have the superuser password!

Brute force may not always be a necessity. There is reportedly a well-known inversion to the encryption algorithm used on certain OSs, including older versions of VMS. Sorry to say, I don't know exactly what this inversion method is. I do know there are ways to algorithmically reverse the effects of a "crypt" command in UNIX. That command uses the World War II Enigma coding algorithm, which was devious for its time but no match for modern supercomputers. Sure, it still takes a while to do the inversion, but it is possible to do it if you have a computer with enough horsepower.

However, the crypt command isn't used all that much because everyone knows how vulnerable it is. Mostly "crypt" is left around for sentimental reasons. The encryptor that is most often used to encode passwords is a version of the federal Data Encryption Standard (DES). The UNIX variation of DES is "defective" in that brute force attacks for encryption keys are close to impossible. How does it defeat brute force attacks?

---

2 Under UNIX, ".login" is the name of the batch file that gets executed once a user logs into his or her account.

As we all know, UNIX password files are openly available for anyone to read, copy, or print out, but the passwords themselves are stored in an encrypted form. Well, that's not exactly right. The password file actually does NOT contain any passwords at all. What happens is, when a user logs in for the first time and enters a password, UNIX uses the first eight characters of the password as an encryption key to encode some constant (say, a long random number).

Another reason why DES was chosen to encrypt passwords is that when the DES algorithm is implemented in software form, it is slow. This means it will take more time to run a brute force attack.

Staying with this topic a bit, it's unsettling to note that the Data Encryption Standard also may not be as secure as it was once believed to be. DES was based on a security system called Lucifer, developed by IBM for the National Bureau of Standards in 1973. Before being released as the USA's official (standard) code, the top-secret National Security Agency had their say in the matter, reducing the complexity of the encoding algorithm and keeping certain aspects of its design under wraps. This looked mighty suspicious! Why would the NSA go out of its way to proclaim the code secure while simultaneously making it less secure? Critics warned that a back door had probably been built into the system.

In early 1992, two Israeli scientists announced that they had found a way to beat the system. If someone knows the encoded message, certain mathematical techniques can be applied to infer the key used to encrypt the message. Then other coded texts which use the same key can be easily read.

In any case, it is well known that much better codes have been produced since the 1970s.

Some systems make it difficult to brute force the plaintext out of an encrypted file, because the encryption key supplied by the user is not what encodes the text. Rather, it is used to encode some random sequence of characters. Those characters encode the text.

You don't have to be smart to be a hacker, you just have to be clever. But to crack data encryption algorithms you must be clever, smart and mathematically-inclined. Lucky for us people who don't have calculators for brains, there are so many other ways to read encrypted files than by breaking the code! I'll stick with Van Eck and his cronies, thank you.

Bit By Bit

Let's say you find yourself in some rinky-dink little account one evening, with just about zero access to anything interesting. On this hypothetical system you are able to read the passwords file, but of course to change it is out of the question.

You can see that your account's password has been encrypted (in the file) as "fg(kk3j2." If you had the ability to load the password file into a text editor, you could replace the sysadmin's encrypted password with yours ("fg(kk3j2"), then save the file. Well, naturally you can't do that. You could get as far as loading the file into a text editor and changing it: but to *save* like that is impossible without superuser status. Or is it?

The system security may be such that it only makes validation checks at the highest level of interaction. So the high level commands to delete, move, execute, or alter files are disallowed if the user does not have a certain security clearance; the actual machine level commands to move the read/write head to a particular location, let's say, may not be halted in the least. If this were true for the whole available storage arena, every file could be completely read or rewritten bit by bit. If programming or disk maintenance software is available to you on-line, you might then be able to use it to alter individual storage locations — to change the system administrator's encrypted password to your own.

On the other hand, you might find that security prevents even low level instructions from being performed. Don't give up too soon! It may be that only parts of the storage arena have been protected, while others — due to forgetfulness, bugs, impossibility or impracticality — have been left unsecure. If so, you may not be able to change the passwords file, but perhaps it would be possible to move files to another user's private directory, or to change files that are already there. This opens up a whole world of possible Trojan horses and back doors.

If security seems to prevent all illegal access from taking place, perhaps it is possible to trick a process with superuser security clearance into doing the work for you. A simple program, such as a game, could be written, containing instructions to secretly alter passwords. Compile and save the program, making access to it available only to superusers. Then move the file into a public directory. Eventually some superuser will come along and execute it, thus enacting the portions of your program which, if you had run them yourself, would have resulted in error messages and perhaps a few more ticks on the security log.

Program Employment

Most programs that are employed by hackers are of the Trojan horse variety. And the classic Trojan horse example is one which uses the faults of others to achieve its goal. Generally this means using undisciplined PATH commands.

Most modern operating systems allow you to arrange your files in an organized fashion by the use of directories and subdirectories. This makes finding where you left a file easy, but it causes problems when you get sick of typing in long pathnames to change from one directory to another.

The solution is in PATH commands. A PATH command says to the OS, "If you don't find that file in the current directory, look over there... Then look there.... And there." In other words, you specify a path which the OS can follow to find files. That way you don't have to be in a file's directory to access that file.

PATH commands are usually put into batch files which are run at login. They are especially used on big machines which contain lots of files and tons of directories. In those cases, especially if the user is a maintenance operator and needs access all over the place, there might be a lot of directories specified in the PATH.

Sloppy search paths, especially ones which look at all or most of the directories on a system are of extreme importance to the hacker. The hacker starts by rewriting a program that gets used often and putting a Trojan horse into it. The program is then put into a directory that is likely to be in a superuser's path. A privileged user or program, such as a superuser shell script, may innocently chance upon, let's say, your "date" program instead of the "official" version stored in the OS directory. It is accessed, and your hidden code does its thing.

Trojan horses can do a lot of things. They can collect passwords, simulate login prompts[3], remove read/write protection from files, or fake system crashes (and when the user shuts off his terminal and walks away, you type in the secret control code which causes the Trojan horse to uncrash back to the user's account). Trojan horses should definitely make up the majority of a hacker's tool kit. But there is another, different means of gaining higher access by employing programs, and that is with the use of computer viruses.

Viruses

A virus is born from the cross breeding of three other families of programs: the Trojan horse, the worm, and the logic bomb.

A logic bomb is a piece of code hidden within a larger program. Usually it is no more than a simple IF/THEN statement. IF such-and-such is true, THEN do something. Judging by the name, logic *bomb,* you can guess what that "something" usually entails.

The classic example of a logic bomb being put to use is when a system programmer is fired for inadequate job performance, or for some other humiliating reason. A few days after he walks away, the head honchos at the firm get a message from the programmer: "Pay me X thousand dollars before July 31st and I'll tell you how to save your software and records from total annihilation." The programmer has, you see, implanted a logic bomb that will detonate at that certain date.

A worm is a program with one purpose: to replicate itself. All it does is look at its environment, see where it can make a copy of itself, and it does so. Then there are two copies of the worm. Each of those reproduces, and there are four. Four quickly become eight, and so on. Soon an entire computer or network is clogged with hundreds or even thousands of unstoppable reproduction machines.

Then there's the virus. A virus comes from the mating of these two other breeds. When a worm takes on a logic bomb aspect to it, you get a program that will replicate as much as it can, and then *explode* when "something" happens. The whole

---

[3] Also, think about Trojan horses in terms of the multi-user games discussed earlier — obtaining those passwords, etc.

thing hides itself within an application program, as a Trojan horse.

Logic bombs are dangerous, but at least they are contained. Worms and viruses on the other hand, are unpredictable. Therefore, I say a true hacker will never release a worm, because they are too destructive with no purpose. A true hacker *may* release a virus if it can move harmlessly throughout a system, erasing itself as it goes, making sure it never backtracks to where it's been before.

A virus can be programmed to e-mail passwords to a specific address, or it can be used as a battering ram to brute force new passageways into computer systems. There are lots of ways in which hackers can use viruses, but it is difficult to use them safely.

There have been rumors of a microcomputer virus which, if it exists, would gladden the heart of many a hacker. The virus is called the AT&Tack Virus. Once it copies itself onto a computer, it tries to find a Hayes brand or compatible modem. If one exists, it silences the modem's speaker and dials a preprogrammed number. Apparently then whoever is at the telephone number it calls has remote access to your computer.

To me, this seems like nothing more than a rumor. Indeed, as of this writing none of the commercially available virus detection software makes any mention of an AT&Tack Virus. Besides, it seems to me this sort of thing would work better as a Trojan horse in a graphics display program, rather than as a virus.

Covert Channels

One of the fun things about using Trojan horses and viruses is the designing of covert channels to get the data they collect back to you in some readable form. Consider a virus that attaches itself to the login program and thus collects passwords. It does no good to have this virus halfway across the world with no way to get back that list of passwords it is reaping. One method has already been mentioned: the virus can periodically e-mail you a list of passwords. Take heed not to have that e-mail sent to any account where you can be identified.

It would also be a good idea to encrypt the mail before it is sent. One problem with encryption is

that a key is required. Anyone finding your virus or Trojan horse will easily figure out what the key is and be able to interpret e-mail or temporary files that the virus/Trojan horse produces. So you have to encrypt the key... which requires another key... which means more hiding needs to be done... another key.... Well, this could go on forever. Make the best of the situation.

If you're going to be encrypting anyway it may be easier to have your virus or Trojan horse send the encoded data to an unmoderated newsgroup. Disadvantage: You have to spoof the post, or someone may notice that this user (who is unknowingly activating your virus or Trojan horse) is posting a lot of "garbage" to the group.

You may also have the encrypted file uploaded to the *incoming* directory of an anonymous FTP site somewhere. Make certain files can be downloaded from that directory, because as mentioned earlier, often the ability to download from such directories is turned off for security reasons.

To send short messages (like a single password[4]) you may have your rogue program rename a world-changeable file to that message. By "world-changeable," I am referring to the security protections placed on that file — set it to very low protection, so that anyone can change its attributes. Your Trojan horse/virus will come into your directory under the disguise of various users from all around the network, and attempt to rename that file to that message. You don't want your Trojan horse/virus to generate an error message. (You can set up a process to constantly run in the background, monitoring the state of that file. As the file's name changes, the background process stores the new name, then gives the file its original name,

---

[4] Normally a Trojan horse or virus would send back to you three pieces of information: username, password, and the address of the computer where that username-/password was valid. However, if you targeted a specific individual by giving that individual sole access to your Trojan horse, then only a password would be needed.

Of course, viruses and Trojan horses don't have to be messengers for only password information. You may be a hacker, but you may also be a spy, a crasher, or who-knows-what-else. As far as I know, the information you need covertly passed back to you could be virtually anything.

thus allowing another copy of your Trojan horse or virus the opportunity to send *its* message.)

Other short messages can be sent a bit at a time. For example, the existence of file X in a certain directory means that your rogue program is sending the digit one. If the directory is empty, the file deleted, a zero bit is being transmitted. A background process is running in your home directory to monitor the appearance and disappearance of that file. When enough zeros and ones accumulate, the program translates them into a character of the message.

The extended ASCII code uses eight bits to define a character. For instance, 01000001 represents the capital letter A. 01000010 is B, and so forth. For your virus or Trojan horse to send an eight character password, 64 deletions and creations of file X would be needed. Those bits would be sent one at a time, whenever the rogue program had the opportunity to do so unnoticed.

Get Out Of Jail Free

Okay, all of that is fine if you've broken in by discovering someone's username and password, but what if the only access you've found to a machine is that of a command account or information setup? Then you have to see what can be done to break out of this jail of a program and get down to the level of the operating system. Probably this will be difficult to do. It will be less so if you've done any serious programming in the past.

As a programmer, you know what kind of bugs and errors crop up, and what kinds of things to look for to make them appear. If you're stuck in an account that runs an info program, let's say, you will want to try *every* unconventional, unexpected thing you can think of, in the hopes that you'll find something the programmer didn't think to guard against. Then hopefully you'll get an error message and crash out to the OS prompt.

Things to try:

Give bad, inappropriate, unrequested, or extremely long input to prompts, especially alphabetic answers to numeric questions. Or when asked to supply a number, that will be analyzed by a function, try an incredibly small or large one. Try responding with break signals, either Control-Z, Control-C, or possibly Control-P. Try executing

"Find" commands that will search out of bounds of available resources, or that will look beyond the alphabet. See if it's possible to set up programs for nonexistent hardware or memory capabilities.

If there is any sort of text editing facility, such as a program to send mail to sysops, do what you can to compose a batch file, and see if it's possible to send your message as a command that must be executed. Also with text editors, try to compose excessively long letters. If the editor has special text revision functions, write up a huge paragraph then cut and paste a copy underneath it. Then cut and paste those two paragraphs underneath, etc., until the program either crashes or doesn't allow you to continue. If the latter, see what happens when you try saving or sending the whole mess.

You may be in a program that is made to look like a simple operating system or control program, essentially a menu with the list of options either unavailable, or callable with a HELP command. Thus, you're given a prompt and asked to enter a command. Some application commands allow appending to them the name of a file on which you intend to work. For instance, to edit STORY.DOC with a word processor, you might type the command "WORD_PROC STORY.DOC," to run the word processor with STORY.DOC already loaded in it. On an on-line system, try to crash a program that allows such execution by giving it too much data, ("WORD_PROC STORY.DOC FILE.ONE FILE.TWO...") or by giving it inappropriate data. Some examples:

```
WORD_PROC WORD_PROC
WORD_PROC \directoryname
WORD_PROC nonexistent-filename
WORD_PROC /etc/date [or other command]
```

The "inappropriate data" tactic has been used successfully in the recent past. Another bug that's been exploited is excess command stacking. Command stacking is the placing of multiple commands on one line. Commands may be separated with spaces, semicolons, slashes, or a number of other punctuation symbols. The parser which interprets the stacked commands may break down if too many commands are given it. The line editor may not allow you to enter so many lines that this occurs, but through programming tricks you can probably get an unwieldy stack of commands sent as though from the keyboard.

If there is a language or compiler available, then it should be possible to POKE some values into places that would be better left unprodded. Alternatively, you might find yourself able to compile code into specific areas of memory, overwriting the code which is impeding your progress. Or your code might cause the program to jump to a new location, where further instructions can be carried out.

Finally, see if you can load a program into a mail writer or other editor, or into a superzap program, and alter it so that when it runs, it will crash.

Bugs in software are most likely to occur if the software in question:

- Is new (i.e., version one or thereabouts, or being Beta tested).
- Was hastily slapped together to make some fast money or to comply with the advertisements or demands.
- Has remained the same for years despite hardware or other changes.
- Is being renovated.
- Is not commercially available.

When you're hopping around on the networks you encounter, stop and read the notes that accompany new versions of old software. These will generally list, not just the improvements made, but sometimes the reasons for the improvements (i.e., if there was an exploitable bug in the earlier version). By the time you read the upgrade note, most sites will probably have already upgraded to the new version, but given the tremendous number of computers running today, more than a few won't have heard that a new version of their software has been released.

Returning To The Scene

The prudent hacker will build himself or herself a trap door to allow easy entry if further penetrations are required. Mainly this means setting up a dummy account to use in successive hacks. After all, there is no guarantee that the account you used the first time will still be valid the next time you login, or that the password or some other critical item won't have been changed, barring your entrance. If you have gained access not through a

password, but through some fluke hidden command or technical means, you will definitely want to add a trap door just so you don't have to go through all that rigmarole the next time you want to get in.

On many operating systems, programs can be set to run even after the user has logged off. Sometimes the program can be put on a timer, to begin execution at a specified future time. Writing a suitable program and then running it under one of these commands can make your return easier to accomplish.

Mission Accomplished... Almost!

Hey! Look at what you've done!

You've done your research, found your computer, broken in, and now, you've dabbled around inside. These four components are what hacking is all about. This is what it means to be a hacker.

But there is also a fifth level of hacking to consider.

These first four parts had to be done in linear order, one following the other. The final part is really not final at all. It is something you should be doing from the very beginning, thinking about every step of the way.

Because you see, this thing you've done, this *hacking*, is illegal. And so you must protect yourself.

So now let's look at what exactly it is about hacking that our society considers wrong. Then we will see how we can keep on hacking forever unscathed. Finally, we will tie up loose ends and look ahead to your future as a hacker.

Part Three
After Hack

Chapter Thirteen:
This Lawful Land

There are lots of fraud investigators, special agents, Secret Service people, FBI guys and all manner of local, state and federal enforcement officials roaming around cyberspace, waiting to trip you up. There are also private citizens who love hacking but don't love the idea of being criminals, so they hack the hackers, building up dossiers, which they then turn over to the authorities.

Getting caught can make you famous, maybe even throw some money your way. It can also take away a good part of your life, your money, your reputation, your computing equipment, and your hopes for the future. Let's take a look at the laws that cause this state of affairs.

State Computer Crime Laws

Every state except Vermont has explicit laws forbidding computer crime. They are all pretty much alike in that they start out by defining what a computer is, and defining various terms relating to computers and computer crime. Then they list the specific offenses the law prohibits, and the penalties associated with those illegal activities.

You can easily find out what the situation is for your state. Just so you know what kind of things cops and lawyers are talking about when they talk about state computer crime laws, let's take a look at a typical anti-hack statute.

The Wisconsin statute on computer crimes ("Chapter 293, Laws of 1981, 943.70" for you lawbook gurus) lists eight possible naughty things a person can do with a computer. The first six have to do with "computer data and programs," the sixth being the willful, knowing, and unauthorized disclosing of "restricted access codes or other restricted access information to unauthorized person[s]." The first five bits of software naughtiness detail the willful, knowing, and unauthorized modification, destruction, accession, possession, or copying of computer data, computer programs, or "supporting documentation."

The final offenses have to do with the hardware aspect. "Whoever willingly, knowingly and without authorization," either modifies, destroys, uses, takes or damages a computer, computer system, network, equipment or supplies related to computers, is guilty under this statute.

There are eight different penalties listed, depending on whether the act in question is considered a misdemeanor or a felony under the law. The magnitude of the crime is based on how much damage was caused money-wise, how much threat to others there was, and whether the hacker did the deed with intent to defraud or obtain property. Penalties range from life imprisonment (sheesh!) to various fines in the $500-$10,000 range.

Traditional State Crime Laws

Just because your state doesn't have a law that specifically forbids snooping around in someone else's computer, doesn't mean what you're doing is completely legal. Prosecutors will try to convict hackers on violations of *any* law, even if there's a large void between the hacker's actions and the original intent of the law. In some circumstances, the prosecutors may feel there is not a good enough case against a hacker using the computer laws. For other reasons — such as a rural jury — prosecutors will press the issue of guilt, but try to sidestep the technical aspect of it. They will charge a hacker with infractions of traditional crime laws, such as malicious mischief, burglary, larceny, and whatever other nasties they can squeeze into play.

There are problems applying traditional laws to modern "crimes," and the focus changes from whether Hacker X is guilty or innocent, to whether Hacker X is guilty of that particular crime. Can hacking be considered a kind of burglary? In a blue collar computer crime, such as the theft of the actual hardware, there is no question whether or not a law has been broken. On the other hand, if a hacker steals records from a database, do the burglary statutes still apply? What if the hacker didn't actually deprive anyone of their information, but only made a *copy* of it for him or herself? Is this a different issue?

These topics have been addressed differently in different court cases. If you are ever unfortunate enough to be tried for hacking-related offenses, the judge's decision will be based on the exact definitions of "software," "burglary," and other key words for your particular state. If the state has no computer crime statutes, then "software" may not be defined; in that case it is up to the judge entirely to decide what these terms mean.

Since we do have 50 states worth of laws to consider, in addition to federal laws, space constraints dictate that we not list every single statute and definition that might apply to a hacker's trial. For the specifics you will have to do your own research into your state's laws. Here is a generalized overview of traditional crimes, and how they can be applied to convict you of computer hacking. I want to stress this point of "generalizations." All the definitions of law to follow are simplifications of the laws throughout the land. Individual states add their own personal quirks and nuances to these laws — minutiae on which both surprise verdicts and legal loopholes are based.

Criminal Mischief

Also called malicious mischief, this is the willful destruction of someone else's property. You may say to yourself, "Gosh, as long as I don't purposely go around acting like a jerk, how can they convict me on *that* one?" Good question.

To be able to say that malicious mischief has occurred, three things must be present: a real human action, evidence that the action has caused damage to someone else's property, and that the damage is observable to a bystander. That's the traditional definition. Well, any bystander can see a smashed storefront window, but how many "average bystanders" can easily see how an algorithm has been changed in a program to allow access to anyone named "Borges"?

The thing is, a hacker may change software or password files to gain entry to a system, but it is often hard to determine whether or not such an action has caused "willful destruction" of that file. Indeed, the software may not actually have been altered to any detectable degree, and the hacker himself may not have done any noticeable actions at all. Can one then honestly say that criminal mischief has occurred? And yet, the hacker may have *left* the software in an altered, "destroyed" state.

The answers to such questions remain to be adequately determined.

Burglary

For most states, burglary is the unauthorized breaking and entering of the real property of another with intent to commit a crime. Again there is a problem, in that we have to decide whether or not to accept an operating computer network as property. The act of entering one's username/password is often metaphorically associated with that of unlocking and opening a door to one's house, but does that analogy exist to such a degree that the unauthorized entry into a computer directory is committing a *burglary*?

It is generally conceded that the attempt to prosecute such an act under traditional burglary statutes becomes futile. It may become slightly less futile if there is a clear intent on the hacker's part to commit a crime. Again, make sure the world knows your intentions are benign, and be sure to follow that path.

Of course, the physical breaking and entering of a building, with the intention of using the computers there to hack, is a more clear-cut matter. Don't expect to wiggle out of *that* one on as many technicalities.

Fraud

Fraud is easy to define: any sort of deception, cheating or unfair behavior that is used to cause injury to another person. Using someone else's password is fraud, since you are falsely representing yourself, and the "injured person" (computer) reasonably believes you to be that person to the extent that you are given privileges you should not have received.

But to be convicted of fraud it must be shown that *because* of the deception, the victim had damage done to him or her. What happens in the case where a computer manager *knows* it's a hacker on the line, and yet the manager is unable to prevent damage from occurring? Since there is no deception, there is no fraud. That may be *intent* to defraud, and perhaps not fraud itself.

Social engineering is clearly fraud if information gained from the exchange is used to enter a computer, and some injury can be proven. Actually, fraud is universally cited in any instance of computer crime, no matter what methods were used or what the outcome of the "crime." You can see then the importance of not causing "injury" to a computer. In all of these cases, it is essential that it can be established that no damage (or alteration) was done, and none was intended.

Larceny

Larceny occurs when two conditions hold true: A piece of property has been criminally taken and carried away from another person, and the intention of so doing was to permanently deprive the owner of his or her property.

Again, problems arise when applying this to computer hacking. Think about a case where a hacker inserts a GOTO statement in a program to bypass the section where the program asks for login information. Has the hacker effectively deprived the administrators on that system of that section of code — that piece of property? Additionally there is the problem of determining if the intent was to leave the GOTO in permanently, and not only that, whether or not such an action constitutes "taking" away of property. After all, the intermittent code is still there, only the access to it has been temporarily eliminated.

Larceny may be applied to the stealing of time on a computer, to stolen telephone service or electrical power. In these cases it would seem the lawyers are doing their best in a trying situation — a situation in which they realize the hacker has not done any harm, and yet they want to symbolically punish the hacker for invading their computers.

Theft Of Trade Secrets

Theft of trade secrets — also called "misappropriation" of trade secrets — may be contained in the larceny laws of the state if a trade secret is defined as a kind of property, or it may be the principal construct of its own statute. Misappropriation of trade secrets might be the better of the two names, as it more accurately reflects the nature of the law: either the physical taking of secrets, or the unauthorized copying of them, may be viewed as a violation.

So if a hacker has printouts of some top secret laboratory reports, that information has been misappropriated, copied by an individual unauthorized to do so.

If this law is subsumed into the general larceny statute, a prosecuting complication might arise. We are then back to the question of whether or not it can be shown that the hacker intended to permanently deprive the owner of his property. We both know that computer hackers generally don't have any intention of deprivation — just learning. *We* know that, but we can't expect judges and juries to understand.

Finally, let's end this section on a good note. If the accused hacker leaves no trace of his or her entering a system, then it is typically the case that theft of trade secrets can not be seriously considered as having taken place. Thus, hackers should make certain that all files and printouts which contain data that one might regard as trade secrets, are either purged, burned or hidden *very* well.

Receipt Of Stolen Property

Let's describe this one by mentioning its three parts: (1) The stolen property must have been received by (2) someone who knows or should reasonably suspect that the property was stolen, and (3) the receiving has been done with the intent of permanently depriving the owner of his property.

As with trade secret theft, ROSP may be included in the larceny laws, or it may have its very own statute to call its own. Regardless, ROSP is a good crime to catch hackers by. Here's why:

ROSP is applicable for almost any stolen property or "property," including trade secrets, information, goods and services, high credit ratings (been hacking TRW lately?), computer time, passwords, and files. If you've got any of these, or anything else for that matter, you've got ROSP to deal with.

Theft Of Services Or Labor Under False Pretenses

Theft of Services Under... Boy, I thought I had to abbreviate when discussing Receipt of Stolen Property! TOSOLUFP is basically a form of larceny whereby you trick someone into letting you have something. For instance, TOSOLUFP might occur when a hacker gets access to an on-site computer by showing a guard a fake ID badge.

Similarly, any false representation of a fact with the intention of obtaining the property of another is TOSOLUFP. Additionally it must be shown that the victim's judgment relied on acceptance of that false representation and because of that reliance, suffered some injury — such as loss of computer time or monies which would be paid by a legal user of the system.

Interference With Use Statutes

If someone does something so another person can't use his or her property (with a resulting loss to the property owner) then it is said that an "interference with use" statute has been broken. In the hacking sense, if a cracker were to change password files so others couldn't log on, or tamper with a piece of source code, or use another person's username and password, an IWUS may be said to have occurred. Sometimes these are called anti-tampering laws.

As we have seen with the other traditional laws as they apply to hacking, there are of course no clear ways to overlay centuries old terminology onto modern situations. An IWUS can apply even if there is no visible damage as a result of tampering. Even the installation of a back door may be punishable, regardless of whether other users know this illegal mode of entry exists.

Traditional Federal Crime Laws

A crime may become a federal crime if it takes place on or involves federal property, or if there is a vested federal interest in the crime. There are federal laws which don't necessarily refer to computers, yet are acceptable for use in the prosecution (persecution?) of computer hackers. Note that these laws, as well as the laws described in following sections, are applicable only when the computers you hack are related to the federal government in some way.

Conspiracy

Conspiracy (aka 18 USC #371, if you like numbers) takes place when two or more individuals combine to agree upon or plot an unlawful act, or to commit a lawful act in an unlawful manner. The law goes on to state it is unlawful for these two or more people to plan to defraud the US government, or any federal agency.

This means that a bunch of criminals who use hacker's techniques to make money appear in their checking accounts will be accused of conspiracy if the bank or financial institution involved is a member of the Federal Deposit Insurance Corporation.

In any case, if you are a member of any sort of group which discusses hacking, or if you've ever discussed hacking or other illegal activities with anyone, you are a potential victim of this law.

661, 2113, 641, 912, 1343, 1361, Etc.

Other federal laws may also apply in select cases of computer hacking. Applicability of these laws depends on the nature of the "crime," what computers were being hacked, where the hacking took place, and how the hacker went about breaking in.

For example, laws 18 USC 661 & 2113 have to do with thefts committed within a special maritime jurisdiction and burglary of a bank respectively. Other laws deal with post offices, fortifications, harbor-defense areas, and federal property in general. These are special laws that will apply only if you have, let's say, "burglarized" the information in a post office database, or committed some other special-area offense.

United States Code 641 applies to the theft of federal property (is information property?) or records. USC 912 makes it unlawful to obtain "a thing of value" by impersonating a federal officer or employee. I would guess entering a federal employee's password is considered impersonation.

Number 1343 on the books says you can't use wire communications to execute or attempt to defraud or scheme to obtain property under false pretenses, when the message crosses state lines. 1361 prohibits malicious injury to federal property, and 2071 disallows the concealment, mutilation or removal of public records. All of which a computer cracker is likely to do, if on a federal computer.

There is law after statute after law, all dealing with specific issues like these. It doesn't seem worthwhile to go through every last one of them. Suffice it to say, if you get caught by the feds, they have a lot of legalese they can use to say why what you were doing was wrong. I'm not saying you should go out and memorize every bill that's ever been passed that might have some remote connec-

tion to computer law. I'm saying you should realize that computer hacking can be a risky business. Use your head. Don't make the mistakes that others have made. If you're lucky, you'll be hacking without harm for as long as you want.

Federal Computer Crime Laws, Or: It's 10:30, Do They Know Where The Hackers Are?

Finally, there are the federal laws which specifically relate to computer crime that one must be wary of. The Counterfeit Access Device and Computer Fraud Act of 1984 (18 USC 1030) was the first law that explicitly talked about computer crime. As you might expect, it is a law that can be applied to just about any government hack. It prohibits unauthorized access to data stored on any "federal interest computer," and specifically mentions financial records and national secrets as info not to mess around with. This law allows for fines up to $10,000 or up to 10 years imprisonment if it's a first offense.

Two years later, two computer crime acts were passed by Congress. The Computer Fraud and Abuse Act of 1986 defined more situations in which hackers could be prosecuted, by talking more about financial houses and medical records, targeting computers involved with interstate crimes, computers belonging to certain financial institutions, and other federally owned computers. There are also provisions for the trafficking in passwords with intent to defraud computer owners. Most interesting to the hacker, I believe, is that The Computer Fraud and Abuse Act of 1986 makes it illegal to use other people's passwords, or even to use one's own password improperly — that's where the "fraud" part of the title comes from.

One sort of strange requirement that this law makes is that it can only be applied to crimes where the victim has lost $1,000 or more due to the crime. Since you are going to be hacking under a set of ethical constraints, this law doesn't apply to you at all then (i.e., no computer you hack will lose anything from your explorations). This facet of the Act is made even more interesting when you realize that the Senate Judiciary Committee, in their report on the Act, explained that a cracker doesn't have to actually steal data to be prosecuted under the law

— he or she only has to read the data. Makes you wonder what they're thinking since it's beyond my comprehension how anyone can prove that reading some data caused $1,000 worth of damage. But then, I'm no lawyer.

The Computer Security Act of 1987 is a do-nothing law that requires security standards to be developed for classified and unclassified federal data, and requires that security plans and periodic security training be implemented on federal computer systems containing sensitive information.

Conclusion

I was going to apologize to all the lawyers out there, for the way I've manhandled these descriptions of all the above laws. But really, why should I apologize to lawyers?

Now let's talk about what we as hackers can do to protect ourselves; then we won't have to worry about any of the above.

Chapter Fourteen:
Hacker Security:
How To Keep From Getting Caught

Hacking is fun. Hell, it's exhilarating. But it's also illegal, sometimes immoral, and usually punishable. Even if what you're doing is perfectly innocent you'll be hard pressed to find an acceptable excuse for it in court. The very least that might happen is the security holes you utilized the first time around might get patched up. More serious punishments inflicted by the courts can include community service, fines and even prison, as we've seen. Informal punishments include the unofficial destruction of your equipment by law enforcement officers, and being blacklisted from tech-related jobs.

Consequently, the prudent hacker has two goals in mind while hacking. Number one: don't get caught. Number two: if you do, don't make it count. This chapter will present strategies the careful hacker will follow to ensure both situations are true.

Hacking — to use one's curiosity about computers to push them beyond their limits — involves not just technical knowledge but also the hacker's mindset. Part of the mindset must deal with keeping oneself safe, or else the rest of it has been all for naught. Accordingly, the strategies here should not just be known rotely and followed, but expanded upon to apply to new situations. Remember, there have been many computer criminals who've been sent to prison. True, some have even hacked while in prison. Some even *learned* to hack in prison. But you don't want to go to prison. So when you're online, in public, in private, or just living through your life, make sure you apply these guidelines.

In Researching

There may be local ordinances in your area forbidding machines or people to continuously dial up numbers and disconnect, as with an autodialer program which searches for dial-in lines. If you make the calls yourself it's better to say a simple, "Sorry, wrong number," than just hanging up and annoying all those people. Remember the "pers-pros" rule: The more people you get angry at you, the more likely it is you'll be *persecuted*, and the more likely it is you'll be *prosecuted*.

In Social Engineering

Some social engineering and most reverse engineering requires authorized user contact over the telephone or through the mail. This is obviously risky since you are giving out your address or telephone number to people whom you are about to defraud. Hackers have utilized several ingenious methods to overcome this problem.

Once I found a small business with a technical-sounding name that would be closed for a few weeks over the summer. By doing some hacking, some research, and rubbing my lucky rabbit's foot I was able to come up with the code that released messages left on their answering machine. That gave me a way to have people contact me without them knowing who I was.

I put up some phony advertising for a computer network, instructing people to call and leave their name and vital data. I could call up the machine whenever I wanted, punch in the magic code and listen to those messages. When the store reopened, I called them up, saying I was from the phone company. I told the store owner that some lines got crossed, so they might get some weird calls.

Some hackers will simply change a pay phone to residential status and work out of there.

In order to work a social engineer through the mails, you could rent a private mail box or mail drop. One hacker found a cheaper solution. He noticed that the P.O. Box underneath his in the college mail room was always empty. Apparently it was unassigned. The mailboxes are open in the back so workers can stuff the mail into them. This hacker took an unbent clothes hanger and a metal clip, fashioned them together into a grabber that he could slide into his box and go fishing into the mailbox below his. Later I showed him how to determine the combination of the box, so he wouldn't have to do all that. For a long while the box remained unused, and he was able to get all the secret mail he wanted sent there.

Dialing In

"If you don't want it known, don't use the phone."
— Nelson Rockefeller

When you're new it may be okay to dial up remote computers from your house, but once you've been around a while you'll never know if your phone is being tapped or your computer usage being monitored. So when you're past your hacking childhood, make sure to never make an illicit call from your own house, or from any number that can be traced to you.

Even when you *are* new to hacking, you could be in trouble. Imagine if you become a regular on the TECHRIME-USA BBS, right about the time an FBI officer is planning to bust the sysops for conducting illegal business on their board! You don't want to get involved with that, especially if you haven't done anything illegal. Even scarier than that are semi-reliable rumors which have been circulating through branches of the technical underground which imply that the phone companies routinely monitor and record modem conversations which pass through their lines. This is supposedly done automatically by detectors which listen for modem tones, and will then turn on a recording device to keep a record of the call. Even if the gossip turns out to be false, consider this: (1) We obviously have the technology to do such a thing and, (2) it is well known that the NSA records many, many phone calls.

So... If you must associate with known computer culprits, or with established hackers, do so as covertly as possible.

Not calling from your house means calling from someplace else. That means you may want to splurge for a portable laptop computer. While you're at it, buy an acoustic coupler and an external modem to go with it. All this should run you about one or two thousand dollars — a lot less than the cost of retaining an attorney to defend you in court.

The acoustic coupler is necessary because not every place you hack will have a telephone jack to plug into. The *external* modem is needed to plug the coupler into. While many laptops come with modems included, they are generally *in*ternal models, and so can not be coupled to a telephone handset.

Now that you have your equipment, where should you take it? There are plenty of places. At night and over the weekend you can sneak into many big office buildings and, if the right door happens to be unlocked, sit yourself down at a cubicle and chug away.

Two summers ago, I was walking past my local municipal center a little past 9 p.m., and I noticed that *every* office had their windows open. *Every* office — at *night*! Their air conditioner must have malfunctioned during the day, as it had been incredibly hot. Needless to say, if I'd been in the hacking mood I would've scrambled through a window and hooked up my portable to a telephone. I could have been making illegal computer B & Es while making a physical B & E, all just a few doors down from a bustling police station — and with no one being the wiser.

If you have money laying around, or if you have a hacking expense account, you can always hole up in a hotel or motel to do your hacking.

The money problem is one which gets to hackers in other ways. Phone bills add up fast, which is why most serious hackers are phreaks too. A phreak is someone who hacks the telephone networks. One of the major aspects of phreaking is the producing of code tones which signal the telephone system to perform special functions, such as place long distance calls for free. Phreaking is definitely a major area for hackers to investigate, and the telephone system — and especially the computers which run the system — is something which all hackers should become intimately familiar with.

Many hackers will say that any hacking *other* than hacking the computers which run the telephone system is child's play. This is true to some extent. The telephone computer networks are incredibly large, sprawling, wonderful masses of intricate functions, enormous databases, technical operations and blinding wizardry which makes hacking anything less look pitiful.

Once the phone line leaves your house it goes to a local switching center. This center controls all phones in your neighborhood, which may mean as many as 15,000 telephone lines. Each neighborhood switch is managed by its own computer. These computers are the essential targets of the phone company hacker; if you can access the computer, you can access every phone that it switches. You can turn phones on and off, reroute calls, change numbers. You could, if you were not a hacker, wreak quite a lot of havoc.

There are also switched networks which connect the computers that run switches. From there you can go to regional maintenance systems such as COSMOS (which sends out instructions to create and kill phone numbers among other things) and MIZAR (the local MIZAR actually does the work that COSMOS sets up).

Once you've gotten familiar with the intricacies of these telephone computers, you can use them in ways to protect yourself. For instance, you know you probably don't want to place hacking phone calls from your house. What you can do is connect to a neighborhood switching computer, take the phone numbers of some local pay phones, and deactivate their need for coins. You then use the pay phones to call or hack any place in the world.

Or you can use a MIZAR — which, as far as is known, does not keep records of its activities, unlike COSMOS — to temporarily change your present phone number to that of a nearby church. If your call gets traced, you'll be sending the feds on a wild goose chase.

I want to make the point that dialing in to a remote computer is not as safe as it feels. Communicating through a telephone or through a computer sometimes gives you a false feeling of protection, especially when you become good at hacking and phreaking, and turn from confident to cocky. Don't let that happen to you. Remember to always follow these safety rules.

Don't set up patterns of behavior. Always call from a different place, at different times of day.

When is a good time to call? Ask hackers this and each one will give you a different answer. Late night is good because system administrators will probably have gone home already — but then, so too have most valid users, so you'll stand out like a clown at a funeral. You can try hiding yourself within the bustle of heavy usage times, like mid-morning and afternoon, but then the mainframes will be at their slowest, your activity can easily still be noticed, and the account you've hacked may be unavailable for your usage. There really isn't any perfect time to call. Some research into how the company structures its computer guard duty may help.

Time how long you're on the phone with a machine. A phone trace is instantaneous if you're local, and takes just a half a tweak longer if you're calling from far away. But it's still not wise to stay on a single line half the day. Move around a lot, calling *from* different phone numbers, *to* different access numbers. If your target has multiple dial-in lines, randomly choose from all of them.

Laptop Hints

Since you'll be calling from who-knows-where on your portable laptop, here are some suggestions to help you get connected.

When in unfamiliar domain, such as an office, hotel, schoolroom after hours, or otherwise, your laptop is of infinite value — so long as you can get it to work. Never plug your modem into an unfamiliar phone setup until you've verified that doing so won't burn out your equipment. Many offices have installed their own electronic phone systems, called PBXs, to facilitate special functions such as in-house dialing and phone menus, or to block certain phones from making long distance calls. Some of these PBXs place a current into the telephone wires that is powerful enough to damage your delicate modem. To see if the line you have in mind is safe, try plugging in a really cheap phone first. If *it* works, your modem should, too.

PBX-networked phones may not work with your modem because of special audible or numeric codes used in local routing procedures. If you get a dial tone on your cheap test phone but your modem won't work, you can assume that it's the PBX system at fault.

To correct the problem you have to plug the modem into the phone jack, and connect the *room* phone (not your cheap one) to the modem (you may need a special double port for this). To use the modem you place the call using the room telephone, and when you hear the remote computer ringing, turn your modem on-line and hang up.

Alternatively, devices can be bought to process signals as they go between the telephone handset and the modem. The device converts ordinary modem signals so they will work on digital systems such as a PBX. This may be a more suitable alternative if you find yourself having to bypass PBX phones a lot.

Sometimes you can find yourself in a place with a telephone, but no plug-in jack for your modem. For instance, if you are using the phone from a public fax or automatic teller machine. In these cases, unscrew or pry off the mouthpiece of the phone and use a cable with attached alligator clips

to connect the red and green wires from your modem wire to the two silver mouthpiece contacts inside the telephone handset. This can easily generate a poor signal, so if you have the actual telephone (not just the handset) available for vandalism, take apart the entire case and clip your red/green modem wires to the red and green cable leads from the telephone's transformer. You will then have to hold down the switchhook on the telephone to place the call.

Your On-The-Road Kit

Make sure you have this stuff with you when you go hacking on the road:

- A laptop, or otherwise portable, computer. Must have a modem. Preferably two: an internal, and an external with acoustic coupling cups.
- One small, cheap, reliable telephone for testing line voltages. You can use a commercial tester for this, but the phone comes in handy in places like motels, where you may want to connect to a telephone but the acoustic coupler won't fit on the phone they supplied.
- An extra phone cord, with an RJ-11 modular clip at one end (the standard, square telephone plug-in thingy) and with alligator clips at the other end.
- Wire cutters, screwdrivers, and assorted coil cords with various size ports.

System Tiptoeing

Even the best intentioned, the most honorable and nondestructive of hackers are thought of as evil by the managerial population. This means that if you're caught breaking into computers that don't belong to you, expect some trouble. Even if the hacking you were doing is completely benign you are likely to be punished in some way. I've seen reports that estimate the cost of computer crime per year is $3 billion to $5 billion dollars — and that's on the low end. Other sources list figures as high as $100 billion.

Even the $3 billion figure, to me, seems pumped up for insurance purposes, but the people who run businesses and government don't see it that way. Government and industry people will realize that most computer crimes go unreported, and so the true cost is likely to be much higher than the official estimate. Even if these dollar amounts are bogus, that's what people believe, and so they will be even more inclined to prosecute someone who they believe is contributing to that multi-billion loss every year.

Let's take a brief interlude here and examine the case of the Greenwood Family Hospital BBS.

"Pretty Theft" is the name of a hacker I used to communicate with infrequently. One day she sent me a message on a BBS asking if I knew how to get into the computers of a certain hospital that was in my area. I was puzzled, because that hospital was the easiest thing in the world to get into — in fact, it was one of my earliest successful hacks.

When you logged onto the system, you were greeted with this informative message (names and numbers are fictitious, of course).

Welcome to GFH-NET!
300-2400 baud
(123)456-7890

GREENWOOD FAMILY HOSPITAL

GFH-NET IS MAINTAINED BY ROGER CORNWALL AND HAROLD LIPNICK QUESTIONS OR COMMENTS? E-MAIL TO THEM!!!

WHAT IS YOUR NAME?
TYPE IN FIRST AND LAST:

WHAT IS YOUR PASSWORD?
TYPE <RETURN> ON A
BLANK LINE IF YOU DON'T HAVE ONE:

A few months after I began actively hacking, I was using my computer and watching the evening news when a story came on about the governor breaking his arm and being rushed by helicopter to a hospital. I thought to myself, "Hey, hospitals must use computers, right? I can probably get into one!" So I got the supposedly private number for the Greenwood Family Hospital Network, and I called up, and I got that welcoming screen. Guess what I did next?

It's not too hard to figure out what I did! Naturally, I typed in ROGER CORNWALL for my name. Unfortunately, the real Roger Cornwall had

a password of some sort; pressing Return on a blank line just got me an error message. So I tried HAROLD LIPNICK. Again, no go.

I went into the kitchen, got out the phone book, looked up the telephone number of Greenwood Family Hospital, and I called it. A woman answered:

"Greenwood, may I help you?"
"Yes, please," I said, "Is Tom there?"
"Who?"
"Uhm... There's some guy there I spoke with earlier... Your supervisor or somebody?"
"Lee Brown, you mean?" she asked.
"Oh yeah, I guess that's it. I don't know where I got Tom from. Uh, is he there?"
"Nope. Lee left at five."
"All right, thanks."
"Bye-bye."

I went back to my computer and called back GFH-NET and tried LEE BROWN for the name. Once again, I was out of luck. However, after a few more phone calls to the various numbers listed for the hospital, I came up with a guy (a resident) who had not bothered with a password.

GFH-NET turned out to be nothing special after all. It had nothing to do with hospital billing, patient records, or anything else pertaining to the actual running of the place. Mostly it was like a doctor BBS. From what I could make of it, it was medical students discussing problems with the doctors on the system. No file transfers or anything; just a very simple messaging system. It was no big deal, but it was fun to get into.

The next day I looked through the doctors in the yellow pages, and I found about eight listed who had Greenwood Hospital addresses. Out of those names, three had no password.

So anyway, I was puzzled as to why Pretty Theft couldn't get on there. I called it up for the first time in years, and to my surprise found this nasty logon screen awaiting me:

USE OF THIS SYSTEM IS
RESTRICTED
TO AUTHORIZED PERSONNEL
ONLY!
EVERYONE ELSE MUST HANG UP
NOW!

All useful information was gone! All that remained was an angry note and a non-useful arrow prompt.

I tried some of the old names I'd figured out way-back-when, and found that all of them had passwords now. I tried some more social engineering, but everyone I spoke to kept their mouths shut about everything. (Later I was able to get onto the real hospital system with the help of some nice receptionists in the administration department.)

I e-mailed a letter back to Pretty Theft. I asked her what had happened there. The next day I got her reply:

Last month a friend of mine was in the hospital, so I wanted to see if I could change his bill. I remembered you giving me the number two years ago or something, so I looked it up in my book and I was surprised I still had it. I knew the name of my friend's doctor, and when I was there visiting him, I got the names of lots more from the paging system (you know, "Calling Dr. Bower...") and from charts on the walls. Then I went on the system and was trying all these names, when the sysop came on and threw me off. Every time I tried getting on after that he kicked me off. Next morning at about 8:00, I finally got on. One of the doctor's names I tried had the name as a password too. Well as I guess you know, I couldn't change my friend's hospital bill, but I couldn't do anything much else either... after giving my name and password, it just froze. That night I tried it again, and there was a message before it asked for your name. It said, MOST OF THE IMPORTANT FILES HAVE BEEN DELETED BY SOMEONE OR SOMETHING. THE SYSTEM WILL BE DOWN FOR A WHILE — ROGER. A week later I tried it again, and the phone just rung. I didn't do anything to it, but I guess the sysop thought I or someone else deleted the files. A few days ago I called back for no reason, and, well, you know. I guess they got smart?

Yes, Pretty Theft was right. They had gotten smart, and because of it, security was tightened. It is for this reason that hackers should not announce their arrival to a system, nor do anything to attract anyone's attention. There is only one case, really, when you would want to show yourself to the system operator, and that is when you've found out everything there is to know about a system and are never going to call back again.

Incidentally, Roger and Harold had gotten smart in some respects, but remained dumb in others. Through continued perseverance I was able to get onto GFH-NET again. As it turns out, I'd gotten smarter too; the medical conversations between doctors and students seemed a lot more comprehensible than they had been just two years before. Maybe it was the students getting dumber?

There was also an old bulletin posted from one of the sysops. It explained as much as he knew about what had happened (which wasn't much). Mostly it said that certain files were deleted, and many of the bulletins were replaced with obscene musings on female anatomy. From what he said, it sounded like the files could have been erased by either a clumsy system operator, or perhaps a malignant hacker. I did a little investigating, and found that although it was not listed in the main menu, pressing "F" brought me to a defunct file transfer system. With a few minutes of thinking, it was easy to see how someone could've uploaded a program that would delete whatever files were in the root directory after a rebooting of the system.

The next day I typed up a long letter to the sysops at the hospital, explaining everything, what they could do to correct the problem, and how other security breaches could be curtailed. I signed it, "Sincerely, Polly Wanza Hacker." Then I called back the BBS and uploaded it to them. Soon after, I got this message from Pretty Theft:

"There's a new logon screen at the hospital. It says: "THANX POLLY! — SIGNED R.C. & H.L.""

I couldn't have been happier.

Lessons From The Hospital

You already know system operators don't want you on their system. That's why you have to hack in the first place. But if you make it known that you're there, you will compound your difficulties considerably.

On GFH-NET, the sysops went crazy when they realized their computers were being abused, and they made it a lot harder to get into. On a little BBS like that, you might not care whether or not you get in, but if you're dealing with something big

— like some government agency — you don't want to start messing around.

If you do show yourself in any way — like by a million log entries of "USER FAILED LOGON PROCEDURE" from when you tried every word in the dictionary as a password — the sysops are going to get concerned, at the very least. Concerned sysops mean no information will be given out over the phone. It may mean changing every legitimate user's password, or cleaning up dead accounts that might otherwise facilitate entry.

Alternately, if you have a nice feeling about a certain system, and don't want to see it get hurt (and you don't mind possibly eliminating your chances of ever getting back on it), you would be wise to consider informing the system operators about all the little quirks you know about their precious system.

Many times, they won't believe you. They won't even bother trying what you suggest they try, either because they have a huge ego that can't be wrong, or because they think it's some kind of a trick, or god knows why else. But if they do believe you, and they take your advice, they will be quite grateful and, if you ask, might give you a low-level account on the system, or some handy tips. Tell them you'll be their unofficial security advisor. Some of them can be quite good about it, though others will think you're up to no good no matter what.

BBS Protection

This section deals with the two issues of security for the hacker involved with BBSs: hacker as user, and hacker as sysop. These are actually intertwined issues, as sysops of one BBS will generally be users of other BBSs. You should take these safety precautions on all BBSs you use and run, and should not hang around systems which do not employ a high degree of hacker security.

Do not post messages concerning illegal activities on any BBS where you don't feel completely secure. This means it's bad practice to brag about your hacking exploits in private e-mail as well as public message bases. If you are actively involved with BBSing, by all means become good friends with non-deviant systems, if only to maintain a balanced perspective of your computorial exis-

tence. But make sure that what you say on those boards does not implicate you in any way with any crime.

Don't get me wrong. I don't want to imply that posting messages about hacking on a hacker BBS guarantees safety, because it doesn't, of course. When you start sharing secrets on a hacker BBS, you'd better make sure the sysop takes all of the following safety precautions: user screenings, a false front and hidden back boards, double blind anonymity, encryption, and affidavits of intent.

The most important aspect of any hacker group, club, or BBS, is secrecy. A true hacker BBS will not advertise, because it does not need new members. A hacker BBS will seem to be a very homey, family-style BBS up front, but type a code word from off the menu, enter a password or two, and you enter the hidden realm. Hacker BBSs should further protect themselves by only allowing specified users to enter the secret parts of its domain, to prevent unauthorized hackers or pseudo-hackers from breaking in to your meeting place.

Any hacker BBS which does not take this minimal precaution of pretending to be legitimate, is juvenile, dangerous, and not something you want to be a part of.

Going up the scale of stupidity just a bit, I've seen plenty of "hacker" BBSs which allow access to the hidden part by entering words like "DEATH" and, yes, even "PASSWORD" as passwords. Needless to say, the information found on such boards is very low content, and usually consists of the various users calling each other dickheads.

No new users should be allowed on a hacker BBS unless one or several existing members can verify that the potential user is not a cop, will abide by the club's law of conduct, has information to share, and will not be a big blabbermouth. As a sysop, you will enjoy composing the list of rules that govern the way the BBS takes in new members. Remember, any new member should not even know that the BBS exists until the time when he or she is accepted into it. That will keep out law enforcement people, and keep in only the best hackers available.

Once a member has been verified as clean, his or her private information should be destroyed from the computer records. In fact, think about the BBSs on which you are a current member. Are there any which are likely to be busted in a raid? Even if you aren't doing anything wrong on the system — even if nobody on the system is doing anything illegal — you know very well how mixed-up the feds get when it comes to computers. You don't want your name brought into a computer crime trial, even if the case is thrown out of court before it begins. So if you're a member of any subculture BBS, tell the sysop to replace your personal information (name, address, phone number) with falsehoods.

If you ever register with a BBS but decide not to call back, make sure to inform the sysop that you want your information deleted. (Verifying that such information *has* been altered or deleted is one legitimate reason for hacking a BBS. Legitimate, that is, from a hacker's ethical point of view.) It *is* important to do all this, because there are impostors out there who are very good at catching hackers when they least expect to be caught. In June of 1987, an AT&T security official logged onto a Texas BBS and found messages from a hacker boasting about how he'd gotten into a certain company's computer system. This led to the hacker's arrest.

Note that since the hacker undoubtedly used a handle on the BBS, and it was a hacker board, the official might have hacked himself to get the hacker's real name. In any case, make sure *your* real name, address and other identifying data never stray to unsafe waters.

Before we start talking more about what you can do as the sysop of a hacker BBS, let's conclude with a real life example of what happens when hackers DON'T follow the advice I've listed above. In 1986 a BBS called simply and arrogantly, "The Board," came into being in Detroit. The Board was run off an HP2000 computer, and attracted hackers and crackers (and would-be hackers and wannabe crackers) from all over. On August 20, the following ominous message appeared on The Board when one logged in:

Welcome to MIKE WENDLAND'S I-TEAM
sting board!
(Computer Services Provided by BOARDSCAN)
66 Megabytes Strong
300/1200 baud - 24 hours.

Three (3) lines = no busy signals!
Rotary hunting on 313-XXX-XXXX

If you called up that day and read the newest messages posted, you would have been surprised to find these little darlings staring you in the face:

Board: General Information & BBS's
Message: 41
Title: YOU'VE BEEN HAD!!!
To: ALL
From: HIGH TECH
Posted: 8/20/86 @ 12.08 hours

Greetings:

You are now on THE BOARD, a "sting" BBS operated by MIKE WENDLAND of the WDIV-TV I-Team. The purpose? To demonstrate and document the extent of criminal and potentially illegal hacking and telephone fraud activity by the so-called "hacking community."

Thanks for your cooperation. In the past month and a half, we've received all sorts of information from you implicating many of you in credit card fraud, telephone billing fraud, vandalism, and possible break-ins to government or public safety computers. And the beauty of this is we have your posts, your E-Mail and — most importantly — your REAL names and addresses.

What are we going to do with it? Stay tuned to News 4. I plan a special series of reports about our experiences with THE BOARD, which saw users check in from coast-to-coast and Canada, users ranging in age from 12 to 48. For our regular users, I have been known as High Tech, among other IDs. John Maxfield of Boardscan served as our consultant and provided the HP2000 that this "sting" ran on. Through call forwarding and other conveniences made possible by telephone technology, the BBS operated remotely here in the Detroit area.

When will our reports be ready? In a few weeks. We now will be contacting many of you directly, talking with law enforcement and security agents from credit card companies and the telephone services.

It should be a hell of a series. Thanks for your help. And don't bother trying any harassment. Remember, we've got YOUR real names.

Mike Wendland
The I-team
WDIV, Detroit, MI.

Board:	General Information & BBS's
Message:	42
Title:	BOARDSCAN
To:	ALL
From:	THE REAPER
Posted:	8/20/86 @ 3.31 hours

This is John Maxfield of Boardscan[1]. Welcome! Please address all letter bombs to Mike Wendland at WDIV-TV Detroit. This board was his idea.

The Reaper (a.k.a. Cable Pair)

Is any comment required?

You can see from this that the people who come after hackers — the people who will be coming after YOU — are not all Keystone Cops. Maxfield knew enough to pick "k001" handles like The Reaper and Cable Pair. The newuser password to get into The Board was HEL-N555,Elite,3 — a quite hip password considering its origin. Maxfield, and others like him, are as into hacking as we are. They are knowledgeable of the culture and the lingo and the way we think. This last is particularly hurtful, and it means you can't allow yourself to think like everyone else. You won't become an elite hacker without the strength of your entire common sense working for you. When you call up BBSs, be sure and exercise that strength.

Now let's talk about exercising First Amendment rights.

We do have the right to run our own BBS, and to exchange information on it. On a hacker board, that information is likely not going to be the kind of thing you'd read to your mother.

Disclaimers, such as, "This BBS will not tolerate any unlawful discussion of blah blah blah..." are

worthless, but you may want to throw them around anyway to complement my next suggestion: Many of the traditional laws which hackers get nailed on have to do with "harmful intent." That is, can it be shown that the hacker or cracker *willingly* caused damage to a computer?

If you are running a hacker BBS or club, you might then consider having members sign an affidavit which makes their good intentions known. Members should sign an agreement stating that they would never willfully damage another's computer or its contents, that any information exchanged on the BBS was for knowledge value only and that none of the illegal activities discussed will be actively pursued, etc. Basically this should be a way to let the members feel they are actively participating in your code of ethical hacker conduct which should be prominently displayed upon login to the BBS. Signing such a goody-two-shoes affidavit may not get you out of legal trouble, but it will do two things. It will stress the point that a member who does not follow the agreement is unworthy to be a part of your hacker BBS or club. And to a jury, it will help convince them that you all are just a bunch of innocent hobbyists being persecuted by the Big Bad System.

It has been suggested that sysops should have their members sign an agreement that, in the event of a raid by law enforcement officials, users would join a lawsuit against the officials to win back monies to pay for destroyed equipment, lost time, false arrests, the hassle, and everything else that goes along with being persecuted by Big Brother.

Current e-mail should always be kept on-hand, so that you can use the terms of the Electronic Communication Privacy Act to your favor. The ECPA ensures that electronic mail that was sent within the past 180 days is private and requires a warrant for an official to search and read it. Note that individual warrants are required for each user who has e-mail stored on your BBS, thus increasing the amount of paperwork required by The Law in going after you and your gang of happy hackers.

So, if your users have signed an agreement, and sample e-mail is stored for each user (it may be fudged e-mail whose time and date of origination gets automatically updated every 180 days), you want to make all of this known to invading officials. Make a message such as the following avail-

---

1 Boardscan is a company headed by John Maxfield, which seeks out and destroys hackers and their ilk.

able to all users when they log in for the first time, and every time they use the system:

A SPECIAL MESSAGE TO ALL
LAW ENFORCEMENT AGENTS:

Some of the material on this computer system is being prepared for public dissemination and is therefore "work product material" protected under The First Amendment Privacy Protection Act of 1980 (USC 42, Section 2000aa).

Violation of this statute by law enforcement agents is very likely to result in a civil suit as provided under Section 2000aa-6. Each and every person who has such "work product material" stored on this system is entitled to recover at least minimum damages of $1000 plus all legal expenses. Agents in some states may NOT be protected from personal civil liability if they violate this statute.

In addition, there is e-mail which has been in storage on this system for less than 180 days. Such stored electronic communications, as defined by the Electronic Communication Privacy Act (ECPA), are protected by the ECPA from unauthorized accesses — such as seizure by government officials — without warrants specific to each person's e-mail. Seizing the computer where this BBS resides would represent such an unauthorized access. There are civil actions which may be taken against law enforcement agents under provisions of the Act. You can find them in USC 18, Section 2707. On this system you can expect up to X people to have stored e-mail. Each of them is entitled to collect a minimum of $1000 plus all legal expenses for violations of Section 2700 and 2703. Note that all users of this system have already agreed in writing that their privacy is well worth the hassles of court. We will sue YOU.

Perhaps the agency you work for might pay your legal fees and judgments against you, but why take chances? If you feel the need to go after our private and legally protected e-mail, or take actions which would deny e-mail access to

our users (such as seizing our hardware), get appropriate warrants.

It is the policy of the sysop of this system to cooperate with law enforcement agents — though we will not be involved in entrapments, and will not respond to idle threats. Please bring it to my attention if you discover illegal activities on this board, because as curator of this museum I will not tolerate it.

"Hacking the hacker is the ultimate hack," John Maxfield has said. Maxfield is a computer security consultant well known as a hacker tracker, and the one who helped organize The Board sting described above. John scans BBSs looking for hacker activity, and when he finds it, he informs the company that is being hacked about the problem. You know how insecure computers can be, and when you post messages or send e-mail on a BBS you are in effect opening yourself up for the world to see. Don't let some hacker tracker see something about you that you'd rather keep private. When you roam around cyberspace, do so discreetly.

Other On-line Security Steps

In real life and detective fiction, the real enemies to a person's well being are patterns in that person's life. Having a regular schedule of activity may make life easier for you, but it also allows others to find you when you are trying to hide, and notice you when you are trying to remain inconspicuous.

As an example, consider the case of the oilman who would ask the system manager to mount temporary backup tapes every time he began a computing session. The oilman would then read from the tapes posted by the system manager before starting his work. The manager got suspicious fast: it was pretty evident that the oilman was looking for data that others before him had backed-up onto those tapes. That industrial spy, like many other hackers and crackers, was caught because he followed a pattern.

Criminals (and hackers) like to formulate plans of action. But remember, any plan you conceive should have elements of randomness to it. Don't allow yourself to always call at a certain time, from the same workstations or telephones, because one day you will arrive at your favorite hacking location and find someone standing there with a pair of handcuffs.

Once I got a list of Social Security numbers from sitting in on a computer class on the first day: the professor handed around a sign-up sheet for students to list their name and number so that accounts could be made for them on the computer system. I waited until the accounts were made, then I had to go in and try them out. But trying them all at one time would have been too suspicious. Instead, I tried a new one every few hours, a different name each time, so it would look as though different people were trying it out.

The system was secure in that it asked me to change my password upon first login. After doing so I was able to use the operating system's password-changing command to go back to the Social Security number so the original user could get in. But in each user's directory I left behind a hidden program that I could use for remote file viewing and playtime later on.

If *you* ever get into a situation where you can't change the password back to its original form, try re-entering the password as some variation on the Social Security number. For 123-45-6789 you might enter 123456789 or 123-45-6780 or 123-45-67890, as if the typist's finger has slipped. If security precautions require a capital letter or something, use one that is close to the last digit in the ID.

It is equally important that your *modus operandi* change as you move from one hack to the next. As you know, once you're into a system you should do what you can to create a new account for yourself. But make sure you always use a different name and password, and make anything you input about your fictional persona as noncommittal as possible. It is a minor point, but one of the things investigators noticed when tracking down computer cracker Kevin Mitnick was that the words he used were often identifiable American vernacular, thus implying that he was in fact American (i.e., a spy from a Third World country probably wouldn't use the password "RENANDSTIMPY").

Security Logs

It is easy to get manufacturers of security products to mail you everything you would ever want to know about the things they sell. Here I am concerned mostly with software which quietly monitors the activity on a system, audits the system resources for misuses and irregularities, and keeps a disk-based or printed log of usage. Someone at the company takes a look at the log, then says to himself, "Hey! Mr. Poultry has been logging on every night at three in the morning. That seems unusual... Better have a chat with him..." Suddenly you're in an unsafe position, and you never even knew it was coming.

From your research into a particular computer you are looking to hack, you will know which security products are in force (by calling system operators feigning that you are a computer consultant, or by looking through the company's library of reference manuals). Get the descriptive literature from the manufacturer so you'll know what silent enemy you are up against.

Security logs — if they are in place and actually attended to — will alert administrators to any patterns which you create. Well, you're not going to create any patterns, but you're probably going to create some problems, and those too, will show up on the security log's report.

If you plan to stay on a given computer for any length of time, for instance if you plan to use that computer as a springboard from which to jump around through the network, you must discover the security auditor and render it useless.

Don't destroy the auditor, simply reprogram it to ignore you when you log on. Or find out how it keeps a record of events and see what can be done to eliminate your own tell-tale traces. This should be piece of cake, considering that if you're in the position to do these sorts of things, you most likely already have root access.

If you have been logging on in a similar way for a while, you might want to change previous log entries to reflect a more random login schedule. You may also be able to use a date or time setting command to control how the security monitor judges your behavior.

WARNING!

There have been many, many instances of hackers carefully editing out personal sections of audit records, only to find to their horror that they've deleted more than they should have. Or hackers who were trying to be helpful by cleaning up a messy program or fixing a typo in a memo, and having some disaster occur. You know you should always keep backups. The backup rule applies *every* time you use a computer, especially computers which aren't yours. If you feel you must alter a file that doesn't belong to you, alter a *backup* of that file. When you're done, make certain your changes are perfect, delete the original file and then rename the backup.

One simple task that most auditors and many secure operating systems will perform is the recording of unsuccessful login attempts. Again, research is needed to see how your particular target computer responds to inaccurate logon inputs. Some programs will let you try three or four username/password combinations before resetting and saving the last attempt. In that case you would try to always make your last login attempt something innocuous. Or to be safer, don't type anything for your last allowed login attempt. Instead, press Control-C or Control-Z or whatever it is you can use to break back to the previous level of interaction.

Auditing programs can be a nuisance if you're running a big job, such as a brute force password generator. If you're able, try to write these programs so that they get around the security logs. Going directly to the hardware may be one solution to this problem. Another, depending on what kinds of things the log is keeping track of, would be to rename suspicious commands, so that the log either won't know to record those commands under their new name, or if the supervisor reads through the log printouts, he or she won't notice any questionable activity going on.

Printed logs are a big problem. Any hacker worth his salt, can go in and fiddle with records which have been stored on a tape or disk. But what if the security monitor makes a real-time printout of events as they occur? Then, my friend, you are stuck. Once a deed is done, it is trapped on that page for life.

The thing to do is catch any mistakes before you make them. Limit the number of illegal or questionable activities you perform until you can find a way to disable the printer. You may be able to use software switches to program the printer to print everything in a nonexistent font, or if it's a multi-color printer, in a color that has no ink cartridge or ribbon. Of course, since you're probably doing all this over the phone, you might not know what equipment is being used. However, it might be possible to reroute print jobs to an electronic storage medium, or to an unused port; that is, tell the computer to print stuff out on a printer that doesn't exist. At times it may even be possible to trick the computer into thinking it's printing to the printer when actually it's printing back through its own modem — and so you end up receiving reports of your own activities as you go about your business.

A more troublesome form of paper log is sometimes used by organizations to keep track of who does what, when, and why. Some companies insist that each employee enter telephone calls in a log. A monthly review and a comparison of the log with phone bills is done — and if anything doesn't match up, well, you can figure out what happens next. If you sneak into an office to make long distance calls, you can be easily trapped with such a log, since you probably won't know about it. Even if you're dialing in from home (or a phone booth), a log can trip you up. If you use a company's computers to call other computers, that might be a toll call which would show up on the phone bill, but not in the employee log.

Companies may keep logs to verify employee comings and goings, and use of equipment. Stay on top of things because the littlest errors lead to the biggest downfalls.

In Public And On-Site

Doing any sort of hacking-related function in public or on-site — altering public access computers (PACs) or public access terminals (PATs), sabotaging for reverse social engineering (RSE), doing in-person social engineering (SE), using a university's computing facilities, or simply doing research at a library — is riskier than doing the same sorts of things at home. Not only do you have all the threats that a home-based hacker has, you have the additional concerns of whether or not you will be recognized or apprehended.

Use proven burglar's techniques when selecting a spot to do public hacking. When a burglar enters a house, the first thing he does is scope out all the exits. Don't sit down at a computer from where you won't be able to escape easily in more than one direction. And just as a burglar is always glad to see tall shrubbery to hide behind, you should try to sit at computers that are hidden in some way; with people or objects sitting in front of you, and hopefully a wall behind you, so no one can look over your shoulder.

Always be ready to leave a public hack at a moment's notice, and never get so involved with your work that you forget where you are. Remember, that's what happens to regular users when shoulder surfing takes place — they forget where they are and they let people see the secret things they're doing. A hacker must always be more security-aware than a regular user.

Take care to have a decent story prepared if you're trespassing, or if your actions will seem fishy to a passer-by. Make sure you dress the part of your story. Regardless of your story, clean dressy clothes are always a plus.

Finally, one should always keep in mind that a computer room is very likely occupied by at least one hacker or cracker at any given moment. Be alert to shoulder surfers, and to other tricks of the trade. When I sit down at a public terminal I always press the Break key a few times, and log off several times before logging in — just in case someone has set up a simulation trap.

Be cautious, too, upon log out. Some terminals, such as the Tektronix 4207 and others, maintain a buffer of the screen display. Often that buffer is not cleared, even after log out. What that means is,

some unsuspecting soul walks away from the terminal, but leaves behind a record of every action taken during his or her session. Anyone can go over to that terminal now and access, read, even print out dozens or hundreds of screenfuls of data.

While Off-Line: Minimizing Losses

Okay, so what if all of this doesn't help you? What if you still get caught? It's good to be prepared for such an emergency so if the feds do catch up to you they at least won't have any evidence on which to base a trial.

Maintaining Your Computer

You should routinely look at the files stored on your computer and destroy those which you illegally acquired. When I say "destroy" I mean it — don't just delete those files: overwrite them with a single repeated character, encrypt them with the lengthiest, twistiest key you can fathom, and only then erase those files. You can use a "Wipefile" or "Wipedisk" program to write over data. That way you won't have compu-cops poking around in your secrets.

Also keep in mind that sometimes pieces of files get lost or unattached from the files to which they belong, or parts of files get duplicated elsewhere on your disks. It's a good idea to regularly check for these orphan text strings and eradicate them if they contain incriminating evidence.

Any computer file which you simply can't destroy must be encrypted and, ideally, hidden under an inconspicuous filename, such as PACMAN.EXE.

There are other matters to consider, other things about your computer that might not directly convict you, but can lead to evidence that will: terminal programs, autodialers, databases of modem numbers and account codes, lists of BBS numbers (especially pirate, phreak or hacking boards), and any other program that could even remotely be linked with a crime.

To play it safe, I use physical locks on my computers along with software "locks." I programmed all my computers to check for a particular key being pressed during the start up procedures. If the computer goes through its entire start up mode without detecting that key, it knows that something's wrong. It will then call a time-and-date sub-routine. The routine shows the correct time and date, and gives me the opportunity to correct them. I must input a certain time and date, otherwise the computer will display a "LOADING MENU" message and remove the directory in which I keep all my naughty stuff. There is an opening menu too, which one can not enter or exit without inputting the proper password.

Luckily, I've never had my computers seized. If I ever do, I pity the untrained lummox who gets to go through my stuff; my systems are all booby trapped to destroy incriminating evidence. And even if he's prepared for that, he still won't know how to prevent it from happening!

Keeping Your Other Stuff

Once a law enforcement official has a warrant for your arrest, he or she can legally steal all of your computers and peripherals, blank disks and audio cassettes, commercial software and documentation, printouts and operating logs, telephones and answering machines, *any* piece of electronic equipment as well as any papers indicating that you are the owner or user of that equipment, wires and loose parts, model rockets, disk boxes, radios, soldering irons, surge protectors, books, journals, magazines, *et cetera*. These things I've listed are all things that have been seized in past raids. Also, if the crimes which you are suspected of committing are related to a specific place or person, they will seize any papers or evidence with which a connection may be made between that place or person and the crime. They purposely write their warrants to allow seizure of a wide range of items, and believe me — they *will* take all of it.

And don't expect to get any of it back in one piece, either. This is yet another reason why, as I said in the beginning, it may not be such a great idea for hackers to even own a computer. It's sad but true, and so you should do your best to hide anything when you're out of your house or not using your equipment. If you have printouts or notes lying around, keep them in folders marked "SCHOOL HOMEWORK" or "CHURCH GROUP". Make the marks big and visible, and innocuous, and maybe they'll overlook the folders' contents.

It is a myth commonly heard that computer printouts can not be used as evidence in court, since they are so easily forged. The truth is, a printout is just as valid as any other piece of written evidence, as long as it can be shown to have been made at or near the time of the criminal act, or during preparation for the act. If a Secret Service thug, after taking your computer, makes a printout of a file contained on it, then *that* printout is invalid evidence, since *he* made it and not you. On the other hand, if there is in fact some accessible incriminating evidence stored on your computer, the prosecuting attorneys will know how they can legally present it to the court (I presume by bringing your computer into the courtroom, plugging it in and firing away). On the other hand, the feds are so good at smashing up seized computer equipment that you probably have nothing to worry about!

It is important that when you hide stuff, you make it look as if the stuff has no connection with computers or electronics. Law enforcement officers are smart enough to get warrants that let them take anything even remotely connected to *electricity*. Let's look at a hypothetical example. Suppose underground information were routinely distributed on audio cassettes. Naturally we would resort to putting that information on store-bought tapes with legitimate names — Beatles, Grateful Dead, whatever. The cops would know that, and thus would want to get their hands on *every* tape we own, including ones that look as harmless as rock and roll.

As hackers, we do exchange information and keep records on disk. So if you have a box of disks containing all your hacker stuff, you can't simply label the disks with names like "Space War" and "Pac Man." They will suspect either that the disks have been labeled misleadingly, or that the games themselves are real. (Think of Steve Jackson.) Besides, in their raid they won't stop to sort seemingly irrelevant belongings from the obviously illegal ones. So you'll have to hide the disks themselves, and hide them in a way that is unrelated to technology. The same goes for your other electronics equipment, and anything else that might reasonably be stolen by the feds. For example, I keep my backup disks in a graham cracker box. Am I being paranoid? I don't think so. I store my laptop in a big corn flakes box up in the closet — it's just as easy to keep it there as anywhere else, and doing so makes me feel more secure.

You already know how companies leave helpful information in their garbage bins, but you should realize that *your* garbage is just as helpful to someone investigating you for computer crime. Anything incriminating you want to discard should be destroyed beyond recoverability first, and discarded from somewhere other than your home. When I say "destroyed" I don't mean putting it through a shredder — I mean completely destroyed. If the Secret Service finds shredded paper in your trash, they WILL piece it back together.

Paper printouts should be soaked in water to wash away the lettering, and *then* shredded. Disk contents should be encrypted, then deleted. Disks should then be zapped with a strong magnet (bulk erasers, called degaussers, are available to do just that) and the disks themselves chopped up.[2] These items can be anonymously deposited in some public garbage can, or in the case of paper, a public recycling bin. I'm serious! You do this and you've just blown away any "theft of trade secrets" indictments they wanted to hang on you!

Conclusion: How To Get Caught

This is a book of methods after all, and so here is a list of methods NOT to follow. If you do these things, you will definitely get in trouble. Because, you see, there are five ways you, the hacker, can get caught hacking:
1. by traces or technical means,
2. by being finked on,
3. by getting many agencies ganged up against you,
4. by making a mistake, or
5. by being made (recognized).

You will get caught by phone line traces and other technical means, such as audit logs. So don't

keep a routine. Switch the phones and computers you call from all the time.

You will get caught by getting ratted on. Maintain contacts with other hackers, but do so discreetly. Don't tell anyone who doesn't need to know about what you're up to. Above all, be nice to the people you come into contact with while sharing hacking tales, doing research, or while performing the hacking itself. Be nice to them, and hopefully they will be nice to you.

You will get caught by getting many agencies ganged up against you. Don't steal or destroy or vandalize. These things make you look bad, and downgrade hacking in the eyes of those investigating it. Hackers have a bad enough image as it is, mainly because hacking's most public practitioners are nerdish eighth grade heavy metal pseudo-anarchists with skin problems. If you remain true to hacking ethics, you will fare better than if you demolish what you hack — because fewer agencies will be willing to pursue you. Tiptoe.

You will get caught by making a mistake. It is a mistake not to take all of these precautions. Always think before you act. Never reveal anything about yourself. Remember to delete backup files. One of the things that tripped up Lt. Col. Oliver North — according to Donn B. Parker in his *Computer Crime: Criminal Justice Resource Manual* — was that he:

> did not understand that using the ERASE command in the White House Executive E-mail system merely removed the name and storage address of an E-mail message from the directory of messages; it did not destroy the contents of the message. In addition, frequent backup copies of all messages were made and stored for later retrieval in the event of a computer failure. As a result, much of his correspondence was retrieved as evidence of possible wrongdoing.

You need to be especially vigilant about timed backups which are made automatically, without your consent.

If you're careful, you will make few mistakes. But the most careful hacker can be tripped up by the mistake of assuming a course of action is infallible when there are, in fact, gaping holes in it. For example, in 1974 a criminal in Tokyo tried to use

---

[2] This behavior is not paranoid enough for the US Department of Defense, which according to Lance Hoffman in his *Modern Methods for Computer Security and Privacy* (Prentice-Hall, Inc., Englewood Cliffs, NJ: 1977) "feels that there are techniques for electronically retrieving overwritten information and thus requires destruction of the recording medium."

one of the fundamental properties of electronic transmission of data in his favor — the delay that comes about from data being shuffled through cables or telephone lines.

The criminal opened a bank account using the false name S. Kobayashi, then proceeded to withdraw small amounts of cash from automatic teller machines (ATMs) scattered around Japan. Each time, after he withdrew some money, he would telephone the bank to find out the status of his account. By doing so, Kobayashi found that it took twenty minutes for the bank's central computer to register a withdrawal from a remote cash-dispensing machine.

Later, Kobayashi used this information after carrying out a kidnapping. He demanded a ransom of 5 million yen to be paid into his account, figuring he would have twenty minutes of getaway time while bank officials waited for the main computer to receive the information regarding from which dispenser the sum had been withdrawn. The plan backfired because of this one assumption. What Kobayashi didn't realize was that programmers at the bank were able to reprogram the central computer to *immediately* identify which machine the criminal was using. Police were stationed close by to each of the bank's 348 ATMs, and when the kidnapper retrieved the money, he was caught.

Look out for the unexpected twists in your plans, and remember that there probably are people on the other side trying to find ways to foil you.

Finally, you will get caught by being recognized. In public places, make sure you stay unobtrusive.

The surest way to NOT get caught is to NOT start hacking. But then, the surest way not to die is to live an inactive life. Part of your life is computers and the things you can do with computers. Without hacking, all you have to do with computers is business stuff or school stuff, a little game playing, and possibly some programming.

But WITH hacking, you have instantaneous control of the world. Enough said. May we all have a good many peaceful, happy hacks!

Chapter 15:
Conclusion

The Hacker's Ethic

Many hackers and non-hackers have given their versions of the "Hacker's Ethic." The versions are all pretty much the same. What's different is the degree to which the ethic is followed. Smart people, like many hackers, start out by following the rules, the moral codes — the Ethic — but then they get sidetracked. They begin to get the feeling that because they *know* about the law, they have the authority to break it: "It's not like we're blindly acting without discretion." That's what smart people do — because they know they're smart, and because of it, they forget that even smart people, even smart hackers, are often very, very dumb.

What I'm about to do is give my own version of the Hacker's Ethic. This is a set of beliefs that I have about the world of computers. It may not be what you believe, but that's all right. Hacking has to do with independence.

However, I urge you to understand why it's important that you formulate a hacker's code of ethics and live by them. Having a code of ethics will help keep you out of trouble. Now, I'm not saying that if you're caught, a judge and jury are going to base their verdict on whether or not you behaved according to your beliefs — especially since some of your beliefs likely involve illegal activities.

What I'm saying is, I like to think that if you have formulated a moral code, and it is well known that you abide by that code, and if all members of your hacker's circle sign affidavits testifying to their loyalty to the code, then in some instances it may allow a judge or jury to honestly say to themselves, "Gee, he meant no harm by it — the damage was not intentional." If you remember our previous discussions of law, many offenses require that, for a criminal action to have occurred, the suspect's conduct must have been intentionally criminal. Well, I would like to think that's the way it would turn out. In real life one can't count on others seeing things from your point of view.

At the very least, one would hope that by providing a code of ethics, you could more easily weed out undesirables from your group, and keep your members safe and happy. More importantly, I feel there is some indescribable underlying goodness about having a code to guide you. If I sound preachy, fine. I'm done.

This is my Hacker's Ethic. These are my beliefs about computers and hacking, as I attempt to live them.

My Code Of Ethics

Computers have enabled a great deal of information to be available to anyone, and quicker and cheaper than ever before. The free flow of information is *good*, but not when it violates human rights. There are two kinds of human rights. There are rights which pertain to individual humans, and rights which pertain to humanity as a group.

All of humanity should have the ability to access virtually any known information. There should be a free flow of information, and information and technology should be used in *moral* ways. People should know how things work, if they choose to know, and such information should not be kept from them. New ideas should be heard, and there should be the capability for ideas to be discussed, and questions answered, from multiple viewpoints. People should be made aware that all this knowledge exists, and can be brought to them. Technology should be used to this end, not for profiteering or political gain.

Individually, people should have the right not to have data pertaining to them available for use in ways which are adverse to them. People should have the right to be notified when information about them is added to a database, when and to whom it is sold or given. Because it is their own personal information, individuals should have the right to control how information about them is distributed.

A person should have the right to examine information about him or herself in a computer file or database, and should be able to do so easily. The person should have the right to easily correct inaccuracies in that data, and to remove information that is offensive to that person. People should be guaranteed that all makers and suppliers of databases will enable these rights to be granted, in a timely fashion.

All of this is what *should* be the case, and in some situations these rights are currently acknowledged. However, most of these rights are almost unanimously ignored. Therefore it is necessary to *hack*. Hacking is using computers (or whatever) to live according to these ideals. Hackers have these ideals about individuals *in general* and humanity *in general*, and I have a set of ideals which I *personally* follow so that the general ideals may be carried out:

- Never harm, alter or damage any computer, software, system, or person in any way.
- If damage has been done, do what is necessary to correct that damage, and to prevent it from occurring in the future.
- Do not let yourself or others profit unfairly from a hack.
- Inform computer managers about lapses in their security.
- Teach when you are asked to teach, share when you have knowledge to spread. This isn't necessary, it is politeness.
- Be aware of your potential vulnerability in all computing environments, including the secret ones you will enter as a hacker. Act discreetly.
- Persevere but don't be stupid and don't take greedy risks.

I am not suggesting that following a code of ethical conduct of this sort makes my hacking moral or right. But I'm also not saying that my hacking is immoral. Don't even raise any arguments along those lines with me because I simply do not care about them. We know what's legal and what isn't. Hacking is something that I am going to do regardless of how I feel about its morality. It is pointless to raise the issue of "Do you honestly think you can justify snooping with your loopy code of ethics?" because if you must consider that issue, you must not have hacking in your blood.

Combining Principles

Throughout this book I've tried to offer general guidelines on the various topics that will prepare you for any computing situation you happen to find yourself in. When it comes to so broad an undertaking as "hacking," there can obviously be no one specific set of steps to follow to achieve one's objectives. Rather, one must call upon a variety of general ideas, overlay them when appropriate, and just hack away until something comes of it.

From knowing what to expect you should know how to react to a new challenge — and your ability to hack will improve.

I want to tell you one final story. This is a story which demonstrates many of the principles you have learned from this book: research, scavenging, shoulder surfing, persistence and logical reasoning, programming methods, brute force, general computing knowledge, social engineering, reverse social engineering, screen analysis, system simulators. It shows how each is played off the other for the final triumphant result of a successful hack.

My One-Person Tiger Team

Recently I was given the opportunity to try my hand at hacking into a newly set up computer system at a special library. The library director was concerned because they had recently transferred to this new system which, unlike previous ones, allowed dial-up access from outside lines. The director wanted to know if it was possible to break out of the search facility, into the restricted areas having to do with overdue fines, patron names and addresses. Or would it be possible to escape entirely from the library program to the operating system and perhaps do some damage?

I told him I would be happy to look into the matter.

Now, he offered to give me one of the dial-in numbers, but I told him there was no need for that. I was a hacker after all! (Actually, I was acting cocky to impress him — I already knew the phone number from watching him give me a demonstration of how the public part of the system worked.)

I called up the system from my home and explored every inch of it. It was a command-run system. The opening screen allowed one to select a function by entering commands such as CAT to search the library catalog, or HOL to place a hold on an item. The proper way to end a session was with the END command. I tried other, unlisted commands to see if any would work. More than you might realize, this is a very common practice on computer setups where part of the system is public and part is private. Almost always the public part of the system will have at least one secret command to allow entry into the private side. So I tested a whole slew of key words: EXIT, BYE, LATER, START, LEAVE, LOGIN, QUIT, USER, PASS, LOG, LOGI, CIRC, and the like. Some of these I have seen used in actual applications. (For example, CIRC is often used to enter the part of a library program that takes care of circulating materials. I discovered LEAVE on a computer that was situated in a museum — typing it in allowed one to exit the menu and enter a special area for museum curators and employees.) None of these, nor any of the other words I tried, worked.

Since it was a brand spanking new system, I was sure there would be lots of bugs hanging around that I could exploit. Indeed, when I spoke to the director, he bemoaned the fact that certain function keys on the terminals had not been set up yet, and that pressing them would exit one to an incomprehensible programmer's environment. Aha! This is what I needed! But when you're calling in over the phone lines, you don't have access to the function keys that are available on the computers in the company offices.

I thought perhaps the function keys were macros for commands which a user would otherwise have to type in by hand, but I didn't know what those commands were. I was doing nightly excavatings of the building's garbage bins to see if anything would turn up, and finally something did — a badly mangled reference card from the company which had supplied the software package. I painstakingly searched every last inch of the trash that night, but could only come up with half of the card.

At home, I saw that among the things listed on the card were indeed the names of commands mapped to the function keys. Only two of them were legible, and the rest were either torn off or smeared beyond readability, but those two turned out to be enough.

What was immediately apparent was that I had made a wrong assumption — not ALL the commands were standard English words or abbreviations of words, like CAT or END. There were two-letter commands and dot commands, too.

When you input a dot command you type a period (.) followed by an alphanumeric command. They are often used in applications where entering the alphanumeric command by itself would be misinterpreted as inputted data. For example, let's say you're using this library system, and at the prompt where it asks for an author to search for, you decide to search for books by title instead. So you type the TITLE command. What's going to happen? The computer thinks that "Title" is the name of the author you want, and starts a search for someone with that name. To get around that sort of problem, this system allows a period to be typed before a command. Now if you type ".TITLE" at the author prompt, the system sees the leading period and recognizes that what follows should be treated as a command.

Programs often use a period before the command because a period is a small, undistracting character and is also very easy to type. But occasionally you will run into "dot" commands which use other characters, most notably, slashes (/ or \), or an apostrophe (').

Anyway, the reference card told me that pressing function key F1 was akin to the .QUIT command, and F2 was the .HELP command. Both seemed promising — .QUIT because it might allow me access to the nether regions, and .HELP because since this was a newly set up system, help was very likely not yet implemented — and might be one of those functions which the director was complaining would crash the system if someone used it.

I was dialing in to the computer from the outside world, and there really isn't any way to transmit a function key press through a modem (function keys are not in the ASCII lineup), so I had to hope that either .QUIT or .HELP would work. Of course I had tried their undotted counterparts before to no avail, but maybe, just maybe, one of them *with* the dot would work....

Nope!

.QUIT simply terminated my session and disconnected me. When I typed .HELP, the screen cleared, and the following line was printed:

<EOF \txt\hlp\help000>

I presumed this meant that the End Of File help000 in the \txt\hlp directory had been reached; in other words, the file existed but was blank.

I was temporarily licked, I thought, though it was interesting that now I knew about a \txt directory which apparently contained various text files, and a \hlp directory within it which held help files. Something else I noticed: every time the screen was redrawn, a line at the top was displayed which read something like this:

<<< J. Smith Co Special Library On-Line >>>
(000)U/SYS v55.6

The three digits in parentheses changed depending on which part of the program I was using. "(000)" presumably signified the opening screen, where I was attempting to launch these unlisted commands. If I tried the .HELP command at, let's say, screen number (013), I figured the system should then search for the file "\txt\hlp\help013." Indeed, that is exactly what happened.

Now, every program has its own style of input and output. One of the things this system used to take input was a command followed by a number. For example, if a search turned up fifty books, you might type "BR12" to see a brief citation for book number 12. I wondered if the same format would apply to the help command as well. I tried ".HELP99999," hoping that 99999 would be a number too big for the system to handle (certainly there was no screen that high). What happened was I got a message informing me that the command was not valid. I tried other variations, such as ".HELP 99999" and ".HELP < 99999" but none of them were valid either. Finally I gave ".HELP99999" one last try and this time it worked! I guess I had made a typo when I tried it the first time, perhaps inserting a space between the "P" and the "9," or whatever. The system crashed, and I found myself launched into the programmer's debugging environment.

It was like a mini-editing system for the text and batch files that the database used. I fooled around a bit with it and came up with nothing much of value except for a copyright notice that gave the initials of the company that made the program. I looked through various directories of software companies, trying to come up with actual words to go with the initials, and finally I found two that fit. I called up the first and found out that they were the ones who had written the program I was interested in. I asked about obtaining replacement documentation for the package. They said sure — all I had to do was supply the serial number that came with my software and they would send me the book for a nominal fee. I tried some bullshitting: "Well, I don't know the serial number because I don't have the instructions." No good; the receptionist informed me that the serial number could be found on a label stuck to the original disks. "I don't have the disks near me right now — I'm calling from my car phone. I'm sure I sent in my registration card, perhaps you could check that? My name is Jonathan Smith from J. Smith Co..." I prayed that the real J. Smith had sent in his card. He had not. I thanked the receptionist and told her I would call back the next day.

I figured the company library must have the documentation, but I couldn't just show up there and ask the director if I could peruse it for a while. Besides, I wanted to do this whole thing as if I were an outside hacker, unconnected with the company, trying to get in; special favors were out of the question.

That meant it was time for some serious social engineering. The only person at the library who really knew anything important about the system was the director himself, and he was out of the question since he would recognize my voice. Anyway, all I needed was this serial number. I called up the library reference desk, and made up a story about how I was a programmer from the company that had installed the new computer system and I was wondering if they had version 8 of the program? Naturally she didn't know, but I kindly explained to her that to find out she would have to look for some disks with labels stuck to the front of them....

She found the disks in the director's office, and told me that the number eight wasn't printed anywhere, just one long serial number. I had her read it to me, and one of the twelve digits was an eight, so I told her yes, everything was fine, that I just wanted to make sure she had the newest version, and that I would send her version nine if we ever got around to releasing it. She couldn't have cared less.

Anyway, I paid extra for overnight delivery of the debugger documentation, and got it late the next day. Poring through it I found out how to move around in the programming environment and — more importantly for my purposes — to exit from it. (All the important commands were abstruse things like KL00 and EE61. This editor was clearly a rush job, created by programmers, *for* programmers.)

Exiting the debugger got me to a login prompt. I quickly found that typing in "circ" at this prompt, and "JSC" at the following password prompt, would bring me one step closer inside. (Here JSC stands for J. Smith Co. Of course that is a fictitious name.) After entering the password correctly I was brought to a second level of security — apparently the circ/JSC was a general login combination that

anyone with legitimate access to the system knew. I know how to put in "your personal 9-digit ID code." Okay, well we know what nine digits means — a social security number!

I knew that the director had been born and raised in Kentucky, so I knew the first three digits of his social security number. I wrote up a program to continuously spit out possibilities for the last six digits, and it wasn't too long before I found one that worked. When it did, I was greeted with, "Good evening Jane Thornbuckle! Please enter your personal password." Jane Thornbuckle was not the library director. Now I needed Jane's password. I went back to brute forcing for a while, looking for Thornbuckle's personal password by trying out the obvious possibilities, until I got sick of it.

I didn't know who Jane Thornbuckle was, but one of the things I had pulled from the garbage was a stack of discarded company newsletters. Buried deep in the stack was the answer: Thornbuckle was a figure in the company's Management Information Services Department (i.e., a computer programmer). I did some more hacking away at her password, but that was fruitless. Finally I restarted my program to try social security numbers, and eventually came up with the library director's. Hacking his password by chance was, like Thornbuckle's, getting me nowhere.

I decided to look back at what I already knew. The programmer's environment was an interesting thing, and I played around with it awhile until I had learned enough about it to use it to edit files to my liking, as well as a few other tricks. I was able to use one of the debugger's find commands to locate every occurrence of the word "circ" in the system files. One of these files contained a bunch of gibberish, the word "minicirc," some more gibberish, and then "circ" followed by more gibberish. I tried analyzing the gibberish after the second circ to see if it could be unencrypted to read "JSC." If it could, then I would be able to use the same procedure on the gibberish following "minicirc." This tactic was to no avail.

Back I went back to that initial login prompt and tried typing "minicirc" with various passwords. The problem was I didn't know what the "mini" part meant. My best guess was that it was some sort of small version of the actual library system — a simulator or training module. I was trying passwords like TRAIN, MINI, MCIRC, MINICIRC,

TUTOR, LEARN, and after a lot of trouble, finally came up with T.CIRC1. This got me to my favorite little message: "Please enter your personal 9-digit ID code."

Within a few seconds I had discovered that the number "555555555" worked like a charm on this mini circulation system. The screen cleared.

"Good morning New User!" my glowing computer screen exclaimed — it must have been three or four in the morning. "Please enter your personal password."

This was, I hoped, the last level of security. Yes it was: a few moments later I was in the minicirc under the password "TRAIN."

I was proud of myself. I had managed to get out of the public side of the dialup system and into the behind-the-scenes area. But my journey was not over yet, because I still had not gotten into the actual circulation system — just the simulated one used for training purposes.

The minicirc was helpful, but it lacked certain features which, if I were an industrial spy, I would have liked to have had access to. I could use minicirc to check out books to patrons, register new patrons, search the databases, etc., but the database contained only imaginary names and addresses. Many of the other features of the system were unimplemented, but just knowledge of their presence helped me. There was a bulletin board service, which would display messages after logging in. A few standard messages had been left by the installers: "Hi, welcome to the system...." From examining these messages carefully, I came up with some important tidbits of information.

Each message began by listing who had sent the message, and who could receive it. Part of the sender data included the word "minicirc," which implied that it was possible to send messages from the minicirc to the circ and vice versa (otherwise, why would they bother putting that in there?). The second important fact was that although messages were apparently sent by default to all users, one could specify a particular user who would be the only one to read a posted message.

I used the editor to write a letter and send it to myself. Then I logged off, called back and broke out to the programming environment as I had been doing. Pushing the debugger to its limits, I was able to use its file editors to find the letter I had written, and alter its contents. Instead of being di-

rected to me on the minicirc, I changed it to be sent to the library director. And where originally the file had stored my own name — "New User" — I altered it to say that it came from some fictitious representative from the database company that had written the software. The bulletin instructed the director to call this person about some new improvements that could be gotten for free now that version nine had been released (*reverse engineering!*). I supplied a phone number to call. The number I gave him was that of a friend of mine, a fellow hacker named Morriskat, whom I had thoroughly briefed on how to act when the library director called. We set up Morriskat's answering machine so that if the director called when he wasn't there, a convincing song-and-dance would tell about the new products this company was offering at the time.

When the director did make the call, Morriskat talked about some upcoming features, then asked him some technical questions about the particular way the software had been installed for his library. The director didn't know the answers but, he said, he had a terminal right in front of him — he could log on...

"Perfect," Morriskat said. "Just go through your usual stuff. Circ. JSC. Uhm, Social Security Number 402-66-0123. Are you still using the personal password we originally set you up with?"

"Yeah, 'Firebird.' Okay I'm in...."

Knowing three out of the four security controls, projecting an air of omniscience, and having the spoofed e-mail as support, getting that final password was easy as pie.

For the last phase of the project, Morriskat and I sat down to see what we could do with the library director's system access. It turns out we could do plenty. We made up new superlevel accounts for ourselves. We were able to toggle access to virtually every aspect of the software to any other user. And we could print out personal information about every employee at the company — because every employee, whether they ever stepped into the company library or not, had a record in the library's computer. We knew what materials they had borrowed, their home and office phone numbers and addresses, and year of birth.

Exiting from this level to the network server was simple to do, and from there we could login to one of the host computers using the library director's name and his password "firebird."

As the *coup de grace*, and to prove conclusively that I had done what I had set out to do, I used the programmer's interactive debugger editor to alter the library program's opening screen so that instead of giving an explanation of commands, it told a dirty joke. Then I left a file inside the library director's directory which explained how I had broken in. This story as I've told it here is pretty much that file, although here I've expanded more on the hackerish side of things.

Principles Combined

If you are to be a truly successful hacker, one who can hack on demand like this, then you must be a hack-of-all-trades.

It's not enough to be a spontaneous and smooth-talking social engineer. It's not enough to be a programming genius. It's not enough to have the perseverance of a marathon runner. You must have all of it and an imaginative, goal-oriented mindset as well. And the ethic. I truly believe that a hacker who lacks the hacker's ethic will be going nowhere fast, because if you don't show an honesty and compassion in what you do, others will not act kindly toward you and that quickly leads to trouble.

Did I display the hacker's ethic when I carried out the hack I've just described? Yeah — I had done nothing more than rename the file that contained the system's opening screen, and put the dirty joke in a new file with the old name. And I showed the library director how to go about switching them back. Later the two of us, along with members of the computing staff of the company held a meeting to discuss what actions would be taken to close up the security holes I had found.

And, I should add, they have done so.

Concluding Thoughts

Ask any enlightened sage about the purpose for the existence of our universe — or ask any burning, age-old philosophic question of the kind — and the response will invariably be something like this:

"I can not say it in words. I know the answer — I can feel it, and I can feel myself knowing it. But to simply use words to describe an indescribable sensation is impossible."

Your natural reaction to this bull is, "What a phony!" And of course, he *is* a phony. But he's also sincere. He truly believes he understands all the mysteries of the universe, and those many and varied teachings that make up the answers to those mysteries are things that must be experienced first hand. Things can be explained to you, but they can't be felt unless you yourself have felt them.

So here is your passport to the world of hacking outside this book. You now know the ideas, the methods, the information and facts that will allow you to begin a hack in a systematic way, and you know what can be done to minimize mistakes and wasted effort, and reduce your chances of getting caught. But naturally, that is not enough. As with any hobby/game/education/occupation it takes trial and error, practice and experience, lots of time and patience and practice and more practice, before things work out as you would like.

Some Thoughts
To The Concerned Administrator

If you have read this book because of your interest in law enforcement, security, or the mindset of the computer delinquent, then you should have by now learned dozens of ways the most seemingly airtight of security systems can be broken and penetrated. You should have, by now, made up a comparable list of ways to protect against each of the methods I've described.

Such a list should include stressing to your system's users the importance of keeping good passwords, regularly changing them, and taking note of the login message which will display the user's last login date, time and place.

Explain to users that they should never reveal any information of a confidential or suspicious nature over the telephone, through the postal service or electronic mail, or in "chat" mode. Tell your users that if they are asked to reveal such things as passwords, they should simply respond, "I can not help you with that," and end all communications. They should not reveal name or phone number, e-mail address or physical address. All that is required is that statement. Any caller with a legitimate complaint or concern will be able to deal with the situation. All others will be hackers.

Set up a means by which legitimate users can question a suspicious character lurking about the offices without seeming to be rude or obnoxious if the "character" has an honest reason for being there.

Don't let your users become complacent about security, but don't overwhelm them with it either. Most people will follow a few rules, even if it inconveniences them slightly. If your demands are too outrageous however (changing passwords at every login, for example), none of your users will comply. Make sure they understand *why* you are concerned. Point out the loss to *them* if security is breached. Make sure they understand how important all of them are in maintaining safety not just for themselves, but for every other member of the organization, and every other member of any group connected with yours.

Finally, to really ensure that security is as close to 100% as possible, set up a regular maintenance and clean-up schedule. Actively look for holes in your system's armor. If you hear of hacker attacks or viruses at other sites, learn about their problems and see that they don't happen to your own site. Fix known bugs immediately and promptly remove all debugging tools and options. One investigator has estimated that a third of the security holes he has found were due to debugging options.

If an employee leaves your organization, immediately erase their access and change everyone else's access codes. Notice that when you erase the ex-employee's account, you must strike a balance between fair-warning and urgency. A disgruntled employee will be even more vengeful if you destroy a year's worth of work in addition to firing him and closing his account. But giving a warning too far in advance allows viruses, time bombs and trap doors to creep into your system.

Numerous pieces of literature are available for any machine detailing specific security measures an administrator should take. Make use of these. They will point out flaws you could never have dreamed existed.

Ultimately, the little bit of extra work this all involves will prove its immense worth.

Some Thoughts To The Concerned Hacker

You've come this far and you still have doubts about success? I guarantee you, if you care about learning to hack, you will become proficient in the art.

If you've tried and tried and tried, but you still haven't managed to get past finding a phone number — or perhaps you can't even get to that — you can still count yourself among one of the few true hackers so long as your intentions are good, you play it safe with hacker security, you intend to act ethically when you *do* come onto a system, and you intend to enjoy your life to its fullest potential.

After all, that's what a hacker is and does.

Congratulations and good luck to you: now you know the Secrets of a Super Hacker!

And you, too, are one.

Further Reading

Hacking begins and ends as an intellectual exercise. What that means is, if you want to continue to experience the thrill of tap dancing through the nation's computer systems, you must have thorough knowledge of what goes on within that playing field of networks, telephones, terminals and users.

If you expect to get in and out of the really big systems — governmental and corporate — you must be intimately familiar with the operating systems, acronyms, weird jargon and the way people think.

I highly recommend — at least for your own enjoyment and to further your interest in the world of deviant computing — the books listed below.

The Books

Berkman, Robert I. *Find it Fast: how to uncover expert information on any subject*. Harper and Row Publishers. New York: 1987. There are many books of this kind; if you can't find this particular one, it might be helpful to see if you can locate others. Berkman lists some good phone numbers and addresses of organizations you can get in touch with to help you get information in lots of areas necessary for a hacker to know about, including: companies, special/company libraries, governmental documents, etc. If for no other reason, find this book to read the last couple chapters. In them Berkman gives you his tips for extracting information from people. It may not all be directly applicable to social engineering, but it will surely help you out.

Cornwall, Hugo. *The Hacker's Handbook*. E. Arthur Brown Company. Alexandria: 1986. This book is geared toward United Kingdom hackers, especially those with knowledge of electronics and ham radio. It often talks in general terms rather than specifics, and is not as handy as the title seems to indicate. (Unless you're in the UK and/or have a technical understanding of electronics. If you're the former, then this book will probably be of some assistance. If the latter, there's probably nothing in here you haven't already thought of yourself.)

Farr, Robert. *The Electronic Criminals*. McGraw-Hill Book Company. New York: 1975. Not too much here about hacking per se, but there are many helpful and exciting anecdotes to aid you in your social engineering and trespassing skills.

Forester, Tom and Morrison, Perry. *Computer Ethics: cautionary tales and ethical dilemmas in computing*. MIT Press. Cambridge, MA: 1990. Computers and ethics. That's what hacking is all about.

Glossbrenner, Alfred. *How to Look it Up Online*. St. Martin's Press. New York: 1987. Includes many useful phone numbers (voice and modem), explanations of the various services offered and how to use them. Glossbrenner's books are often called "The Bible of X." X being whatever topic he is currently writing about. Check out his other books, too.

Hafner, Katie and Markoff, John. *Cyberpunk: outlaws and hackers on the computer frontier*. Simon & Schuster. New York: 1991. Learn from their mistakes! Profiles of three "outlaws and hackers" are given here. Sprinkled throughout are helpful hacker hints, interesting histories and revelations of behind-the-scenes goings-ons at your favorite hack targets. Possibly more important than all that is to see how these master hackers got caught, so you can do just the opposite of what they did.

Landreth, Bill. *Out of the Inner Circle*. Microsoft Press. New York: 1984. "Reformed" hacker Bill Landreth uses his expertise to show system operators and computer managers how they can prevent their security from being breached. Because Landreth has had actual hacking experience, this book is more useful to the hacker than other books of its kind. Includes some interesting anecdotes and useful information.

Parker, Donn B. *Computer Crime: criminal justice resource manual*. SRI International. 1988. A National Institute of Justice publication intended for feds and phone cops. Some useful hacker tips can be found here and there, but more importantly, it is essential for you to learn how you will be investigated so you can protect against it.

Rothman, David H. *The Complete Laptop Computer Guide*. St. Martin's Press. New York: 1990. This book is a must-read for out-of-towners. Handy information is given on the laptop and modem laws in countries all over the world. This is done without neglecting the United States. If you need a good source for any portable computer information, this book is the place to find it.

Sterling, Bruce. *The Hacker Crackdown: law and disorder on the electronic frontier*. Bantam Books. New York: 1992. There's a lot of history and homages herein. Much ado about many topics related to hacking, cracking, phreaking, partying and wild boys having a good time cruising through computer networks. Also, Sterling is a good writer.

Stoll, Clifford. *The Cuckoo's Egg*. An instant classic, this book is an intriguing mix of detective story and cracker espionage. Don't ask questions: just read it.

Zarozny, Sharon. *The Federal Database Finder: a directory of free and fee-based databases and files available from the federal government*. Information USA, Inc. Chevy Chase: 1987. Lists governmental contacts to find out about various databases. Many such directories exist, this being just one.

Other Sources

Keep up to date with all the above-ground computer mags and newspapers, college and company newsletters, and computing service pamphlets from various sources. You will find that most of this information is totally useless and/or bogus, but every once in a while you'll get a lead or a good idea. And you can use straight computer magazines to get tons of free literature from companies. You can even get the magazines for free if you convince the subscription department that you are someone in the industry. There are two ways to do this. The way I do it is I go to the library and borrow some computer magazines. I tear out the "Reader Information Postcard" from the back, and as I'm going through the issue, circle the numbers for products which interest me. I get information from a lot of different companies, as well as free disks and posters. When I fill in my name and address, I put myself down as president of some made-up company. (There are usually spaces on these cards to enter your title and company.) After awhile, the magazine subscription department goes through its mailing list, finds President so-and-so, and sends me a form to fill out which entitles me to a free subscription to their journal! (Note: The form they send you usually contains a lot of nosy questions.)

If your library doesn't carry a magazine you'd like to receive, you can always just type up a letter to the subscription department of that magazine, and ask about rates for "buyers." You see, they are only interested in giving away free mags to people who spend a lot of money at their companies. By the way, if your library does get one of these magazines, there's no sense in using these tricks to *steal* a subscription, is there?

In any case, for the real inside dope on the hacker scene, you want to go to the underground press. There are many, many hacker/phreak/-anarchist journals flying around. Most of these can be found on-line. That is, you get them from anonymous FTP, or download them from BBSs. They are all *free*, and *legally* free. Certain nefarious presses have been selling this stuff through mail order for exorbitant prices. If you've bought any of it, you've been screwed. There's no reason to buy it when you can download these journals yourself and print out the good parts.

These zines are often written by cocky, spaced-out adolescent weirdos who don't know much except that they hate everyone and everything. Sometimes they contain decent information, but often it is just a bunch of how-to-be-an-asshole. A lot of the articles ("philes") you'll find in these journals are simply rehashings of mainstream works, such as down-to-earth retellings of technical articles. But I have come across useful stuff in these things. In the very least, reading these journals makes you feel good, because you'll end up thinking to yourself, "Gosh, these so-called hackers don't know much more than I do."

And it's true. You can know a lot about computers; you can learn a lot about hacking, but ultimately, the greatest hackers are the ones who are most dedicated to what they set out to do. There are no algorithms to follow to become a good hacker. There is only trial and error, continued patience, and a loyalty to one's own ethics.

Glossary

acoustic coupler — A device consisting of two cups mounted on a base, into which one inserts a telephone handset. The acoustic coupler is connected to a modem, which sends its signals directly through the mouthpiece of the phone, and receives signals through the earpiece. Useful for hacking on-the-run, such as from telephone booths and public fax machines.

amplifier — A device for increasing the amplitude of a signal without altering its quality.

analog signal — An output that changes in proportion with changes in the input producing it.

anonymous FTP — The ability to transfer a file from a remote computer connected to Internet without having an account on the remote computer. (Though the remote system actually does know who is logged in.) One enters "anonymous" for username, and usually one's e-mail address for the password. The program that performs the file transfer is called FTP.

application program — Any software that is not part of the operating system. A word processor is an application program. These are where you hide Trojan horses. Sometimes called "app" for short.

archive — Several files grouped together and generally compressed into a single file. This is done to facilitate uploading and downloading those perhaps unwieldly files to other sites. Archive also refers to a computer or drive which acts as a repository for files, especially a drive which can be accessed via FTP.

asynchronous — Multiple programs or processes overlapping each other in execution and possible memory. An asynchronous attack on a system involves one program attempting to change the parameters that the other has checked as valid but has not yet used. For example, it is illegal for just any old user to invoke the "su" command to make himself a superuser — doing so gets an error message. But if the contents of memory that hold the "reject request for superuser status" are changed to "accept request for superuser status" by another process, then the original "su" command will execute.

avatar — Alternative name for the root or superuser on a (usually UNIX) system. In Hindu mythology, an avatar is the incarnation of a god.

backbone site — Key USENET and e-mail site which processes a large amount of third-party traffic. That is, it receives and sends news and messages to other sites.

back door — Synonym for trapdoor.

baud — Pulses per second (pps), with the assumption that each pulse is identical in amplitude. One baud is considered to equal one bit per second. Thus, when all pulses have the same amplitude, baud refers to bits transmitted per second.

BIOS — Basic Input/Output System. Consists of a piece of code used to govern the elementary system-level functions of a computer.

bit — The smallest unit of data that a computer can understand.

BITNET — A network of normally mini or mainframe computers. BITNET connects many universities and colleges together. It provides e-mail and file transfer capabilities. It does not have the ability to do remote login (telnet sessions).

BBS — Bulletin Board System. A computer set up to receive modem calls. Users dial in, then have access to various features including e-mail, message exchanges, games, and text files.

boffin — Term used circa World War II to refer with admiration to hacker-like folk who wanted to understand how the world worked, and used their knowledge to invent accouterments for the world. Now we refer to ourselves as hackers.

browsing — To ferret out data that has been left behind in computer memory or on storage media after the termination of a critical program or process.

bps — Short for "bits per second."

buffer overflow — A buffer is a (usually temporary) holding area for data. Overflow happens when excess data is fed to a buffer, without giving it time to digest previous intake. Two reasons for buffer overflow: The buffer may not be sufficiently large to contain all the data that is needed before processing of that data can begin, or there may be a mismatch in the rates of data production to data consumption. A person might try and hack his way out of a program by inducing buffer overflow.

byte — 8 bits. Informally, a byte is a small amount of memory, just enough to hold a single letter, digit, or other character.

C — A popular programming language that, along with its cousin C++, any hacker should have at least a passing familiarity with. UNIX is written in C.

chat — To talk to another user online. In BBS circles, chat would imply talking with the sysop on a single-user system.

CCTV — Closed Circuit TeleVision. Security cameras set up in office buildings and elsewhere are monitored on CCTV.

CD-ROM — Compact Disc Read Only Memory. Some computers use compact discs the way other computers use floppy disks. Often large databases are distributed on compact discs.

CIO — Chief Information Officer.

console — On a mainframe, the station which the system operator uses to control the computer, or whichever tty the system was booted from. Also, cty and ctty.

console PBX — Desktop switching service.

covert channel — A way to secretly communicate information out of a private domain of a system, such as an account.

cracker — A hacker who does not respect the computers he or she hacks.

cty — Console tty. (Also ctty).

daemon — Short for Disk And Execution MONitor. A program that is not explicitly started either by the user or the program the user is using, but rather one that lies dormant, watching for a set of conditions to hold true, then it will start itself. Pronounced "day-min" or "dee-min." Also, demon.

demodulation — The process of removing an audio signal from its high frequency carrier. When a modem demodulates those funny beeps coming over the phone line, it is shedding the high pitched, waste portion, and retrieving the usable information.

demon — Similar to a daemon, except this program is invoked by a user or another program.

DES — Data Encryption Standard. A standard encryption technique for scrambling data.

detector — An electrical circuit used to remove the modulation from a carrier signal. Also a device which makes use of such a circuit.

DOS — Disk Operating System. Term used to refer to operating systems in general, or to the operating system of the Apple II series. Also used loosely to mean either MS-DOS or PC-DOS.

dual-tone multifrequency dialing — A dialing method using a pair of tones, one high and one low. Touch Tone phones use this method.

dumb terminal — A device that allows input to a computer (such as through a keyboard) and output from the computer (through a video screen) — and nothing else. Contrast with smart terminal.

duplex — Simultaneous communication in two directions. Two telephones connected together make a duplex system, but if one of the telephones has its mouthpiece broken off, it becomes a simplex system.

EDP — Electronic Data Processing.

e-mail — Short for electronic mail. Sometimes seen as email. The ability to have a private message exchange between two or more users on a BBS, network, or other computer system. Also refers to the message itself.

firewall machine — A machine equipped with various security features, used as a gateway to protect the main computers. Users must get through the safety features of the firewall in order to access the important computer or network beyond.

FOIM — Field Office Information Management System, computer used by the FBI to automate the routine administrative and record keeping functions of their field and resident offices.

FTP — File Transfer Protocol. A set of protocols by which files can be transferred from one computer to another. FTP is also the name of a program that uses the file transfer protocols to move files back and forth between computers.

FTS — Federal Telecommunications System. A direct-dialing phone system used by agencies of the federal government for voice, scrambled voice, high-speed data, fax, and teletype communications.

group accounts — A single computer directory or account protected by passwords, where the passwords are distributed to a number of users. For instance, all secretaries at an office might use the same account.

hacker — Time for a pop quiz! Read this book, then use your own judgment to compose a definition for the word.

handle — An assumed name; an alias. Often used on BBSs.

handshaking — The process or activity by which two separate pieces of hardware coordinate their signals so that they can work together, usually to send messages between them. When you call another computer on your modem, the two modems must handshake to synchronize their responses.

intelligent terminal — A smart terminal.

interactive question and answer sequence — Access control system using a random list of questions. Because of their personal nature, the answers should be known only by the correct user and the system itself, thus authenticating account ownership.

Internet — A very large network that connects just about any type of computer together. It supports e-mail, file transfer protocol (FTP), and remote login (telnet).

interoffice telephone — A telephone not able to call the outside world. Or one which only seems to be so because the security code is not known.

iron box — Perhaps not too accurate a name, since any hacker falling into a literal iron box would certainly know about it! An iron box is a restrictive or otherwise special environment set up on a system to trap unwary hackers into staying on the line long enough to trace. The trap may be a simulation of the actual system, or an abundance of groovy text files to read, or something simple like slowing down the system to a crawl.

ISIS — Investigative Support Information System, used by the FBI as a massive database of important ongoing investigations. Every piece of known data about a case is entered, which can then be cross referenced and checked instantly.

Joe — An account which has the username, or a variation of the username, as the password (regardless of whether that username is, in fact, "Joe"). Joe accounts have been called the "single most common cause of password problems in the modern world."

LAN — Local Area Network. A network that is linked locally, that is, within the same room, the same building, or perhaps between adjacent buildings. Usually machines in a LAN are connected via cables (such as in an office). Contrast with WAN.

letterbomb — A piece of e-mail that contains live data, with the purpose of causing harm to the recipient's system. Might also be called a nastygram.

limited-use passwords — A passwording system that combines the standard reusable password with once-only codes. These passwords may only be used a set number of times, or until a certain date.

line — Pairs of connecting wires from a telephone to a central office. Also, loop, telephone line.

Listserv — A program available on many BITNET computers that sends mail and files to other computers. For example, if you want to start a mailing list, the Listserv would send the files you want mailed to the appropriate destinations.

live data — Information in a data file which, under certain circumstances, gets interpreted as instructions to the computer. For example: On the Apple IIe it is possible to turn an innocuous REM statement in an Applesoft BASIC program into a nightmare. Slip a Control-D into the REM so that when someone lists the program the ^D will be printed on the first screen column. Any DOS command following that character will be executed. One could write a program that does nothing, but if anyone tries to list it, their disk gets initialized. More commonly, one thinks of live data as control instructions to the terminal.

log — A record kept of computer activity; may be printed or stored to disk. System operators are fond of reading through their logs to spot hacker activity. If you find one detailing your exploits, you'll want to remove the incriminating parts of it.

login — To gain access to a computer, usually by entering the required username and password.

logic bomb — A subversive piece of code in an application program that is executed when specific conditions hold true. A disgruntled employee might, before quitting his job, insert a line that says, "IF Joe Smith's account is deleted from the system THEN instruct payroll program to combine all paychecks into one and mail them to Joe Smith." A logic bomb is also called a time bomb.

lounging — See passive computing.

macro — A keystroke or short name that is used to reference a longer piece of text or a series of instructions. For example, if you were writing a book about Hieronymous Bosch, you might set up a macro in your word processor to insert his name whenever you typed "Alt-H."

modulation — A process of loading a voice or other signal (wave) on a much higher frequency carrier wave. When a modem modulates your data as you type on your keyboard, it is converting the computer's digital pulses into frequencies within the audio range that the telephone transmits.

modem — MOdulator-DEModulator. A device that modulates computer data into a format that can be sent through telephone wires, and can demodulate information that has been sent to it from another computer.

MS-DOS — Generic version of PC-DOS, operating system software that runs on IBM PCs, clones and compatibles.

MULTICS — Short for MULTiplexed Information and Computing Service. An antique operating system that was built with security in mind.

multiplexing — The use of different modulating frequencies for the simultaneous transmission of signals.

NCIC — National Crime Information Computer, run by the FBI and containing information about stolen vehicles, missing and wanted persons, and arrest records. NCIC is linked with TECS — the computer system of the Treasury Department — as well as many state computers.

net — Short form of network. Often used as part of words that refer to a specific network, such as the Internet.

network — Two or more machines connected together for the purpose of exchanging data.

newsgroup — A section of USENET devoted to the discussion of a particular topic.

node — An individual machine (such as a computer or printer) that is connected to other machines in a network.

OCIS — Organized Crime Information Systems, run by the FBI. Allows FBI field offices in separate locations to read and share information collected.

once-only codes — A password that can only be used for one access.

operating system — (Abbreviated OS). The control program of the computer which oversees how the system interfaces with the user and peripherals. Examples: DOS, MULTICS, MS-DOS, PC-DOS, PRIMOS, UNIX, VMS.

OS — Operating System.

PAD — Packet Assembler/Disassembler.

PABX — Private Automatic Branch eXchange. A PAX with outside-dialing capabilities.

packet assembler/disassembler — One of the node computers of a public data network.

packet switching — A method of transmitting data along computers in a network. Each intermittent computer is a PAD that receives chunks of data (128 bits long, following the X.25 standard) and routes them onward along a path to the receiving computer.

parser — A program that looks at some inputted text and tries to make sense of what it means. For instance, when you are using MS-DOS, you might type "del filename." The parser inside MS-DOS figures out that what you want to do is erase the file called "filename." A parser in an adventure game looks at commands such as "Walk to the door and knock on it," and, if it was a good parser, would, for example, interpret the word "it" as referring to the door.

passive computing — To monitor the contents of a computer screen through surreptitious means, using one of several methods such as Van Eck phreaking, or cabling the target computer to a second, secret monitor or VCR. Also, lounging.

pass phrase — A series of words or syllables used for access control instead of a password.

password — A word, phrase or other series of characters needed as part of the login procedures to access a computer system.

PAX — Short for Private Automatic eXchange. A network of phones, not connected to outside lines. Used for faster and more secure communication.

PBX — Short for Public Branch eXchange. A network of telephones, each equipped with its own switching arrangement, instead of requiring switching to be done from a separate switchboard. Multiple phone numbers may ring each phone, and special function buttons are pressed on the telephone to either answer a call or transfer it to another telephone.

PC-DOS — Operating system supplied by IBM for use with its personal computers.

PDN — Short for Public Data Network.

phreak — One who hacks the telephone system, usually to obtain free long distance calling and other services such as conference calling. In the original sense, phreaks used blue boxes, black boxes, green boxes, etc. — specific pieces of hardware they had built to generate signals that would cause the phone network to do their bidding. The phone companies have taken precautions and nowadays the boxes will usually not work (and will usually get you arrested). Phreaking has become more code-oriented; stealing calling card numbers and otherwise charging phone perks to another's bill. Phreaking is related to hacking yet it is entirely different, a field of expertise unto itself. It has its own set of rules and jargon, and even a knowledgeable hacker who stumbles upon a phreak BBS is likely to be confused by the discussion. As they say, it's good to know a foreign language. For hackers, that language is phreak.

piggybacking — In the physical sense, to get into a locked building by following in another person who has the key, card, or security clearance to enter. In the computing world, to login to a system by tapping into another user's communication with the computer. Usually done at the end of the user's call, and usually by chance, piggybacking can only be done when the computer doesn't realize that the first person has disconnected.

plaintext — In encryption, the message (or file) that is encoded.

PLE — Public Local Exchange. A local network of telephones usually in separate buildings, houses or offices, and operated by an outside phone company.

post — To publish a letter, article, essay, story, graphic image, computer file or whatever — but usually a letter or article — electronically, by sending it to the public message area of a BBS or newsgroup.

PPN — Project-Programmer Number. The TOPS-10 operating system used PPN to refer to a user's

ID number. PPN may at times be applied to other systems.

pps — Pulses Per Second.

premises wiring — The wires inside a building that are used to connect telephones to phone company lines.

PRIMOS — An operating system for PRIME computers.

process — A program that a computer is currently running.

process command — A command to the operating system that requests a listing of all active processes. For instance, under UNIX one can type "ps -f" to see what everybody else logged on is doing.

protocol — A set of rules used by software to interact with hardware. When two pieces of hardware must interact (such as when two modems connect), they must follow the same protocol, else communication between them will be impossible.

public data network — A network, such as Telenet or Tymnet, that uses packet switching to connect computers; generally follows an international standard called X.25.

pulse — A momentary flow of current, characterized by a sharp rise and fall.

pulse frequency — Number of pulses per second.

receive only telephone — A phone that does not have a ringing circuit, and probably doesn't have a dial or keypad; cannot normally be used for placing calls. These can be found at public fax machines and some automatic teller machines. A hacker would whip out his tone generator, hook it up to the telephone, and immediately call China.

reverse social engineering — Tactic whereby the system user contacts the hacker for advice, and in the process of problem-solving, divulges confidential data.

root — The superuser account, the top level of a hierarchical directory structure, or, in programming, the top node of a tree. For hacking purposes, we talk about the superuser aspect of it. It is often the hacker's goal to obtain root access to a system.

salami technique — A method used to steal large sums of money over a long period of time, based on the assumption that little amounts won't be missed. A computer that handles financial transactions is reprogrammed so that when fractions of pennies accrue in an account due to interest earned, those fractions are rounded down, and are placed into a dummy account. The criminal then makes off with the account.

scavenging — To look through garbage bins in search of discarded, but still useful, information. Also, trashing.

script — A command file that is executed automatically following handshaking by the caller's communications software; eliminates the need for the caller to remember his or her terminal type, login procedures, and whatever other input is required by the remote computer.

security through obscurity — Here is a pre-login message that exemplifies the opposite of security through obscurity: "Thanks for calling Hey There Travel Agency Network. Please enter your five character password in the form ABC-12 where ABC stands for uppercase letters and 12 stands for digits. If you need help, call Cheryl in data processing at (818)-XXX-XXXX." Obviously there are a lot of security holes in this message. One would want to obscure it, by changing it all to one cryptic character, such as >. Security through obscurity can also refer to known bugs being left undocumented in the hopes that no one discovers them.

serial — Passing information one bit at a time in sequential order.

shell — An interface or command interpreter between the user and computer. Basically, whenever you input a command to a computer you are using some kind of shell.

shoulder surfing — Finding out what a user is typing by looking over his or her shoulder, and watching the keyboard or monitor.

simplex — One-way communications. (Compare with duplex.)

simulation — A program set up by a hacker that mimics a legitimate aspect of the system, such as login screens.

smart terminal — A terminal that has memory, editing commands, graphics, computational ability, security features, or is somehow otherwise a computer in its own right, and not just the input/output to a mainframe. Also called an intelligent terminal.

social engineering — To use lies, deceit, play acting and verbal cleverness to trick a legitimate user into divulging the secrets of the system.

source code — The list of instructions that a programmer types in that make up a computer program. This list is the "source" text that the computer will use when it translates the program into machine language.

stand-alone — A computer or computer system that will operate without requiring additional equipment. A terminal is not a stand-alone device, since it must be connected to a computer for it to work. A Macintosh is a stand-alone device.

superuser — The sysop, system administrator (sysadmin) or system manager, or any person who has no restrictions on usage on a machine. The superuser can create and delete accounts, view and change passwords and files, and is usually responsible for machine maintenance.

superzap — To use special debugging or computer maintenance software tools to modify data. Usually to do so constitutes a security breach, or in the very least, violates the intended usage of the software one is altering.

switch — To make a connection; or a system of connecting pairs of telephone lines. In surveillance, the redirection of output of two or more cameras to the available viewing monitors.

startup file — A file that is executed when a computer is booted, or when one logs into an account. Usually this is a plain ASCII text file containing shell commands which are run as a batch. On MS-DOS and PC-DOS machines it is the AUTOEXEC.BAT. UNIX uses .login ("dot login").

sysadmin — SYStem ADMINistrator. The overseer of a computer or network.

sysop — SYStem OPerator. The person who takes care of and controls a BBS. The people who help the sysop are "co-sysops," or simply "co's." Pronounced "sis-op" or "sy-zop." Often written as "SysOp", and sometimes as "sys-op" though this latter version is pretty lame.

talk mode — To engage in on-line conversation with another user. What you type appears not only on your screen, but on his or her screen as well, and vice versa. If you were on a UNIX system and you knew that user Smuggy was logged in also, you would type "talk smuggy" and Smuggy would receive a message saying you wished to talk. Smuggy would respond with "talk yourname," and the conversation would begin. In the BBS world, this is more commonly known as chat mode.

TAP — Technological Assistance Program.

telnet — A set of protocols used to access one machine through another. There are two types of programs used to do this. One, called telnet, establishes a VT100 type terminal emulation to the remote computer. The second, TN3270, establishes a full screen connection.

terminal — Usually refers to a dumb terminal. In general, it is a combination input/output device (a monitor and keyboard) connected to a remote computer.

TG — Technical Guide.

tiger team — A hacker or group of hackers who are engaged by an organization to find the security flaws in that organization's computer system.

tone generator — A device which includes two exterior components — an acoustic coupling device and a telephone keypad — with interior electronics that generate tones needed to operate a telephone. Often seen as a portable tone dialer, these devices are small enough that they will generally include a clip so that they can be hooked to one's belt and easily carried. Also called "tone dialer."

trapdoor — An undocumented way of gaining access to a computer system, usually thought of as a method of entry put in by a system programmer who wants to break into the computer after he is no longer employed by the company. A trapdoor may also lead to hidden areas of a system. A different kind of trapdoor may be unintentional; for example, a laxness in encryption procedure that allows one to determine the plaintext without knowing the key. Synonym for back door.

tracking — An investigator's use of system logs and other audit trails to look and see where a hacker has been and what the hacker has done.

trashing — To scavenge through the garbage of a business or organization, in the hopes of finding useful information, discarded manuals and the like.

Trojan horse — A section of code hidden inside an application program that performs some secret action.

trusted hosts — On some UNIX implementations, it is a list of other computers and users who require no password for entry.

TSR program — Short for Terminate and Stay Resident program. A TSR program is one that is put into memory and stays there, even after other programs are loaded in. The TSR usually stays "hidden" in the background until a person or the computer decides to use it. For example, a program to keep track of what keys are being pressed might be loaded into memory as a TSR. As the user switches from one application to the next, the TSR continues to run silently in the background, capturing keystrokes.

UNIX — An operating system originated by Ken Thompson and Dennis Ritchie at the Computer Research Group at Bell Labs. True hackers, they wrote what would become one of the most predominant operating systems so they could play *Space Travel* without getting a jerky response from the MULTICS time-sharing system they had been forced to use.

USENET — A huge Internet-based message exchange. Users from all over the world read and exchange news, notes, comments, stories, files, humor and help on all topics under — and above — the sun.

username — The name one uses on a computer network or system to identify oneself. Usually it is some variation on the person's real name.

vandal — A cracker, and probably a not-too-talented one, who tries to delete files, crash systems, leave nasty messages everywhere and generally is a big pain in the ass.

virus — A worm implemented as a Trojan horse that contains a logic bomb.

VMB — Voice Mail Box. Voice mail is a computerized phone answering setup that stores incoming messages in digitized form, on disk.

VMS — Virtual Memory System, the operating system used on VAX minicomputers, made by DEC.

WAN — Wide Area Network. A network where the linked machines are greatly separated from each other, usually not within walking distance. Computers in a WAN are generally connected via phone lines (such as Internet). Contrast with LAN.

Warez d00d — A silly name for people who trade or sell pirated software. Warez d00d = (Soft) wares dude.

WATS — Wide Area Telecommunications Service. Service which allows calling within a (possibly interstate) geographic region, often toll free.

worm — A program whose purpose is to reproduce. A worm will copy itself endlessly into multiple directories and onto any disk that presents itself.

Appendices

Appendix A:
Explanation Of Some ASCII Codes

ASCII character code tables are very popular in computer books. Hardly a computer book has been written that doesn't have a list of ASCII codes, even if ASCII has nothing whatsoever to do with the book.

Since ASCII tables *are* so prevalent, I'm not including a full one here. However, I'm giving you something much more useful to use in your hacking endeavors: an explanation of the non-printing ASCII characters. It's just about impossible to find a listing anywhere that tells you what these things do or mean. Usually you just see the abbreviations listed — cryptic codes like "ENQ," "SI" and "DC1."

As you read through the list, try to think of ways you can use the information in your hacking. Remember, these codes may not be acknowledged by all remote computers, but often they will be valid, and can be strategically sent to make a computer think something is happening when in fact it is not.

0 NUL NULl
No character — used for filling time in synchronous communication, or for filling in extra spaces on disk/tape when there is no data.

1 SOH Start Of Heading
Indicates the start of a heading which contains addresses or routing information that applies to the text that follows the heading. (Control-A)

2 STX Start of TeXt
Specifies the end of the heading, and the beginning of a block of text to which the heading applies. (Control-B)

3 ETX End of TeXt
Indicates the end of the text that STX started. Often used as a break key. (Control-C)

4 EOT End Of Transmission
A transmission may have included one or more "texts," each with a heading. Indicates the last

text has been sent. Often used under UNIX to indicate the end of input. (Control-D)

5   ENQ   ENQuiry
A request for a response from the other end. It can be used as a "Who are you?" request for a station to identify itself. Might also be used to ask if a message has been received. (Control-E)

6   ACK   ACKnowledge
Character transmitted by a receiving device as affirmative response to sender. (Says, "Yep. I got the message.") Used as a positive response to an ENQ. (Control-F)

7   BEL   BEL1
Used when there is need to call personnel's attention; may control alarm or attention devices. (Control-G)

8   BS   Back Space
Indicates the movement of the printing mechanism or display cursor one position back. (Control-H)

9   HT   Horizontal Tabulation
Moves cursor or print mechanism to next preassigned "tab" or stopping position. Often the same as pressing the Tab key. (Control-I)

10   LF   Line Feed
Move printing mechanism or display cursor to start of next line. (Control-J)

11   VT   Vertical Tabulation
Print mechanism or display cursor to next series of preassigned printing lines. (Control-K)

12   FF   Form Feed
Moves printing mechanism or cursor to starting position of next page, screen or form. Often clears the display screen. (Control-L)

13   CR   Carriage Return
Moves to starting position of same line. Often corresponds to the Enter or Return key, or Control-M.

14   SO   Shift Out
Indicates that the code combinations which follow should be interpreted outside standard character set until an SI is reached. (Control-N)

15   SI   Shift In
Indicates the code combinations which follow should be interpreted according to standard character set. Sometimes aborts output while allowing program to continue. (Control-O)

16   DLE   Data-Link Escape
Indicates the following character is a control code rather than data. (Control-P)

17   DC1
18   DC2
19   DC3
20   DC4   Device Controls
Characters for the control of ancillary devices or special terminal features. DC3 (Control-S) usually pauses local reception of output until a DC1 (Control-Q) is given. DC2 is Control-R. DC4 is Control-T.

21   NAK   Negative AcKnowledgment
Character transmitted by a receiving device as a negative response to an ENQ. A NAK says, "What'd ya say? I didn't quite catch it." (Control-U)

22   SYN   SYNchronous/idle
Used in synchronous transmission systems to achieve synchronization. When no data is being sent, synchronous transmission system may send SYN characters continuously. (Control-V)

23   ETB   End of Transmission Block
Indicates the end of a data block for communication purposes. Used for blocking data where block structure is not necessarily related to processing format. (Control-W)

24   CAN   CANcel
Data preceding it in a message or block should be disregarded, usually because an error has been detected. Sometimes used as an "abort transmission" command. (Control-X)

25 EM   End of Medium
Indicates physical end of a disk, tape or other medium, or end of required or used portion of that storage medium. (Control-Y)

26 SUB   SUBstitute
Substituted for character found to be erroneous or invalid. Sometimes used as a break command. (Control-Z)

27 ESC   ESCape
Character intended to provide code extension by giving alternate (usually control) meaning to characters that follow.

28 FS File Separator
29 GS Group Separator
30 RS Record Separator
31 US Unit Separator
Information separators may be used in an optional manner except that their hierarchy is FS (most inclusive) to US (least inclusive).

32 SP SPacebar

127 DEL   DELete

Appendix B:
Common Defaults

These are words that are often used as default names and passwords. Try using various combinations of them as both name and password, then one as name and a different one as password, etc. Besides these, try using variations on the company name and the type of service it offers as names and/or passwords. Try things like putting a slash in front of words (such as "/guest"), or separating two words with a slash, as in "MAIL/company name." Also try putting spaces in the words (i.e., "New user") and varying capitalization (i.e., "NewUser," "newUser," etc.).

Also worth trying are easily remembered numbers (1000, 99999, 12345, 101010, etc.), and repeated letters — if a password can be up to eight characters, try "XXXXXXXX," and other things like it.

Don't forget single letters and digits, asterisks and other above-number characters, and plain 'n simple blank line Returns.

guest	start	account	supruser
visitor	su	default	superuser
visit	0	a	anonymous
intro	email	x	user

demo	use	q	demonstration
mail	enter	z	instructions
new	newuser	sysop	introduction
manager	1	password	name
test	sys	system	systest
field	temp	instr	passwd
pswrd	9	startup	id
tty	root	go	train
trainer	tempy	training	info
testing	mini	hello	techsupport

Now here is a whole slew of defaults, common passwords and account names for different operating systems and other kinds of computers. Most are probably out of date or otherwise inoperable, but it gives you an idea of what is expected in these environments.

Credit Bureaus

TRW uses a password of the form:

"LLLNNNNNNNLNL"

where L is a letter of the alphabet, and N is a digit. Note that the actual password does not have spaces between each letter and number.

For CBI, the passwords are:

"N N N L L N N N - ? ?"

Again, the Ns are numbers and the Ls are letters. A question mark refers to any character. Note the hyphen placed between the last digit and the first wild character.

DEC-10

UIC (User Identification Code):	Passwords:
1,2	syslib, operator, manager
2,7	maintain
5,30	games

FTP
Accounts: anonymous, guest, visitor
Password: Carriage Return

HP-x000 (MPS OS)
Login using "Hello [Job ID],[Username][User Password].[Account Name],[Group Name][Group Password]"

Accounts:	Mgr.Telesup,hp3	
	Mgr.Telesup,hponly	
	Mgr.Telesup,pub	
	Mgr.Hpoffice,pub	
	Mgr.Rje,Pub	
	Manager.itf3000,pub	
	Field.support,pub	(password: fld, field)
	Mail.telesup,pub	(password: mail)
	Mgr.rje	
	Field.hpp187	
	Field.hpp189	
	Field.hpp196	
	Field.support,pub	
	Hpoffice,pub	

IRIS
Account names or passwords: manager, boss, software, demo, PDP8, PDP11, accounting

Libraries
Account names or passwords: library, syslib, lib, circ, cat, bib, biblio, catalog, file, minicirc

NOS
Accounts: $system, systemv

PRIMOS
Account names: admin, guest, prime, primenet, test, system, lib, dos
Passwords: system, sysman, netlink, primenet, manager, operator, prime, primos, primos_cs, test, guest

UNIX
Accounts or passwords: root, admin, sysadmin, unix, uucp, rje, guest, demo, daemon, sysbin, who, whois, time, date, ftp, anonymous

VM/CMS
Accounts or passwords: autolog1, autolog, cms, cmsbatch, erep, maintain, maint, operatns, operator, rscs, smart, sna, vmtest, vmutil, vtam, dial

VMS
Accounts or passwords: system, guest, default, operator, manager, syslib, uetp, sysmaint, service, digital, field, service, guest, demo, decnet, dec

Appendix C:
Common Commands

What would you do if you dialed a number, got connected, and saw nothing but this:

#

on the screen? Out of security interests, many systems will not identify themselves or offer any text at all except a cursor and possibly a strange prompt. This is called "security through obscurity." In these frustrating instances you will have to try typing in every possible command you can think of until something works.

This is a list of all the commands I remember being able to use in this sort of situation. Besides these words, if the system gives you any information at all, like company initials or weird words, try feeding back to it what it says to you. Sometimes commands must be preceded by a control character. For example, instead of typing "login," one types "/login."

Unless the system specifically asks for something (like a log-on ID in a particular format) it's a good idea to try these commands, because you never know when one of them will work.

date	list	log	man	connect	public
page	time	load	trace	dir	info
open	net	login	call	begin	sys
a	go	h	logon	l	i
show	q	state	phone(s)	help	link
mail	print	x	control	tele	
?	buy	show	@	bye	
email	shell	menu	sell	hint	
quit	demo	access	demo	start	
intro	exit	end	run	sched	
who	whois	on	games	calendar	

Appendix D:
Novice Word List

This is a list of words that turn up frequently as passwords. Using one of these as a password usually indicates a novice or disinterested computer user. In other words, if you happen to know a certain user is new to computing, either due to postings on a bulletin board, age, or whatever, then these are the words you would want to try.

In addition to these words, you will want to try the letters of the alphabet, various combinations of letters, and numbers, and things easily typed on a standard keyboard, such as "poiuy" and "yhnujm". Also for novices, try names and team names, cars, colors, animals, job-related words, pet names, music groups, local popular radio station call letters, local slang, names of cities or towns, company names, and names or type of computer.

For parents, try things like "dad," "daddy," "mother," or "mommy." For people of certain occupations, something like "Dr. Daddy" may be more appropriate.

Two lists of words are given. The first is my own. The second, written by Robert Morris Jr., was used by the worm program that blazed through the Internet in 1988. Many of the words he used seem oddly chosen and superfluous, and there are many others which I can't understand why he did not

include. I have it listed here mostly for historical reasons. I also think it's interesting to see how another hacker handles a situation. Duplications between the lists have been removed from *my* list.

My List:

account	birthday	disk
adventure	black	diskette
aid	blue	dollar
aids	book/s	dumb
alpha	bowling	earth
angel	brain	eat
ass	breast	fish
asshole	car/s	force
bach	Christmas	Friday
bard	code	fuck
barf	comp	fucku
baseball	cow	fuckyou
basic	crazy	games
basketball	cunt	go
bboard	darkstar	god
bbs	dead	golf
beam	death	ham
beta	dick	happy
big	disc	hell

hi	nazi	strike	atmosphere	clusters	establish
hitler	no	striker	aztecs	coffee	estate
hockey	o.k.	stupid	azure	coke	euclid
home	okay	suck	bacchus	collins	evelyn
hope	open	sun	bailey	commrades	extension
horses	oreo	sunshine	banana	computer	fairway
hump	overload	superbowl	bandit	condo	felicia
id	pass	superman	banks	cookie	fender
ident	penis	system	barber	cooper	fermat
identify	Pepsi	talk	baritone	cornelius	fidelity
identity	play	television	bass	couscous	finite
in	please	tennis	bassoon	creation	fishers
intro	print	terminal	batman	creosote	flakes
keyboard	printer	test	beater	cretin	float
kill	pswd	tester	beauty	daemon	flower
king	qwerty	thanks	beethoven	dancer	flowers
kiss	radar	thunder	beloved	daniel	foolproof
later	radio	thunderbolt	benz	danny	football
life	real	tiger	beowulf	dave	foresight
lion	red	tincan	berkeley	december	format
little	rex	tits	berliner	defoe	forsythe
login	run	tv	beryl	deluge	fourier
logon	Saturday	tyger	beverly	desperate	fred
love	sex	universe	bicameral	develop	friend
manager	shit	user	bob	dieter	frighten
marijuana	skull	vagina	brenda	digital	fun
me	smart	white	brian	discovery	fungible
mensa	snoopy	who	bridget	disney	gabriel
Mickey	soccer	word	broadway	dog	gardner
mine	space	world	bumbling	drought	garfield
modem	spacebar	yes	burgess	duncan	fauss
Monday	starlight	you	campanile	eager	george
money	stars	zoo	cantor	easier	gertrude
moon	start		cardinal	edges	ginger
mouse	startup		carmen	edinburgh	glacier
music	stop		carolina	edwin	gnu
			caroline	edwina	golpher
			cascades	egghead	gorgeous
			castle	eiderdown	gorges
			cat	eileen	gosling
			cayuga	einstein	gouge
			celtics	elephant	graham
			cerulean	elizabeth	gryphon
			change	ellen	guest
			charles	emerald	guitar
			charming	engine	gumption
			charon	engineer	guntis
			chester	enterprise	hacker
			cigar	enzyme	hamlet
			classic	ersatz	handily

Morris's List:

aaa	algebra	answer
academia	aliases	anthropoge
aerobics	alphabet	anvils
airplane	ama	anything
albany	amorphous	aria
albatross	analog	ariadne
albert	anchor	arrow
alex	andromache	arthur
alexander	animals	athena

happening	lynne	patricia	sal	target
harmony	macintosh	peoria	saxon	tarragon
harold	mack	penguin	scamper	taylor
harvey	maggot	persona	scheme	telephone
hebrides	malcolm	percolate	scott	temptation
heinlein	mark	persimmon	scotty	thailand
hello	markus	pete	secret	tiger
help	marty	peter	sensor	toggle
herbert	marvin	phoenix	serenity	tomato
hibernia	master	philip	sharks	topography
honey	maurice	pierre	sharon	tortoise
horus	mellon	pizza	sheffield	toyota
hutchins	merlin	plover	sheldon	trails
imbroglio	mets	plymouth	shiva	trivial
imperial	michael	polynomial	shivers	trombone
include	michelle	pondering	shuttle	tubas
ingres	mike	pork	signature	tuttle
inna	minimum	poster	simon	umesh
innocuous	minsky	praise	simple	unhappy
irishman	moguls	precious	singer	unicorn
isis	moose	prelude	single	unknown
japan	morley	prince	smile	urchin
jessica	mozart	princeton	smiles	utility
jester	nancy	protect	smooch	vacant
jixian	napoleon	protozoa	smother	vertigo
johnny	nepenthe	pumpkin	snatch	vicky
joseph	ness	puneet	snoopy	village
joshua	network	puppet	soap	virginia
judith	newton	rabbit	socrates	warren
juggle	next	rachmaninoff	sossina	weenie
julia	nic	rainbox	sparrows	whatnot
kathleen	noxious	raindrop	spit	whiting
kermit	nutrition	raleigh	spring	whitney
kernel	nyquist	random	springer	will
kirkland	oceanography	rascal	squires	william
knight	ocelot	really	strangle	williamsburg
ladle	olivetti	rebecca	stratford	willie
lambda	olivia	remote	stuttgart	winston
lamination	oracle	rick	subway	wisconsin
larkin	orca	ripple	success	wizard
larry	orwell	robotics	summer	wombat
lazarus	osiris	rochester	super	woodwind
lebesgue	outlaw	rolex	superstage	wormwood
lee	oxford	romano	support	yaco
leland	pacific	ronald	supported	yang
leroy	painless	rosebud	surfer	yellowstone
lewis	pakistan	rosemary	suzanne	yosemite
light	pam	roses	swearer	zap
lisa	papers	ruben	symmetry	zimmerman
louis	password	rules	tangerine	

Appendix E:
Job-Related Word List

These are passwords that might come up in a secretarial or office clerk setting. If the system you're attempting to get into is an office, it's a good idea to try these words before the novice list.

For office settings, also try the company name and variations (initials, abbreviations), titles of software programs they might use there, and words related to that particular job.

spread	memo	info	work	spread-sheet/s
wp	comp	job	office	word
file	doc	paper/s	file/s	busy
notes	report/s	sheet/s	type	docu-ment/s
txt	text	enter	dbase	printer
database	print	journal	process	desk
desktop	data	write	folders	secretary
computer	term	terminal	news	processor
letter/s	mail	mailing	business	docs
read	stuff	project	labor	public

week	day	phone/s	lotus	123
disk	disc	level	service	admin
pc	net	network	protect	safe
boss	software	IBM	Friday	account-ing
Monday	book/s	writer	begin	secretery
margin	list	field	record	check
sec	pres	manage	table	clock

Appendix F:
Technical Word List

Most people who use computers are just casual users, but then there are the powerusers — people like you — who know what they're doing and love doing it. These sorts of people are also often fond of ham radio, science fiction and fantasy, electronics, mathematics, chess, programming, and other related things. This list is comprised of words taken from some of these categories. Also try words from the Glossary. You'll notice that a lot of *Star Trek* words have been included here, as *Star Trek* is big among computer users.

abort	ambassador	atheist
abortion	anarchism	attack
absolut	anarchy	avatar
absolute	analog	baggins
access	application	band
address	arc	bandwidth
ai	archive	bang
algorithm	ascii	barf
alias	async	baud
alpha	atheism	bbaggins

bboard	chomp	erotics
beam	Christmas	expert
beamup	cluster	external
berserk/er	connect	female
biff	cowboy	foobar
bilbo	crack/er	fractal
blast	crunchy	freq
board	crusher	frequency
bogon	data	frodo
bomb	date	fronteir
bones	dbms	frontier
bridge	demigod	function
broadcast	demo	gene
buzz	devil	generation
cable	diana	genius
cage	digital	go
captain	dipole	god
central	director	green
chang	dos	grep
channel	dump	grok
chaos	dvorak	gronk
chen	ebdic	group
chess	enterprise	hack/er
chief	enterprize	ham
choke	erotica	hamradio

hobbit	oscillator	szone
home	output	tasha
horizontal	overheat	tech
host	overload	technical
hotkey	picard	technician
human	piggy	test
index	power	time
input	pres	tng
iris	primos	transport
isis	procedure	transporter
jlp	prodigy	travel
kermit	protocol	trek
king	quartz	treker
kirk	quattro	trekie
klingon	query	trekker
lan	quit	trekkie
lang	qwerty	trekky
language	radio	tribble/s
laser	random	troy
lee	ravel	tsupport
lord	register	tyar
male	riker	unix
man	robot	var
mark	romulan	variable
mask	romulon	vax
master	romulun	vector
matrix	rtty	virus
memory	ryker	vms
mensa	scotty	vulcan
menu	scraft	wan
modal	shuttle	wang
mode	shuttlecraft	warf
model	skip	warp
modem	skipzone	wc
modulate	space	wheel
moon	speed	wizard
msdos	spock	worf
nc-101	star	worm
net.god	stars	xmodem
network	startrek	xterm
next	sting	ymodem
nil	strek	zmodem
nill	sttng	yar
nim	su	zero
node	sundevil	zoo
null	super	
object	superuser	
ohm	support	
oop	swl	
operation	synch	

Appendix G:
Social Security Number Listing And ICAO Alphabet

The Social Security number has pretty much become the Great American Serial Number. The Social Security Administration (there's that SS again!) wants to have a number issued to every American newborn. In addition to maintaining records on virtually every American, the SSA keeps track of millions of foreigners who work in this country or who once worked in this country and have since retired to live outside the US.

Except for a few numbers issued in the mid-1970s to military recruits, all Social Security numbers contain nine digits. Those military SSNs contained ten digits beginning with zero. There are very few of those ten-digit numbers around.

The first three numerals are known as "area numbers" because they indicate from which state the subject applied for a number. Remember, SS records are confidential and not available for public or even law-enforcement review.

Very few SSNs above 595 have been issued, so stay away from brute forcing those. The 700-729 range was issued by the Railroad Retirement Agency years ago, and so any SSN beginning with 700 or above would belong to older people. New numbers in that range have not been assigned since

1963. 596-599 has been reserved for Puerto Rico, 600-601 for Arizona, and 602-626 for California — although no numbers in any of these ranges has yet been assigned. (That is, there are currently no SSNs between 596-626.)

Alabama	416-424
Alaska	574
American Samoa	581-585
Arizona	526-527, 600-601
Arkansas	429-432
California	545-573, 602-626
Colorado	521-524
Connecticut	040-049
Delaware	221-222
District of Columbia	577-579
Florida	261-267, 589-595
Georgia	252-260
Guam	581-585
Hawaii	575-576
Idaho	518-519
Illinois	318-361
Indiana	303-317
Iowa	478-485
Kansas	509-515

Kentucky	400-407	Maryland	212-220
Louisiana	433-439	Delaware	221-222
Maine	004-007	Virginia	223-231
Maryland	212-220	West Virginia	232-236
Massachusetts	010-034	North Carolina	237-246
Michigan	362-386	South Carolina	247-251
Minnesota	468-477	Georgia	252-260
Mississippi	425-428, 587-588	Florida	261-267
Missouri	486-500	Ohio	268-302
Montana	516-517	Indiana	303-317
Nebraska	505-508	Illinois	318-361
Nevada	530	Michigan	362-386
New Hampshire	001-003	Wisconsin	387-399
New Jersey	135-158	Kentucky	400-407
New Mexico	525,585	Tennessee	408-415
New York	050-134	Alabama	416-424
North Carolina	237-246	Mississippi	425-428
North Dakota	501-502	Arkansas	429-432
Ohio	268-302	Louisiana	433-439
Oklahoma	440-448	Oklahoma	440-448
Oregon	540-544	Texas	449-467
Pennsylvania	159-211	Minnesota	468-477
Philippine Islands	581-585	Iowa	478-485
Puerto Rico	581-585	Missouri	486-500
Railroad	700-729	North Dakota	501-502
Rhode Island	035-039	South Dakota	503-504
South Carolina	247-251	Nebraska	505-508
South Dakota	503-504	Kansas	509-515
Tennessee	408-415	Montana	516-517
Texas	449-467	Idaho	518-519
Utah	528-529	Wyoming	520
Vermont	008-009	Colorado	521-524
Virgin Islands	580	New Mexico	525,585
Virginia	223-231	Arizona	526-527
Washington	531-539	Utah	528-529
West Virginia	232-236	Nevada	530
Wisconsin	387-399	Washington	531-539
Wyoming	520	Oregon	540-544
		California	545-573
◆ ◆ ◆ ◆ ◆ ◆ ◆ ◆ ◆ ◆ ◆ ◆ ◆ ◆ ◆		Alaska	574
		Hawaii	575-576
New Hampshire	001-003	District of Columbia	577-579
Maine	004-007	Virgin Islands	580
Vermont	008-009	American Samoa	581-585
Massachusetts	010-034	Guam	581-585
Rhode Island	035-039	Puerto Rico	581-585
Connecticut	040-049	Philippine Islands	581-585
New York	050-134	Railroad	700-729
New Jersey	135-158		
Pennsylvania	159-211		

INVALID SSNs

1. Ending in four zeros
2. Leading numbers 73 through 79
3. Leading number 6 or 8
4. Leading number 9 is suspect — very few ever issued

Spelled Speech

The International Civil Aviation Organization has a standard list of words used for international communication among pilots and air traffic controllers to substitute for letters and digits when appropriate. The chosen words are easy to understand regardless of accent. (The words in parentheses on the following chart are words used by the US Military before the ICAO agreement was reached.)

The ICAO words should be added to any novice and technical word list. And of course, no brute force attack of a military installation or aeronautics-related site would be complete without them.

Alpha/Alfa (Able)	November (Nan)
Bravo (Baker)	Oscar (Oboe)
Charlie	Papa (Peter)
Delta (Dog)	Quebec
Echo (Easy)	Romeo (Roger)
Foxtrot (Fox)	Sierra (Sugar)
Golf (George)	Tango (Tare)
Hotel (How)	Uniform (Uncle)
India (Item)	Victor
Juliet (Jig)	Whisky (William)
Kilo (King)	Xray
Lima (Love)	Yankee (Yoke)
Mike	Zulu (Zebra)

Numbers: Wun, Too, Thuh-ree, Fo-wer, Fi-yiv, Six, Seven, Ate, Niner, Zero.

Appendix H:
Additional R/SE
Role Playing Situations

- Classic social engineering excuse: "Hey, I forgot the password and this work has got to get done. Can you help me out?"
- Call and ask for a naive user. Ask if they want to take a break from work for a little bit. Say you want to test a new help system or tutorial that will help them learn. Ask the user to shut down and login under some made-up password. When it doesn't work, act surprised and say, "Gee, what do you normally do here?" Then tell the user you'll fix it and call back later. You do: On your modem.
- Place fliers in the college computer room: "We need system managers immediately! Looks good on resume! Name____ Password____ We will upgrade you to blah blah..." Or work this on, say, Psychology or Economics students — tell them there's a special project they can enroll in for credit or money.
- Send a memo out saying the dial-in number for a local BBS has changed. Set up your own computer with a simulator. When they phone in and enter their login data, instruct them that the original number is to be used for people in their area code, and that they should re-dial.
- Call a system manager after an incident and say you are a legitimate user who has been locked out, or who's had an account destroyed. (Do your research first, and find the name of a legitimate user.) If software failure was involved with the incident, you will want to talk to the software company and see if you can find out what the bugs were and how they were exploited or repaired.
- Tag team. You are in your target's office with the account holder. An accomplice makes a phone call, says he's the parking attendant calling from the garage. He thinks the account holder's car was broken into. The target leaves, and you are alone with the computer.

SECRETS OF A SUPER HACKER
by The Knightmare
With an Introduction by Gareth Branwyn

This is the most amazing book on computer hacking we have ever seen! The Knightmare is the kind of Super Hacker that keeps security managers from sleeping at night. He's not motivated by money or malice — he's in it for the hack. And if your computer has any link whatsoever to the outside world it is vulnerable to his attack.

Secrets of a Super Hacker reveals in step-by-step, illustrated detail the techniques used by hackers to get at your data. Here are some of the methods covered in this extraordinary manual:

- **Brute Force Attacks:** Hurling passwords at a system until it cracks.

- **Social Engineering and Reverse Social Engineering:** Seducing legitimate users into revealing their passwords.

- **Spoofing:** Designing dummy screens; Delivering fake e-mail.

- **Superuser Abuser:** How to get system managers to do your dirty work for you!

- **Screen Stealing:** How to secretly record every image that appears on a computer screen.

- **Data Delivery:** How to hide the information you've collected; How to e-mail it to your computer.

- **Stair Stepping:** How to use a low-level account to gain ever-higher levels of access.

- **And Much More!** Including a brief history of hacking, lists of likely passwords, and a summary of computer crime laws

The Super Hacker reveals all his tricks: Trojan Horses, Viruses, Worms, Trap Doors and Dummy Accounts. The how-to text is highlighted with bare-knuckle tales of The Knightmare's hacks, including on-site hacking, remote-access hacking and bulletin board busting.

Chapters include: • Researching the Hack • Passwords and Access Control • Social Engineering • Reverse Social Engineering • Public Access Computers and Terminals • On-Site Hacking: The Trespasser-Hacker • Hacking at Home: Dialing Up Computers with Your Modem • Electronic Bulletin Boards • What to Do When Inside • How to Keep from Getting Caught • The Hacker's Code of Ethics • Bibliography • Glossary • And Much, Much More!!!

No system can withstand the ingenious, unrelenting assaults of The Knightmare. And no person concerned with computer security should miss this amazing manual of mayhem.

To order more copies of this book, please include $19.95 per copy plus $4.00 for the shipping and handling of 1 to 3 books, $6.00 for 4 or more. Be sure to enclose your name and shipping address with your request. Send your order to: Loompanics Unlimited, PO Box 1197, Port Townsend, WA 98368. Washington residents please include 7.9% sales tax. Also see the You Will Also Want To Read Section and the Catalog Ad at the end of this book.

YOU WILL ALSO WANT TO READ: